"These essays address the ideological challe
forms and what can be done about it. It is a much needed exposition of the
details of this fundamental problem of the 21st century."

—**John M. Poindexter**, Former National Security Advisor
to President Reagan

"There is no greater need in foreign policy today than the need to understand
Islamism. Western governments are making decisions without any real
knowledge of what they are dealing with – a fact made evident in their
response to the so-called 'Arab spring' and the rise of IS in the Levant. We are
facing a situation more dangerous than any that has arisen since the end of
the Cold War, and our politicians seem to have no settled idea of how to deal
with it. This book is therefore of the first importance for all thinking people
and all policy makers in our time, since it explores the roots of Islamism and
its long-term goals and strategies and, in a calm and considered way, shows
how we might confront the problem that it poses, and how we might find
allies among Muslims who are as appalled as we are by the threat."

—**Roger Scruton**, author of *The West and the Rest*

"Timely and incisive, this is a smart, clear-eyed reading on understanding
and combating the radical Islamist worldview."

—**Ambassador Alberto Fernandez**, former Coordinator, Center for
Strategic Counterterrorism Communications, U. S. State Department

"*Meeting the Ideological Challenge of Islamism* corrects the politically correct
premise that Islamism must be understood and combated as a phenomenon
apart from Islam. But, as Reilly shows, Islamism's grip on its adherents
derives from 'prov[iding] the interpretation of daily events' in terms of orthodox Islam. Waller shows how the Muslim Brotherhood ties secular political

techniques to that orthodoxy. Ulph, by outlining the theological hurdles that continue to marginalize Muslim moderates, removes all doubt that the challenge of Islamism is fundamentally that of Islamic civilization. Valuable lessons all."

—**Angelo M. Codevilla,** Professor Emeritus, International Relations
at Boston University

"President Obama blames internal bureaucratic inertia for his administration's lack of a strategy to defeat the Islamic State. But he has repeatedly insisted that he will not dignify the Islamic State's association with Islam by characterizing it in religious terms. Is either of these rationales defensible or are both mere rhetorical tactics to obscure the cosmic failure of the administration's approach to counterterrorism in general and the Islamist threat in particular? By its publication of *Meeting the Ideological Challenge of Islamism,* The Westminster Institute has assembled five world class authorities to educate us on such questions. Their thoughtful reflections must be understood by every participant in the current debate, especially those seeking an American strategy of victory over the pre-eminent national security challenge of our time."

—**Joseph DeSutter,** Founding Director, National Defense University
College of International Security Affairs

MEETING THE IDEOLOGICAL CHALLENGE OF ISLAMISM

MEETING THE IDEOLOGICAL CHALLENGE OF ISLAMISM

HOW TO COMBAT MODERN RADICAL ISLAM

ESSAYS BY

Patrick Sookhdeo
Robert R. Reilly
J. Michael Waller
Anna Bekele
Stephen Ulph

EDITED BY

Anna Bekele
Patrick Sookhdeo

The Westminster Institute
Isaac Publishing

Meeting the Ideological Challenge of Islamism:
How to Combat Modern Radical Islam

Published in the United States by Isaac Publishing
6729 Curran Street, McLean, Virginia 22101

For more information about obtaining copies of this Westminster Institute
publication, please visit the Institute's website at
www.westminster-institute.org or call 1-703-288-2885.

Library of Congress Control Number: 2015943636

ISBN: 978-0-9916145-9-2

Book design by Lee Lewis Walsh, Words Plus Design

Printed in the United States of America

CONTENTS

INTRODUCTION:
THE IDEOLOGICAL CHALLENGE OF ISLAMISM

Anna Bekele
and Patrick Sookhdeo

The advance of the Islamic State (IS) or the Islamic State of Iraq and Syria (ISIS) in the Middle East caught many by surprise. Its brutality and viciousness has outpaced al-Qaeda, and its gains quickly raised concern among its immediate neighbors and the West. The actions of the IS have been motivated by the leadership's ideology and convictions, deeply infused with ideas of the caliphate in the present and an apocalyptic vision of the future. An attempt to compartmentalize the Islamic State and to declare it unIslamic echoes attempts at condemnations of other radical Islamist organizations such as Boko Haram or the Taliban. It is, though, hard to answer the question, what exactly is unIslamic in the ideology and actions of the IS and some other radical groups? Their claims, attitudes, and actions can be traced back to the origin of Islam, its founding texts and early proscriptions and prescriptions. The followers of the IS and other radical groups have deliberately chosen a radical interpretation and they have been using Islamic theology to justify their actions. Ideology matters, and by ignoring it one may draw an inaccurate picture of the motivations and actions of the Islamic State and other radicalized groups and individuals.

It is no accident that ideology has been underplayed and even avoided in the discourse on extremist Islam. Political correctness is one of the explanations for this, but there are some deeper dynamics behind a sanitized approach to Islam. There has been a tendency to explain violence and the rise

1

of some radical groups by providing a range of sociopolitical and historical explanations. Poverty or relative deprivation has been at the top of the list. Crusades and centuries of colonial suppression have supplied another popular narrative. The modern geopolitical reality, and especially the wars in Afghanistan and Iraq, as well as conflicts in Bosnia, Chechnya and Kashmir are also often invoked. However, any explanation that deliberately disregards the ideological component implies different motivations. It may reflect a staunchly secularist approach and a consequent unwillingness to engage with any religious aspects. It may indicate a fear of criticizing Islam. It may be an attempt to whitewash Islam and intentionally to disassociate it from violence.

The story of the Islamic State (IS) is instructive. Its emergence and its quick expansion in 2014 brought the controversy over ideology to the fore. The Islamic State's ideology and interpretation of Islam was so drastic and troubling that political leaders in the West quickly pronounced it unIslamic. Tony Blair commented on the Islamic State, "It's an ideology based in a complete perversion of the proper faith of Islam."[1] Barak Obama's statement became the most quoted, "Now let's make two things clear: ISIL is not 'Islamic'. No religion condones the killing of innocents. And the vast majority of ISIL's victims have been Muslim. And ISIL is certainly not a state."[2] IS ideology also exposed divisions within the Muslim community. While some explicitly condemned the Islamic State and found their actions repulsive, others could relate to and even sympathize with the IS. Indeed, a steady stream of recruits for the IS in 2013-2014 suggested ideological support for the Islamic State in different parts of the world. Certain target groups readily identified themselves with the IS and did not see it as an aberration. According to the result of the opinion polls in Saudi Arabia 92% of the target group believed that "IS conforms to the values of Islam and Islamic law."[3]

However, the actions of the Islamic State, especially against other Islamic factions and local Muslims, also provoked strong reactions from within the Muslim community. There were numerous individual attempts to condemn the Islamic State and its actions. Sheikh Abdul Aziz al-Fawzan described the Islamic State as "a rogue, external criminal organization".[4] Sheikh Adnan Mohammed al-Aroor and Sheikh Abu Basir al-Tartusi compared ISIS to Kharijites, a radical breakaway group of the 7th century. Sheikh Adnan Mohammed al-Aroor suggested that "ISIS are either Khawārij or infiltrated by the [Syrian] regime. It is composed of three groups of people: brutal Takfīrīs, wicked infiltrators and people deceived by them."[5] In September 2014 about 120 Muslim scholars and leaders cosigned the "Open Letter to al-Baghdadi", where they tried to rebut many theological claims and interpretations made by the IS. For instance they stressed that the Islamic State misappropriated jihad: "Jihad without legitimate cause, legitimate goals, legitimate purpose, legitimate methodology and legitimate intention is not jihad at all, but rather, warmongering and criminality."[6]

Despite the strong ideological component underpinning the actions of some Islamic groups, a grievance based explanation of violence continues to dominate the narrative, whether in politics, in the media or among Muslims themselves. Grievances are important and one cannot simply discard the discontent of the Muslim community, especially of its young people, whose numbers are growing significantly. In fact, the youth "bulge", high levels of unemployment, social upheaval and political instability, corruption, and dysfunctional governments are all important catalysts to the volatility of the Middle East and elsewhere. However, an explanation which reduces the reasons for the rise of extremist Islamist groups to political and economic factors can be misleading. Members of other religious communities often suffer in the same way as their Muslim neighbors from corruption and nepotism, unemployment and poverty, yet they do not resort to employing their religion as a mobilizing force for violence and bigotry. They do not justify an onslaught by referring to religious teaching and instructions, and they do not encourage intolerance by expelling or slaughtering other minorities. Furthermore, some Muslims themselves have become targets of their coreligionists who have espoused extremist views and interpretations. It is striking, and important to understand, that a particular ideology may encourage violence against others or, conversely, negate it.

Different Islamist groups have excelled in combining a variety of tactics they deem appropriate with a narrative that articulates their grievances and sense of outright injustice, and with a proposed Islamic solution. Organizations ranging from al-Qaeda to the Muslim Brotherhood and Hizb ut-Tahrir have been riding on the rhetoric of grievance with enthusiasm and vigor. They may well scorn Western solutions such as democracy, liberalism and the capitalist marketplace. Instead they advocate the comprehensive agenda of the Islamic society and state: a shari'a-ruled world where everything, from jurisprudence to everyday life, from economics to politics, and from literature to science, is defined and regulated by Islamic scripture and the life of Muhammad.

The range of tactics is often contingent on the preferred methodology of the group (an imposed revolutionary strategy or a gradualist approach from within a society), and on whether the Muslims are a majority or minority in a particular region. It also depends on the leadership and their decisions, on what they are willing to do and how far they are willing to go on a range of issues (for instance Zawahiri's stance on bombing and beheadings versus that of Zarqawi's propensity for violence and brutality[7]). There are also pragmatic factors that influence the choice of tactics, and the adoption or abandonment of particular tactics. Boko Haram in Nigeria has been mimicking the approaches employed by al-Shabaab and the Islamic State or ISIS. Thus it is becoming increasingly brutal and seeking to seize territory. In turn the Taliban's tactics have evolved and these now include PR operations, outreach to civilians, and even strategic employment of the Internet and social media.

There is a popular notion that though Islamist groups may differ in tactics, they still share the same goal. They ultimately strive for the establishment of an Islamic state. Palmer and Palmer differentiate between two main approaches, identifying "jihadists" (e.g. al-Qaeda) and "radical moderates" (e.g. Muslim Brotherhood, Hamas, Hizbullah). They suggest,

> The jihadists test the limits of Islamic theology, while the radical moderates come perilously close to being mainstream. ... The jihadist vision of an Islamic state bears much in common with the Spanish Inquisition. The radical-moderate vision of an Islamic state is seductively modern.[8]

Islamists' tactics range from processes of grassroots Islamization to more radical actions such as bombing and insurgency. What may be misleading is that their tactics often mirror the tactics of other movements, and these may not necessarily be Islamic ones. Hassan al-Banna, the founder of the Muslim Brotherhood, copied the Christian missionaries' approaches to working in the community; he also adopted the tactics and practices of the Nazi party and of Communists.[9] Suicide attacks are not limited to radical Islamist groups, but also feature in the history of Japan with the *kamikaze* pilots of World War II, who reflected a tradition of honorable death rather than acceptance of defeat that has roots in samurai culture. Some modern terrorist tactics (bombings, assassinations and other forms of political violence) were initially associated with radical underground activism among students in Tsarist Russia.

The U.S. strategy over the past decade has been to engage and partner with the second group, the gradualist Islamist organizations which prefer nonconfrontational methods and may openly condemn terrorism and violence in the name of Islam. There is a certain logic to this approach, though it may yet prove to be shortsighted. The problem is not only with the ultimate goal of Islamist organizations that is shared by both sides of the spectrum, but also with the difficulty of defining what may or may not be moderate. Those who gradually but consistently promote their agenda are considered to be moderates because they do not resort to violence. However, such groups never ask hard questions about their faith, and never truly engage in reasoning, or in reforming Islam. Their agenda remains deeply fundamentalist because they are driven by faith, and faith alone.

The U.S. strategy for combating terrorism was released under the Obama Administration in 2011 (for an overview of the counterterrorism policies and strategies in the West see Appendix 1). The main premise of the document *Empowering Local Partners to Prevent Violent Extremism in the United States* (August 2011) and a follow up document *Strategic Implementation Plan for Empowering Local Partners to Prevent Violent Extremism in the United States* (December 2011), also known as SIP, is to engage with grassroots communities in order to deter the "ideologically inspired" violence. The strategy became commonly known as Countering Violent Extremism (CVE) and it was the first attempt to provide guidelines for preventing violent extremism. Both documents may be read as examples of political correctness since their language is carefully crafted to avoid either any reference to Islam (as in the case of the SIP which mentions "Muslims" only once) or to mention it only in a positive light. The emphasis in the documents is placed squarely on partnership, communities, engagement, activities and training.[10]

Frank Gaffney was among the first vocal critics of this strategy. In his piece "Enemy inside the Wire" published in the *Washington Times* he objects to the influence of the Muslim Brotherhood on the Obama Administration and to the unhelpful term "Countering Violent Extremism". He believes that a definition loophole has allowed the unrestrained operation of "nonviolent" Islamic groups such as the Muslim Brotherhood. Gaffney explains that:

> "Countering violent extremism" is problematic for reasons beyond its lack of clarity about the threat. It also explicitly excludes a facet of the menace posed by Shariah that is at least as dangerous to an open, tolerant, liberal democracy as the violent sort of jihad: the stealthy insinuation of this doctrine in ways that are nonviolent or, more accurately, pre-violent. The Muslim Brotherhood specializes in this sort of covert warfare, which it has dubbed "civilization jihad".[11]

The release of the strategy documents also coincided with a review of training for law enforcement and military officers in the U.S, and the black-listing of instructors considered to be anti-Islamic. This has greatly under-mined the training process as it has created a reluctance to address the question of ideology. In his critical review of CVE strategy Bjelopera, notes that while ideology is central to radicalization, the CVE training guidance is "silent regarding radical ideologies".[12]

There is a pressing need to address both the ideology of Islamists and their rhetoric, and to understand the motivations both of Islamist extremist groups and of those pursuing a gradualist approach. It is an ideological battle and by ignoring its central component, one is bound to face an even worse crisis than ever before. There is a tectonic shift taking place, as extremist Islamist groups gain ever increasing numbers of recruits, turn ever more violent and audacious, and even seize territory. There is also pressure on states and societies from nonviolent Islamic groups who show a tendency to approach Islam, its Scripture and its prophet within the prescribed parameters of the regulations that Islamists seek to impose.

This collection addresses the ideological challenge of Islamism in its various forms. In Chapter 1, "The Role of Religion in the Battle Space since 9/11", Patrick Sookhdeo provides a very helpful foundation for understanding the importance of religion in the ideological, theological, cultural, and sociopolitical realms. He approaches ideology within a historical context and outlines its main components. Drawing on his experience in training military and law enforcement personnel, he identifies a lack of any overarching strategy and a number of erroneous approaches. He believes that it is counterproductive to separate violent and nonviolent Islamists, and thus to engage with Muslim groups who actually should not be empowered, and to follow an outdated UK model of preventing terrorism. He also notes that religion and its role are grossly misunderstood when a secular approach is adopted or/and it is reduced to Psychological Operations (PSYOP). Patrick Sookhdeo also provides a number of case studies from Afghanistan, Iraq, Lybia and Syria – all seemingly unquenchable hotspots. Finally, he dwells on the implications for current policy and suggests a plan of action.

Robert Reilly analyzes the war on ideas in Chapter 2, "Information Operations: Successes and Failures". He writes from his personal experience in "information operations" as a former Senior Advisor for Information Strategy in the Office of The Secretary of Defense. He cites Voice of America (VOA) as an example and stresses the necessity of broadcasting to the most critical regions of Brazil, China, Russia, and the Middle East. He also high-lights the failure to engage at the religious level in countries like Afghanistan. He particularly dwells on events in Iraq and the attempts to provide broad-casting coverage for the local population there. The main thesis of Robert Reilly's essay is that military strategy should be planned along with commu-nication strategy. Current attempts to do this are episodic and reactionary; they are also inadequate and unproductive.

In Chapter 3, "The Muslim Brotherhood: Doctrine, Strategy, Operations and Vulnerabilities", Michael Waller draws an extensive profile of the Muslim Brotherhood organization. Perhaps one of the most controversial bodies, the Muslim Brotherhood deserves special attention. Michael Waller not only fol-lows its historical development and clarifies its strategic culture, but also tackles such issues as violence and ties to al-Qaeda. He emphasizes the doc-trinal commitment of the Muslim Brotherhood and the fact that the organ-ization does not differentiate between religion and politics. He focuses on its means of warfare from violent to political, ideological and even psychologi-cal. He also exposes the so-called "Civilization Jihad", a stealthy practice of infiltrating and using front organizations. The discursive dimension of the Muslim Brotherhood is evaluated through the work of ISNA and CAIR, key front organizations for the Muslim Brotherhood in the United States. The analysis concludes with an exploration of the vulnerabilities of the Muslim Brotherhood and argues for a different approach to this organization which poses a national security threat to the United States.

In Chapter 4, "Islamic Activism through the Lens of Social Science", Anna Bekele demonstrates how Social Movement Theory (SMT) may be applied to the study of Islamic activism. Poverty or relative deprivation often emerge and re-emerge in debates about the causes of terrorism. However, social scientists have increasingly been trying to debunk this justification and to highlight other factors that play a role. Some Islamic groups have been building up their support base with the help of Social Movement Organizations (SMOs) such as mosques, NGOs and various student organi-zations. The Muslim Brotherhood in particular is known for spawning its support networks at the grassroots level. Networks are critical, as their dynamic nature plays an important role in mobilization and identity forma-tion. While the ideological aspect has been understated in social science, SMT does provide valuable insights into the process of frame alignment, i.e. how Islamist movements make their message resonate with the audience. In order to understand the processes within an Islamic organization, and the group's successes (or failures) in recruiting and mobilizing others, one needs to draw from multiple sources, whether social science, anthropology, theology or ideology.

Finally, in Chapter 5, "The Importance of Progressive Arab Reformers", Stephen Ulph offers an engaging introduction to the world of Muslim advocates of reform. It is vital to understand this critical perspective if one is prepared to acknowledge that the war on terror has failed. Not only has it failed but the world is now in a worse condition than before. Since 2001 the voices of genuinely progressive Muslim scholars have been ignored. Some of these intellectuals have been particularly disadvantaged due to the language barrier. Stephen Ulph methodically helps to amplify their voices by providing an overview of the key issues and offering a glimpse of debate among progressive Arab scholars. Some of these arguments are controversial, not for lack of evidence but because of the dominance of the narrative that is being challenged. Stephen Ulph extensively quotes such Arab scholars as Lafif Lakhdar, Muhammad Sanduk, Abdelmadjid Charfi, and Hashem Saleh, among others, who promote the re-evaluation of Islamic tradition, the revisioning of the history and legacy of Islam, and even textual criticism.

These progressive Arab intellectuals are already fighting the ideological battle. Their ideas need not only to be aired, considered, discussed and promoted, but also implemented if extremism is to be dealt with effectively. The battle may take place in geographic locations, the media, legal and political institutions and even among friends and family members. However, the original and most influential battleground is not geographical or physical, it is ideological. It is fought in people's minds. Thus, an understanding of ideology and its role is essential. The contributors to this collection offer a challenge to the widespread and regrettable dismissal of the importance of religion and ideology in the debate about political Islam – a dismissal especially evident in the media and in academia. They wish to enhance and extend that debate. Enabling progressive Muslim scholars represents one way of countering extremism and its ideological narrative. An honest and engaging discussion of political Islam in its violent as well as gradualist forms should lead to new and pragmatic solutions.

Notes

1   "Tony Blair: West Must Fight not only ISIS, but its Ideology", *CNN*, 21 September 2014, www.cnn.com/2014/09/21/world/europe/tony-blair-isis-islam/ (viewed 30 September 2014).

2 "Statement by the President on ISIL", *White House*, 10 September 2014, www.whitehouse.gov/the-press-office/2014/09/10/statement-president-isil-1 (viewed 30 September 2014).

3 "Saudi Poll to Reveal Public's Level of Sympathy for IS", *Al-Monitor*, 29 June 2014, http://www.al-monitor.com/pulse/ar/politics/2014/07/saudi-families-refuse-condolences-isis-position.html (viewed 30 September 2014).

4 "Conclusive Scholarly Opinions on ISIS", *Islam 21C*, 10 July 2014, www.islam21c.com/politics/conclusive-scholarly-opinions-on-isis/ (viewed 30 September 2014).

5 "Conclusive Scholarly Opinions on ISIS".

6 "Open Letter to al-Baghdadi", http://lettertobaghdadi.com/ (viewed 30 September 2014).

7 "English Translation of Ayman al-Zawahiri's letter to Abu Musab al-Zarqawi", October 2005, www.weeklystandard.com/Content/Public/Articles/000/000/006/203gpuul.as (viewed 15 May 2015).

8 Monte Palmer and Princess Palmer, *Islamic Extremism: Causes, Diversity, and Challenges*. Lanham: Rowman & Littlefield Publishers, 2008, p. 249.

9 Mansoor Moaddel, *Islamic Modernism, Nationalism, and Fundamentalism: Episode and Discourse*. Chicago: University of Chicago Press, 2005, p. 210.

10 "Empowering Local Partners to Prevent Violent Extremism in the United States", *White House*, August 2011, http://www.whitehouse.gov/sites/default/files/empowering_local_partners.pdf (viewed 20 September 2014); "Strategic Implementation Plan for Empowering Local Partners to Prevent Violent Extremism in the United States", *White House*, December 2011, http://www.whitehouse.gov/sites/default/files/sip-final.pdf (viewed 20 September 2014). Both documents were analyzed with the Text Analyser (http://textalyser.net/).

11 Frank J. Gaffney, "Enemy Inside the Wire", *The Washington Times*, 31 October 2014.

12 Jerome P. Bjelopera, "Countering Violent Extremism in the United States", Washington: Congressional Research Service, 19 February 2014, p. 17, fas.org/sgp/crs/homesec/R42553.pdf (viewed 20 September 2014).

— 1 —

THE ROLE OF RELIGION IN THE BATTLE SPACE SINCE 9/11

Patrick Sookhdeo

Islamic terrorist attacks serve a clear and focused ideology, a set of beliefs and goals that are evil, but not insane. Some call this evil Islamic radicalism; others, militant Jihadism; still others, Islamo-fascism. Whatever it's called, this ideology is very different from the religion of Islam.
—President George W. Bush, October 2005[1]

...we reject the notion that al-Qaïda represents any religious authority. They are not religious leaders, they are killers; and neither Islam nor any other religion condones the slaughter of innocents.
—President Barack Obama, May 2010[2]

This is a religious ideology, a strain within the worldwide religion of Islam, as far removed from its essential decency and truth as Protestant gunmen who kill Catholics or vice versa, are from Christianity.
—Prime Minister Tony Blair, July 2005[3]

Introduction: Understanding the Threat

Understanding a threat is key to being able to counter it effectively. The threat that violent Islamism poses to the West must be understood as a cultural battle, an ideological battle, a political battle, and a theological battle.

The concept of the cultural battle – Huntington's "clash of civilizations"[4] – is now being more widely recognized, despite its original rejection by many. Yet, it covers only one element of the truth. In recent years, American and other Western policymakers have also come to recognize the importance of ideology in the struggle against violent Islamism. But an equally crucial step has yet to be taken by many, namely, to acquire a correct understanding of the religious ideology of the Islamists. A correct understanding of the ideology is possible only by means of a correct understanding of the theology that undergirds it.

Historical Misunderstandings

Forgetting the Theology Behind the Ideology

Most Americans – experts, officials, and civilians – have still not addressed the role of Islam in bin Laden's activities and message in a frank and analytic manner. While since September there has been more discussion of the role of religion in the war in which the United States is engaged, this discussion continues to occur within the confines of what a British journalist has described as the West's "suffocating atmosphere of multicultural political correctness." Bin Laden's supporters are said to "pray to the God of hate ... [and are] driven by pure hate and nihilism," their faith is decried as "terrorist fundamentalism," and they are demonized as "fiends ... [and] dedicated fanatics" who hate "with every fiber of their twisted soul".[5]

The quotations cited by Michael Scheuer were all from the first four months after 9/11. But, as can be seen from the quotations at the head of this paper, serious misunderstandings regarding the role of Islam in Islamist terrorism continued over the next decade. President Bush, President Obama and Prime Minister Blair all expressed their belief that there is no relationship between Islam and Islamist terrorism or its guiding ideology. They failed to recognize that it is an interpretation of the theology of Islam that validates the terrorism of al-Qaeda (AQ) and its associates in their own eyes.

After 9/11 Henry A. Crumpton, who was Deputy Chief (Operations) of the CIA's Counterterrorist Center, was tasked by President George W. Bush with defeating AQ and Osama bin Laden. Crumpton recalls in his memoir how he considered many Muslims to be America's allies in the struggle against AQ and its affiliates:

Our focus should be on al-Qaeda and their affiliates. We must define our enemy in very specific, very narrow terms. This is not a war of us against Islam. It's just the opposite. Our Muslim allies are the most important allies that we have. We must reach out to them, reassure them, empower them, and build alliances across the true Islamic faith. And not just with Muslim governments but with Muslim institutions and leaders from all sectors. This conflict is against al-Qaeda, a non-state actor. We must forge alliances with other nonstate actors. We and our Muslim allies must defeat al-Qaeda together.[6]

Crumpton rightly affirms that Muslims should be our allies, but how did he conceive that AQ had emerged from the wider Muslim culture? He does not appear to understand that religion had motivated both bin Laden and the entity that bin Laden created. Indeed, his comment about building alliances "across the true Islamic faith" suggests an assumption that whatever kind of religious ideology inspired and drove bin Laden and his followers, it was not derived from "the true Islamic faith". How did he envisage that Muslim allies could defeat them without tackling the religious ideology that motivated and drove bin Laden and his followers? Crumpton even adds that Muslim clerics would be included amongst America's allies.

A few weeks after 9/11, Crumpton attended a briefing with President Bush at Camp David to discuss a strategy for a response to AQ in Afghanistan. At the briefing, CIA analyst Emile Nakhleh described the ideological impact of AQ on Muslims around the world.[7] Nakhleh, a Palestinian Christian, had joined the CIA in 1993 and eventually became Director of the Political Islam Strategic Analysis Program in the Directorate of Intelligence. He often gave solo briefings to senior policymakers. Nakhleh's fascinating book, *A Necessary Engagement*,[8] written after his retirement in 2006, focuses on the ideology of Islamism but without recognizing any link with the theology of Islam itself. He holds that Muslims living in nonMuslim-majority countries "should be able to reconcile their faith and their citizenship in these countries".[9] We can be very thankful that large numbers of Muslims living in minority contexts of this kind do indeed succeed in reconciling their two identities as Muslims and as citizens of a nonMuslim-majority country. But it should be acknowledged that this reconciliation is not necessarily straight-forward and automatic, for a Muslim who is a good citizen in a nonMuslim context can follow only certain interpretations of Islam and not others.

Nakhleh appears to care mainly about whether any particular Islamic group accepts or eschews violence as a method of achieving its goals. He

13

shows little interest in knowing what the goals are, an attitude shared more generally by the American policymakers whom he briefed.[10] To focus on the means and not the end is extraordinarily short sighted. Islamists all share the same aim – the recreation of the Caliphate, ruled by shari'a – and this is an end result completely incompatible with freedom, equality or democracy. Daniel Pipes asserts that "nonviolent Islamists pose a greater threat than the violent ones", arguing that the nonviolent methods are more effective than the violent.[11] He will certainly be proved right if the U.S. government is content to let nonviolent Islamists have their way in remolding politics, economics and society in their countries, while focusing all their attention on restraining the violence of the violent Islamists.

Nakhleh writes much about ideology but little about theology. Similarly, *The 9/11 Commission Report* recognized that the AQ ideology was a root cause of Islamist terrorism, but failed to acknowledge that the ideology was itself rooted in the classical interpretation of the religion of Islam, as formulated in Islam's first three centuries by the consensus of scholars of the main schools of Islam. As the Report stated:

> The enemy is not Islam, the great world faith, but a perversion of Islam. The enemy goes beyond al-Qaeda to include the radical ideological movement, inspired in part by al-Qaeda, that has spawned other terrorist groups and violence. Thus our strategy must match our means to two ends: dismantling the al-Qaeda network and, in the long term, prevailing over the ideology that contributes to Islamist terrorism.[12]

The 9/11 Commission, Nakhleh, and Crumpton all optimistically asserted that it is possible to develop a strategy that separates AQ violence from the religion of Islam. Crumpton was right in asserting that the U.S. and the West are not at war with Islam. This point must continue to be affirmed, for the Western nations cannot be at war with a religion. However, what he and Nakhleh have failed to appreciate fully is that a religion can have multiple interpretations. If any of those interpretations leads to religious violence, then those interpretations must be addressed, which makes addressing the religion itself unavoidable. There has to be a battle of ideas, and it has to include theology.

Trying to Fight the Battle of Ideas Without Using Theology

As Walid Phares has written, "[A] War of Ideas is raging, relentlessly, behind the War on Terror. The outcome of the second is ineluctably conditioned by the consequences of the first."[13]

Donald Rumsfeld was much mocked in some quarters when, in 2002, as Secretary of Defense, he sought to distinguish "known unknowns" from "unknown unknowns". But his realism and his humility in acknowledging the administration's lack of knowledge and understanding and its inability to change other people's thinking should be commended. In 2009 he said:

> If I were grading, I would say we probably deserve a "D" or "D-plus" as a country as to how well we're doing in the battle of ideas that's taking place in the world today.[14]

The 9/11 Commission Report, issued on July 22, 2004, had urged the need for the U.S. to use public diplomacy to counter the insurgent ideology. A year later, Karen Hughes, a former television reporter who had been a close advisor of President George W. Bush, was appointed to head up efforts to do this, despite the fact that she appears to have had no background knowledge of the Islamic theology that she needed to counter.[15]

The lack of success of American public diplomacy in changing Islamist ideas can be attributed in part at least to the inefficacy of some of the methods attempted. One example is Radio Sawa, a 24 hour Arabic language service that was launched in 2002 to replace Voice of America's twelve hour, content rich Arabic service. Radio Sawa plays mainly pop music, both Arab and Western. It has large audiences amongst young people in the Middle East and is therefore deemed successful, but does it have any kind of relevant effect in the war of ideas when the ideas to be changed are based on theology? Robert Reilly comments:

> In a war of ideas, performing a lobotomy on your enemy might be a good move. It is almost unheard of to perform a lobotomy on yourself, and then declare it a success. How would you like to have a superpower adolescent in your neighborhood?[16]

Ideology

Mohamed al-Zawahiri, brother of AQ's leader Ayman al-Zawahiri, has said that "the strength of Al Qaeda is not in its leaders but in its ideology".[17] Western leaders now understand this point too. But what exactly is the ideology that gives AQ its strength?

The ideology of Islamism is derived directly from the theology of Islam itself. It would be dangerously misleading to draw a line of separation between one and the other, for they are intimately connected.

Historical Roots of Ideology

All of the main Islamic sources can be used to justify violence. The Qur'an itself, the Islamic source of primary importance, contains some very peaceable verses, but these are contradicted by some very belligerent verses, such as the "sword verse" in the Qur'an: "When the sacred months are past, kill the idolaters wherever you find them, and seize them, besiege them, and lie in wait for them in every place of ambush..." (Q 9:5). And also:

> Fight those who believe not in God nor the Last day, nor hold that forbidden which hath been forbidden by God and His Apostle, nor acknowledge the Religion of Truth, (even if they are) of the People of the Book, until they pay the jizya with willing submission, and feel themselves subdued (Q 9:29).

The standard Islamic doctrine of abrogation teaches that, in cases of conflicting teaching within the Qur'an, the later verses take precedence over the earlier verses. Although the relative dating of certain Qur'anic verses has never been settled by Islamic scholars, there is no debate over the general statement that the peaceable verses date from Muhammad's early days in Mecca, while the aggressive verses date from Medina, where he lived for the last ten years of his life. According to classical Islam, it is therefore the hostile verses calling for war and violence against nonMuslims that must be followed.

The well-known Egyptian scholar, Nasr Hamid Abu Zayd (1943-2010), has noted:

> If we follow the rules of interpretation developed from the classical "science of Koranic interpretation", *it is not possible to condemn terror-*

ism in religious terms. It remains completely true to the classical rules in its evolution of sanctity for its own justification. This is where the secret of its theological strength lies.[18]

Second in importance to the Qur'an are the *hadith*, various collections of traditions recording the words and deeds of Muhammad and his earliest followers. These *hadith*, though varying in authenticity and therefore in authority, are extremely influential in guiding devout Muslims, especially on subjects where the Qur'an may be silent or ambiguous. But on the question of violence, they fully back up the teaching of the later verses of the Qur'an, since they include many stories of violence by Muhammad and the first Muslims.

The importance of Muhammad's model (*sira*) cannot be overstated, for devout Muslims set themselves to imitate every aspect of his life. The *hadith* record his involvement in raids, wars and assassinations, particularly targeting pagans and Jews. Often he explicitly commanded such violence.

The influential Islamist Abdallah 'Azzam (1941-1989) celebrates Muhammad's role as a military leader:

> Jihad was a way of life for the Pious Predecessors (Salaf-us-Salih), and the Prophet (SAWS) was a master of the Mujahideen and a model for fortunate inexperienced people...
>
> The total number of military excursions which he (SAWS) accompanied was 27...
>
> He himself fought in nine of these; namely Badr; Uhud, Al-Muraysi, The Trench, Qurayzah, Khaybar, The Conquest of Makkah, Hunayn and Taif... This means that the Messenger of Allah (SAWS) used to go out on military expeditions or send out an army at least every two months.[19]

From the Qur'an and the *hadith*, the classical Islamic scholars derived a detailed set of laws, the shari'a, to guide Muslims in their personal devotional life, their family life and every aspect of society and governance, including relations between the Islamic state and other states. Such relations were to be based primarily on conquest and military subjugation, and within the shari'a are carefully codified rules on how to achieve this.

The example of war-fighting set by Muhammad continued without a break after his death in 622 A.D. and led to a breathtakingly rapid expansion of Islamic power by the conquest of nonMuslims across the Middle East, North Africa and parts of Europe and Asia. Alongside this were internal wars amongst Muslims, often over dynastic, leadership and tribal issues. Barely 20 years after Muhammad's death, a civil war had split the Muslims into three groups: the Kharijis, the Shi'as and the main body, now called the Sunnis.

Theological Components of Ideology

The resurgence of Islamism began in the first half of the 20th century and has particularly accelerated and spread since the 1970s. Starting with the basic Islamic doctrine that Allah is one, Islamism argues from divine unity to divine sovereignty to divine law. The one Allah is sovereign over the whole world and his law (shari'a) should govern every place and person.

Islamism views the religion of Islam as inherently political. It sees a unity of religion (*din*) and state (*dawla*); there is no dichotomy or "church-state" separation. The Qu'ran and shari'a contain the perfect recipe for a complete social and political system (*nizam*). Sayyid Qutb (1906-1966), the main ide-ologue of the Muslim Brotherhood, defined the goal of Islamism as: "the restoration of Islamic life in an Islamic society governed by the Islamic creed and the Islamic conception as well as by the Islamic Shar'iah and the Islamic system."[20] In other words, the ultimate aim of Islamism is for Islam to achieve worldwide political dominance. The state is considered to be the best tool for implementing Allah's law, shari'a, by which all humans should govern their lives. If Islam can gain political power in the state, then it will be able to enforce shari'a. There can be no permanent peace except under Islamic rule. Therefore there will be perpetual jihad, fighting "in Allah's way", until every part of the globe is ruled by shari'a.

Islamists make much use of certain theological concepts within Islam. One of these is *jahiliyya*, the ignorance and idolatry of preIslamic Arabia. Islamists see *jahiliyya* wherever a society is not run in strict accordance with shari'a. They therefore feel obligated to attack it, just as Muhammad attacked, subdued and converted the Arab pagans, Jews and Christians of his day. Many Muslim political leaders and governments of Muslim-majority countries are condemned by Islamists for not conducting themselves as prop-er Muslims should. By a process known as *takfir*, the nonIslamist Muslims are condemned by the Islamists as apostates and heretics, not Muslims at all, and this status makes them legitimate targets for jihad.

For instance, Abd al-Salam Faraj, founder of the Egyptian *Jihad* organization that assassinated President Sadat in 1982, taught that while the Egyptian masses are composed of both Muslims and *jahilis* intermixed, the rulers are all *jahili* and under *takfir* because while claiming to be Islamic they rule according to their own whims and not according to shari'a.[21]

So Islamists find theological justification for waging jihad against internal enemies such as "apostate" secular Muslim regimes as well as against external enemies such as the infidel West. While other Muslims may debate whether "jihad" means "warfare" or whether it means the personal struggle with sin and the struggle to right wrongs in society, Islamists have no doubt that actual violence is involved in jihad. While other Muslims may debate whether jihad is a communal duty or an individual duty, Islamists have no doubt that each and every Muslim should be personally active in jihad in some capacity or another. Indeed the duty of jihad is elevated by some to become a sixth "pillar" alongside the standard five pillars of Islam, the compulsory duties required of every Muslim: reciting the creed, praying, fasting, giving alms and going on pilgrimage to Mecca.[22] In the words of Faraj, "Know that when jihad is an individual duty, there is no need to ask permission of your parents... as the jurists have said, it is thus similar to prayer and fasting."[23]

Other theological concepts on which Islamists focus include *istishad*, the glorification of martyrdom, recalling in particular the principle of assassinations established by the Kharijis in the 7th century and the principle of suicide missions and assassinations established by the Assassins in the 11th and 12th centuries. The memory of the *Khilafa* (Caliphate) is very dear to their hearts, and they long to see it restored; indeed, they see it as a shari'a duty to work towards this end.

As already mentioned, they place great emphasis on the theological concept of *tawhid*, that is, the unitary and uniform vision of Allah, universe and society: one god, one people, one law. This concept teaches that as Allah's physical laws are imposed on the universe, so Allah's religious laws (shari'a) should be imposed on society. In other words, Allah's unity should be imposed on all by means of a unitary system of shari'a. Related to this is the concept of *hakimiyya* (*rabbaniyya*), meaning the implementation of *tawhid* by Allah's sovereignty. Again the practical outworking is that all legal and political systems must be based on shari'a.

As the above has made clear, Islamism is very much centered on shari'a, which is seen as the only criterion of legitimacy. Islamists are driven to seek to implement shari'a in every state in order to fulfil God's will. Hasan al-Banna, founder of the Muslim Brotherhood, demanded that legislation in Muslim states be derived from the prescriptions of shari'a as derived from Qur'an and Sunna. Shari'a is a comprehensive system that includes all spheres of life and al-Banna defined the movement's goal as establishing an Islamic state under shari'a.[24] According to Sayyid Qutb, the greatest sin of the modern world, both Western and Muslim, is the usurping of God's sovereignty and legislative authority. Man has no authority to make laws, only to interpret and apply God's law, shari'a: "Sharia is best because it comes from Allah." True Islam means unquestioningly accepting shari'a because it is God's revealed will. Any group, society, or regime that fails to implement shari'a is to be declared apostate, and jihad by force is legitimate in annihilating it and replacing it with a true Islamic state on the model of Medina under the Prophet.[25]

Islamism is also characterized by its view of Islam as revolution, the protest of the poor and oppressed, the "wretched of the earth". Violence is seen as a purifying force. This is effectively a type of liberation theology. Ali Shariati, ideologue of the Islamist revolution in Iran, developed a discourse very similar to Christian Liberation Theology. He maintained that Islam is a revolutionary ideology because from its inception it sided with the oppressed. Muhammad had fought for social equality and surrounded himself with the deprived of society.[26] Islam is biased towards the poor because its founding liberating document, the Qur'an, states that "God is the God of the oppressed" and the "God of the deprived".[27]

Alison Pargeter for example comments that Qutb's doctrines resonated with young Islamists across the world who eagerly responded to his radical ideas stimulated by the student revolutions in Europe in the 1960s and western radical leftist thought (as exemplified by Fanon's *Wretched of the Earth)* which they sought to integrate into Islamist ideology.[28]

Islamists have what many would consider a naïve and utopian view of man's inherent goodness (*fitra*), which in itself is based on Islamic theology. They believe that humans will flourish under a worldwide Islamic system that ensures Allah's will is done on earth. They see the world in terms of dichotomies: good and evil, Allah and Satan. Everyone must choose sides; there is no neutral ground, and there are no innocent civilians. They are given to scapegoating and to conspiracy theories, identifying evil enemies who are set on destroying them at all times and in all places. Thus Sayyid Qutb senses a worldwide conspiracy of the Crusading Christian West, Marxist Communism, and World Jewry against true Islam. These three forces are *jahiliyya* at its worst, enemies of God always plotting the destruction of Islam. Qutb sees hostility to Islam as inherited, inherent and latent in the West since Crusader days. Orientalism transmitted the distorted versions of Islam absorbed during the Crusades, the Spanish *Reconquista*, the fall of Constantinople, and the Reformation to secular Europe who inherited the contempt for all things Islamic. This anti-Islamic spirit continues to unite all contemporary Western states and cultures.[29]

Policies of Engagement: No Overarching Strategy and Erroneous Approaches

Three Arenas of Policies

After 9/11, the U.S. very quickly developed counterterrorist strategies relating primarily to the homeland. Furthermore, in its attacks and invasions of both Afghanistan in 2001 and Iraq in 2003, it had to develop a counterinsurgency strategy of engagement. But there was a third and wider engagement into which the U.S. also had to enter, and that was with the Muslim world at large.

Yet while recognizing that there was a war of ideas, the U.S. has struggled to make the necessary policy decisions. The homeland policy, as I was told in an international conference on counterterrorism by the U.S. delegates, was not allowed to address issues of religion because of the current understanding of church-state separation, or what could effectively be considered a misunderstanding of church-state separation. This has meant that only societal structures can be addressed, i.e. the organizations that extremists may be using, while the theological and ideological underpinnings are deliberately ignored. As a result, the core ideology is never addressed.

However, in overseas theaters and with the global Muslim community, the military and intelligence communities have felt able to address religion at its source, including deconstructing its core ideology. It is greatly to the detriment of homeland security that they do not feel able to do the same within the U.S. itself.

In the early development of counterterrorism (under the name the "War on Terror," which later came to be so derided), the primary objective was to seek out and destroy the terrorist networks as well as to address the perceived grievances that were thought to give rise to terrorism. This policy was adopted not only by the U.S. itself but by other countries as well, as the U.S.'s reach developed.

Another strand of engagement had to do with moving on from the first stage of battle, in which the "enemy" was fairly speedily defeated. After this had happened, the question arose of how to engage in a sustained counterinsurgency war, which included winning over the population while still pursuing the insurgents.

In the third type of engagement, the U.S. recognized that it had to find some way of neutralizing the "hatred" that it felt many in the Muslim world had for the U.S. and in particular to deal with the many who were supportive of bin Laden or at least sympathetic towards him. This meant the U.S. had to engage in a policy of public diplomacy and eventually even to develop a policy of engaging with the Islamists.

Despite this official homeland policy, in practice a strategy of understanding religion was active in the CIA from at least 1996.[30] Also, according to Ali Soufan, an FBI advisory special agent from 1997 to 2005, at least some in the FBI were also concerned with the ideology of AQ, even if not with Islam itself.

Ali Soufan has been tracking AQ since the 1990s and recognizes that it is the potent Islamist ideology of AQ that allows it to continue successfully recruiting to its ranks, replacing the members killed or captured by the U.S. The U.S., says Soufan, has focused on dealing with the central AQ body and has tackled neither its ideology nor its regional and national affiliates.[31] These local affiliates, such as al-Qaeda in the Arabian Peninsula or the Nigerian group known as Boko Haram, promote the AQ message. This failure of understanding has cost the U.S. dearly.

"Terrorists who endorse Osama bin Laden's jihadist message inevitably move on to the global war against the West," Soufan states. Even bin Laden began by focusing on a local issue: the presence of American troops in his homeland, Saudi Arabia. Soufan therefore urges that the U.S. should use not only military and intelligence tools against the AQ network, but also educational tools to rebut the religious ideology that motivates all the member groups.[32] This ideology is summed up by Soufan as "blaming the West for the Muslim world's problems, rejecting anyone who doesn't follow al-Qaeda's specific beliefs and claiming that terrorism is the only way to deal with opponents".[33] Whilst Soufan is right in emphasizing the need to tackle ideology, and he explains the al-Qaeda mobilization rhetoric, he, too, omits the need to look at the theological underpinning of that ideology.[34]

Over the years, many experts were brought in to advise both President Bush and President Obama on how the U.S. should engage with the Muslim world and on how it should deal with AQ. These included academics, politicians, military personnel and even retired missionaries. Yet despite these efforts, it is still difficult to see a successful strategy emerging, one that would address both the terrorist threats to the U.S. and the position in the Muslim world, where some governments are allied to Islamist extremism, or where Islamist extremism is taking hold within the population.

Of course, much was attempted with the U.S.'s partners, particularly in the West. Counterterrorism strategies were developed at the UN, the OSCE and other international entities. But to have an overarching policy set by the U.S. government that would not just address the immediate problems but also have long-term efficacy has been difficult to achieve. This is partly due to the fact that different contexts require different solutions, and so to develop a single solution would not have been possible. Equally, politicians are only in office for a fixed period of time, and so, while one could develop structures that could last beyond each presidency, policies would be subject to the administration of the day. All this has made it difficult to develop a single line of approach. As a result, multiple approaches have been developed, depending on the context and the time period. But this has left the U.S. vulnerable to uncertainty about exactly how to deal with AQ and Islamist extremism.

Counterterrorist Strategies Abroad and At Home

Separating Violent and Nonviolent Islamists?

This problem is further confused by the growing argument that we must separate the non-violent Islamists from the violent Islamists. The Brookings Institution argued strongly in 2010 that the U.S. was in a state of confusion in addressing the issue of Islamism, and urged a major shift in policy so that the U.S. could engage with the nonviolent Islamists.

The United States has long shown confusion in its policies toward Islamist political movements in the Middle East. By conflating moderates and hardliners, and believing that moderate Islamists pose a threat to U.S. strategic interests in the region, the United States has opted to support regimes that limit democratic participation. American administrations have backed, with limited exceptions during the presidency of George W. Bush, authoritarian regimes that not only impose restrictions on, but use intimidation and violence against Islamist groups and parties.[35]

The idea was to strengthen relationships with nonviolent Islamists, and potentially look to their coming to power, to achieve stability in their countries and regions. Violent extremists would be excluded from this process and be rendered ineffective by legal means. While commanding ISAF forces in Iraq (July 2010-July 2011), General David Petraeus created the policy of "reconciling the reconcilables" and neutralizing the irreconcilables, then using the reconcilables against the irreconcilables.

Engaging With the Wrong Muslims?

The feasibility of Petraeus's doctrine depends entirely on where the line is drawn between reconcilables and irreconcilables. It should not be drawn between moderate, peaceable Islamists and hardline, violent Islamists, as suggested by the Brookings Institution. For all Islamists have the same strategic aim, that is, the establishing of a worldwide Islamic state under shari'a. The peaceable and the violent differ only in the tactics they are willing to use for achieving this aim. Peaceable Islamists should not be viewed as "reconcilable", for they are as implacably opposed to Western values of freedom and democracy as are their violent comrades. Attempts to "reconcile" the peaceable Islamists are therefore likely to prove fruitless.

Engaging primarily with "moderate" Islamists, as advised by the Brookings Institution, would be a sadly and dangerously misguided policy. The Muslims to engage with in the first instance are the moderate, reformed Muslims who reject the idea of establishing a shari'a-run Islamic state in which Muslims subjugate nonMuslims and men dominate women, but who embrace American and Western democratic ideals, such as the separation of church and state and the freedom and autonomy of the individual.

The American policy of supporting the Muslim Brotherhood in Egypt is a prime example of misguided engagement with the "wrong" Muslims. During their short time in power, the Brotherhood made great strides towards the establishment of an Islamic state ruled by shari'a, with all the negative consequences that entails for women, for nonMuslims, for liberty, for equality, for freedom of speech. It is their ultimate aim to establish such rule across the entire globe.

Of course, there may come a time and a place for discreet engagement with Islamists, in order to try to achieve a lasting solution to the challenge they pose. It makes little difference whether the Islamists engaged are violent or nonviolent, because it is their shared Islamist goals that are the ultimate challenge to the West. If such an engagement occurs, it is essential that those who take part on behalf of the West recognize the nature of the people with whom they are doing business and the nature of their aims and motivation. The nature of these aims and motivations remains linked to their ultimate goal of the establishment of a hegemonic Islamic world order under the rule of shariʻa. It is also essential that such negotiators have recognized the non-negotiables of the West; that is, they know which principles and aspects of the Western worldview cannot be sacrificed, in the pursuit of peace, to Islamist desires. Ultimately there is a battle of ideologies taking place. Patricia Harrison, Assistant Secretary of State for Educational and Cultural Affairs, has rightly highlighted the importance of knowing ourselves in the battle of ideas, which is in effect the battle for truth: "If we do not define ourselves, others will do it for us."[36]

Following an Outdated UK Model

After 9/11, the UK developed a counterterrorism strategy called CON-TEST, which had four components: Prevent, Pursue, Protect and Prepare.[37] After some time it became clear that there were serious flaws in Prevent because it had failed to tackle ideology and was sometimes even funding the extremist organizations it should have been confronting. In June 2011, there-fore, a revised CONTEST strategy was launched, in which Prevent now focused on ideology, institutions and individuals.[38] Specifically, ideology was to be challenged by a more sustained and more focused counterterrorist mes-sage, with much attention being given to the "exploitation" of the internet by extremists for radicalization and recruitment.

The focus on institutions concerned places where people "may be espe-cially vulnerable to the influence of charismatic radicalizers," for example, universities and colleges, prisons, mosques. The new plan was to work with a broad range of partners – governmental and nongovernmental – to ensure these places did not become "incubators of extremism".

With regard to individuals, the strategy was to put people at the center of a "more granular strategy". Community empowerment and engagement were held to be vital, and a cost-effective flagship program called Channel was used. This new framework is a multiagency approach aimed at protecting individuals at risk from radicalization and of being drawn into terrorist-related activities. It uses existing collaboration between local authorities, statutory partners, the police and the local community in order to assess risks and vulnerabilities of the specific individual. This is based on understanding her/his engagement with terrorist ideology, their intention to cause harm and their capability to do so. It then develops the most appropriate support plan for these individuals.[39]

Meanwhile, at the request of the American embassy in London, Quintan Wiktorowicz, a U.S. academic, was sent over from the States to study UK counterterrorism strategy. In January 2011, he returned to the U.S. and joined the National Security Council as Senior Director for Global Engagement.[40] Seven months later, in August 2011, the White House issued its strategy document *Empowering Local Partners to Prevent Violent Extremism in the United States.* This was based on the original, failed Prevent model, which had been abandoned by the British between Wiktorowicz's return to the U.S. and the White House's announcement of its new strategy on violent extremism.

Approaches to Religion

Misunderstanding Culture, Misunderstanding Ourselves?

It is important to understand the relationship between religion and culture. Twenty-six centuries ago, the Chinese general Sun Tzu wrote, "It is said that if you know your enemies and know yourself, you will not be imperiled in a hundred battles." A good general will know his own side's strengths and weaknesses, as well as those of the enemy. Likewise, in the battle of ideas, it is vital to understand our own cultural starting point, and to recognize the different cultural inputs that shape us. Western rationalism is based on culture-bound values and not dictated by universal norms. Many concepts strongly ingrained in Westerners are far from universal amongst humankind; for example, the notion of a separation between church and state is still uniquely Western.

As culture entered the battle space, in particular following the initial failure of the U.S. and coalition forces in engaging the insurgents in Iraq, General Petraeus's prestigious work on counterinsurgency recognized the importance of culture:

> Cultural knowledge is essential to waging a successful counterinsurgency. American ideas of what is "normal" or "rational" are not universal. To the contrary, members of other societies often have different notions of rationality, appropriate behavior, level of religious devotion, and norms concerning gender… For this reason, counterinsurgents – especially commanders, planners, and small-unit leaders – should strive to avoid imposing their ideals of normalcy on a foreign cultural problem.[41]

A characteristic of our highly secularized Western culture is a tendency to see religion as a product of culture, rather than the other way round. By contrast, for many in the developing world, not least the Muslim-majority world, culture emanates from religion. The Western assumption that religion emanates from culture has had serious ramifications as the military have sought to engage the culture but found themselves unable fully to grapple with religion. It is telling that David Kilcullen's "three pillars of insurgency" comprise security, politics and economics, with neither religion nor even culture regarded as a component.[42]

Misunderstanding Religion by Taking a Secular Approach

The U.S. sought to understand religion through social structure; consequently, in military theaters today, religion is treated under the heading of culture. Likewise, understanding of religion is built on the basis of religious phenomenology. The focus lies on the institutions that make up the religion, in the hope that an understanding of these will lead to an understanding of the religion. This was the approach taken by many scholars of comparative religion in the 1960s and 1970s.

I would argue, however, that this approach is mistaken and therefore unlikely to bring a true understanding. The basic fault with this methodology is that cause and effect are the other way round. In reality, social structure is derived from religion, not religion from social structure. This is particularly true of religions such as Islam and Christianity, religions that claim to be based on revelation. Social structure, culture and institutions are derived from the religious principles of this revelation. Furthermore if a religion, such as Islam, does not separate sacred from secular or spiritual from social, in particular in its classical and legal formulations, then it is not possible to deal simply with social structure, that is, with the organizations that are the vessels for terrorism and violence. It is essential to deal also with the inner core, which is the essential theology that gives rise to the ideology that gives rise to the institutions.

If one does not deal with a religion as it is understood by its own followers but rather views religion through the lens of modern secularists, there is bound to be a failure of understanding. Writing about the UK context, Alan Judd, in a review of Peter Bergen's book *Manhunt: From 9/11 to Abbottabad*, pointed out that not only do secularists struggle to understand the immensely formative power of personal religious belief, but also those who do grasp its potency are quickly in danger of paralysis and despair, as there seems to be no effective way to respond:

> There has been a tendency, in the British bureaucracy at least, to play down the religious and to play up everything else. This is partly because a secular culture finds it difficult to comprehend true religious enthusiasm and partly because if you do admit it, you can see no end to it – there's nothing to negotiate.[43]

Misunderstanding Religion by Reducing It to the PSYOP

In 2005 the Department of Defense issued a directive concerning stability operations, which were to be executed primarily by the U.S. Army Civil Affairs and Psychological Operations Command (PSYOP), headed at the time by Major General Herbert Altshuler. Altshuler described his unit's mission as:

> ...the bridge between the military commander on the ground and the civilian population in his area of operations. This includes the population, its leadership, elected, appointed or assumed, and the institutions of government and culture of that population.[44]

It is notable that the vital area of religion is not mentioned in this remit so must be deemed to be embedded within culture. Religion was thus considered part of culture, which was dealt with under psychological operations, which was in turn put under strategic communications (See below.).

Nevertheless, religion was taken very seriously. In both Afghanistan and Iraq there were informers in mosques to analyze the sermons and spot whether people were being radicalized and incited to launch an attack. The theological implications of dates and events were considered.[45] Conversely civilian-military (CIMIC) activities took place to engage and befriend, for example, meeting with clerics and providing resources for the Ramadan fasting month. Above all else, troops were trained to be sensitive to the Muslim religion and not to offend Muslim sensibilities.

χ Involvement in religious matters was the prerogative of individual commanders. There was no overall policy. Some chose to become very actively involved and others much less so. Some military, including a colonel I met from CENTCOM, believed religion had no part to play and focused only on the political aspects. But failing to take religion seriously allowed for crucial mistakes to be made; for example, the disastrous burning of the Qur'ans in Afghanistan in February 2012 was sanctioned by U.S. officers and resulted in the retaliatory killing of American soldiers.

It is worth noting also the position of the chaplains. While British chaplains did not get involved in anything with a military objective, seeing their work as purely spiritual and the pastoral care of the troops as their only responsibility, American chaplains were intimately involved with their commanders. American chaplains therefore did become involved in matters of religion, for example, advising their commanders on religious matters and supporting Muslim chaplains in the Afghan and Iraqi military.

Let us consider four case studies of military engagement with religious issues.

Case Studies

Afghanistan

In the ten-year period between 2001 and 2010, NATO had no official, coherent and strategic approach to religion in Afghanistan, but rather they responded on an ad hoc basis. They sought to build schools, which included Islamic religious teaching and so would be in effect partial madrasas; they also ran the mullahs' conference, but without an overarching strategy. In order to defeat the Taliban, they adopted a strategy that combined development (including education), kinetic attack to neutralize the Taliban, and psychological warfare to deconstruct the Taliban's ideology and methodology.

NATO did this by engaging in Friday mosque listening, in which the weekly mosque sermon was analyzed for ideological content with reference to jihad and violence, by paying the *ulema* (clerics) to write *fatwas* and distribute them across Afghanistan, and by involving radio, television and newspapers in disseminating a deconstructed message. This was done through psychological operations, which were a part of strategic communications.

Furthermore, NATO became involved in the *haj* pilgrimage, providing security for those who wanted to go on *haj*. They also provided protection for mullahs, particularly those engaged in children's schooling, and during Ramadan they ensured that appropriate food and sufficient fuel were available as well as people's other requirements. These were all aspects of a piecemeal policy to engage and befriend. To implement this strategy and develop the Human Terrain teams to guide it, the choice fell on social scientists, psychologists, anthropologists and others. Tellingly, there were no theologians employed. As a result, data pertaining to social structures could be acquired, but there was little theological understanding of its inner meaning and implications.

Increasingly, interpreters were used to provide theological interpretation, however in many instances the interpreters were ultraconservative Sunni Muslims who rejected Shi'ism and folk Islam. The problem with this was that interpreters often did not interpret literally but sought to communicate a speaker's meaning as they understood it, colored by their own theological convictions. The following example demonstrates the naivety sometimes shown by Western military and other personnel when engaging with such ultraconservatives. A U.S. Special Operations major once boasted how wonderfully spiritual and moderate his interpreter was, adding, as proof of the man's spirituality, that he had said if anyone were to desecrate his Qur'an he would strap explosives on himself, his wife and his children and blow everyone up. One has to ask how such a threat, surely expressing a dangerous fanaticism, could ever have been interpreted as evidence of spirituality and moderation. Presumably the major interpreted the man's remark as hyperbole, and not to be taken literally, but what grounds had he for making such an assumption?

Iraq

As in Afghanistan, mosque monitoring was employed, but there was a much more acute awareness, especially in southern Iraq, of theological issues, such as the relationship between Sunni and Shi'a Muslims, their different origins and theology, the Shi'a doctrine of the Mahdi and Messianism,[46] and the particular threat this could pose to coalition forces. Work was done on dates and times in the Islamic calendar and on the potential risks these could pose. Soldiers were trained not to offend Muslim sensibilities and were given a basic understanding of the nature of Islam.

Yet in spite of the greater attention paid to religious issues in Iraq, there were still major failings. There was a serious British failure to understand Moqtada al-Sadr, a charismatic Shi'a religious and political leader. Al-Sadr commanded the Mahdi Army militia and had a strong following amongst the poor and downtrodden Shi'a in areas such as the Sadr City neighborhood of Baghdad. The U.S. very rightly wanted to move against him in 2007-8, but the British opposed this. British intelligence analysts argued that Moqtada al-Sadr posed no threat to the coalition forces or to internal stability. He had requested two ministries within the then government: Education and Social Services. British Analysts did not understand the Shi'a doctrine of liberation theology and how Moqtada al-Sadr was able to use education to recruit and train a potent militia force and to use mosques as centers for providing social services, thereby welding the people to the mosque. He posed a threat that could not be neutralized. Yet intelligence dismissed him, arguing that because he was young, he must be insignificant. They failed to recognize that his black turban showed his direct descent from Muhammad, the importance of his father's position as a revered Grand Ayatollah who was considered by many Iraqi Shi'as to be a saint, the potential impact of liberation theology, the theocratic nature of Shi'ism, and the powerful concept of *bay'a* (the oath of personal loyalty). His Shi'a followers saw Moqtada al-Sadr as the *khalifa*, that is, the representative of Imam Muhammad al-Mahdi, the twelfth Imam, who disappeared near Baghdad in 874 and whom Shi'a Muslims expect to return and establish divine justice on earth. Thus, although young and relatively untrained, Moqtada al-Sadr was a major figure with huge influence.

Libya

Perhaps nowhere has the failure of the West to understand the religious dimension been more marked than in NATO's involvement in Libya, which saw the removal of Colonel Gaddafi. The main question is whether NATO breached the UN security resolution, which, while giving permission to overfly and protect, did not give permission to fund, train and arm rebel forces and militias on the ground. Another important question, which has arisen particularly since the killing of Ambassador Stevens in Libya,[47] is: how closely did NATO work with Saudi Arabia and in particular Qatar to encourage – however unwittingly – the development of AQ? A strange partnership was allowed to develop, whereby the U.S. and its allies, particularly the Gulf States, developed new allies on the ground, who sadly turned out to be elements of AQ. The West turned against Gaddafi, even though he had relinquished his nuclear program, paid compensation for the downed *Pan Am* plane, and suppressed the radical Islamists. Western governments, including Britain, decided to support Islamists of various types who helped bring down the Gaddafi regime by violent means. The West thus turned Gaddafi into an enemy to be destroyed, although he was firmly opposed to AQ. The West also embraced Qatar, which was hosting radical Islamist and terrorist leaders. Thus we ended up *de facto* supporting the very people who wanted to destroy us. After the fall of Gaddafi, Islamist and terrorist militias became the dominant entities within Libya, and it is currently suggested that AQ effectively controls southern Libya. Furthermore, sources have reported that arms, money and materials ferried out of Libya by Qatar into Mali are now fuelling the war there as more Islamists and extremists are deployed in West African nations.[48]

Syria

The pattern developed in Libya is now holding true for Syria. Not only are arms moving into Syria, funded by Gulf States and with logistics provided by the UK, France and the U.S., but also these arms are moving to radical sections within the Free Syrian Army and to al Nusra and AQ terrorists. Furthermore, there are suggestions that antiaircraft missiles, antitank missiles, sniper rifles and other weaponry are coming into Syria from Sudan,[49] which has good relations with Iran, the Syrian regime's main backer, but still seems willing for financial support to also supply the Sunni Islamist rebels. The British *Independent* daily newspaper recently carried an intriguing article about whether the U.S. government is now allied with AQ in Syria.[50] The U.S. and the UK, in developing a military and counterterrorist strategy, have embraced nations such as Saudi Arabia, with its Salafist Islam, and Qatar, which hosts the Muslim Brotherhood. Due to their postmodern secularist worldviews they have failed to take seriously the ideological aspects of these alliances, and this has resulted in the development of a flawed policy.

Analysis

Positively, we have seen that the U.S. military recognized the necessity to engage with religion in battlefield contexts, knowing that this would assist in their counterterrorism and counterinsurgency strategies. Furthermore, they addressed motivation, including the theological undergirding and the ideological expression of Islam in relation to warfare.

The military's main weaknesses, I would suggest, were twofold. First, they did not create a coherent approach at a strategic level but left it to individual commanders to act or not as they thought fit. Secondly, it was recognized that religion crosses many departments in the military, yet it was embedded in PSYOP. A more effective approach would have been to embed it in stabilization or, as in the UK, to develop a PRISM cell that would have been both academic and cross-departmental. The PRISM cell was a multidisciplinary cell made up of academics embedded in the command HQ with the purpose of advising the senior commanding officer on sensitive issues e.g. economics, social, political and cultural issues, and governing institutions.

In the homeland context, I would argue that the U.S. counterterrorism policy has been fatally flawed by the refusal to take seriously and address at an official level the theological underpinning and motivation of the terrorists; this is all the more surprising given that these factors have been recognized clearly in external theaters such as Afghanistan and Iraq.

The third type of engagement, that is, with the global Muslim community, has been fatally undermined by the U.S.'s activities around the world. President Obama's key speech in 2009 in Cairo signaled his intention to reach out to the Muslim world:

> We meet at a time of tension between the United States and Muslims around the world... I have come here to Cairo to seek a new beginning between the United States and Muslims around the world; one based upon mutual interest and mutual respect; and one based upon the truth that America and Islam are not exclusive, and need not be in competition.[51]

However, the speech has been largely dismissed, not only in Egypt but also in other Muslim-majority countries, and has come to be seen as complete hypocrisy and duplicity. This is because of a number of issues, including America's drone policy in Pakistan, the expansion of U.S. military engagement in Muslim-majority countries, with significant numbers of

Muslim women and children being killed, and the seeming betrayal of Egyptian President Mubarak and support for the Muslim Brotherhood. It has to be accepted that many Muslims of all persuasions around the world, not only Islamists, feel that America cannot be trusted.

There has been much confusion as to the exact role of religion in counterterrorism. While it is absolutely correct that the U.S. and her allies are not at war with Islam, they are at war with an interpretation of Islam that allows for violence and terrorism. The U.S. and her allies, including her Muslim allies, must have the courage to face up to this with honesty and truthfulness.

Some Suggested Responses

A variety of suggested responses to terrorism have been made and are detailed below. Many were ill-conceived, and some bordered on wishful thinking. A number were guided by a desire to address the issue of Islam, as if by sleight of hand, without naming it and without linking it to violence.

1. Encourage Muslims to return to Muhammad and the Qur'an. This response is based on the belief that Islamic violence started with the teachings of Ibn Taymiyya (1263-1328) and that if Muslims could return to the initial period of their faith they would drop the violent aspects. We shall see later, when we consider the teachings of classical Islam, that there is no logical basis for this approach.

2. Encourage Muslims to return to shari'a, for example in Indonesia and Nigeria. This response is based on the belief that if young men are encouraged to return to shari'a and live according to its principles, then they will not engage in violence, conflict and terrorism. This suggestion betrays a complete ignorance of the content of shari'a, as we shall see, and could have been made only by someone with no theological knowledge of Islam.

3. Create a new lexicon.[52] The idea here is to undercut the theology of jihad and violence and to remove their credibility amongst Muslims by not using traditional Islamic terminology. It requires that another vocabulary be developed, for example, speaking of Qutbi instead of jihadi, referring to Sayyid Qutb, whose books *Milestones* and *In the Shade of the Qur'an* are considered foundational for many contemporary Islamists. The hope is that if the elephant in the room is not mentioned, no one will realize it is there.

John O. Brennan, Barack Obama's assistant for Homeland Security and Counterterrorism, explained the theory as follows:

> Using the legitimate term jihad, which means to purify oneself or to wage a holy struggle for a moral goal, risks giving these murderers the religious legitimacy they desperately seek but in no way deserve.[53]

The 9/11 Commission Report, issued in July 2004, used the word "Islam" 322 times, "Muslim" 145 times, "jihad" 126 times and "jihadist" 32 times. Five years later, however, the National Intelligence Strategy of the United States, issued in August 2009, used none of these terms. Similarly, the FBI Counterterrorism Analytical Lexicon, published in 2008, the purpose of which is "to standardize the terms used in FBI analytical products dealing with counterterrorism," does not contain the words "Islam", "Muslim" or "jihad".

It is significant to note that the Muslim Public Affairs Council (MPAC), an advocacy and public policy organization, had themselves requested a new lexicon, although their motive may have been more to do with concern for the image of Islam:

> Terminology is important in defining our goals as well as removing roadblocks into hearts and minds. The 9/11 Commission identified Islamist terrorism as the threat. The MPAC recommends that the U.S. government find other terminology.[54]

4. Reject all linkage between Islam and violence. In 2012, U.S. General Martin Dempsey, Chairman of the Joint Chiefs of Staff, issued a memorandum to the Chiefs of the military services, the Commanders of the Combatant Commands and the Chief of the National Guard Bureau, requesting a second review of counterterrorism (countering violent extremism) training materials and lecturers used by the Department of Defense. The memorandum expressed concern that nothing should be "disrespectful of the Islamic religion" and that there should be no particular focus on Islamic radicalism.[55] This was a response to complaints by Islamists that the training provided had an anti-Islam bias.[56] Effectively, it banned lecturers from mentioning the concept of Islamic ideology.

5. Embrace the extremists in order to kill the terrorists. This is the policy already considered in some detail, namely, that of drawing a distinction between the nonviolent extremists (such as the Muslim Brotherhood) and violent extremists, using the former against the latter. It depends on the assumption that alienation, poverty and poor governance are the source of terrorism. As I have sought to make clear above, the two groups have the same goal, based on theology and ideology, so this policy cannot succeed.

Issues that Hamper Responses

The approach of U.S. and other Western governments and policy-makers is hampered by a number of factors, including the following:

- Political correctness
- Postcolonial guilt
- Wishful thinking
- Wars in the Islamic world that influence policy
- Misguided attempts to gain popularity in the Muslim world
- The priority given to searching for a quick fix, and the reluctance to recognize that the struggle is long-term

Whilst putting religion under PSYOP and so within CIMIC created its own set of difficulties, I would like to suggest six very practical reasons that would have made developing any overarching policy difficult:

1. In the first phase of the war in Iraq, cultural/religious issues were not a focus of interest; naturally all energies were directed to establishing control through Rumsfeld's 'shock and awe' option.
2. There was a lack of personnel with the appropriate training.
3. Academics who might have been involved would have been required to have top-level security clearance; many academics would not wish to bind themselves in this way and thus to sacrifice their academic freedom.
4. Recognizing their lack of expertise in a sensitive area, many commanders were reluctant to enter the religious field.
5. Any potential Muslim religious advisor would be liable to be killed by fellow-Muslims for serving the enemy.
6. There was a concern that if it ever became known that the military had tried to address Islam and become directly involved in religious matters,

this could have dire consequences in terms of accusations by Muslims that the American military were tampering with their religion. It would also alienate the allied Muslim governments they were engaged with.

Engaging with Islamists

Both in the wake of 9/11 and during the Arab Spring there were calls for the U.S. to engage positively with some Islamists. In fact, the U.S. already had a history of engaging with and supporting Islamists across the world.

During the Soviet-Afghan war of 1979-89, the American Operation Cyclone provided funding of up to $630 million a year, which was distributed through the Pakistani security services. The funds empowered violent Islamists such as Gulbuddin Hekmatyar and Osama bin Laden and helped to destroy secular-nationalist groups. According to *The Independent* "The US and Saudi Arabia both sent about $500m (pounds 300 m) annually between 1986 and 1989 to fund the mujahedin".[57]

According to Peter Mandaville:

In the 1980s and even part of the 1990s, U.S. diplomats in Egypt had fairly regular meetings with Islamists. In fact, regular engagement with Islamists has been a fact of life in U.S. foreign policy for a couple of decades across both Democratic and Republican administrations. U.S. embassies in countries like Morocco, Jordan, Yemen, Algeria, Kuwait, Pakistan, Bangladesh, Malaysia, and Indonesia have long had routine meetings with representatives of those countries' Islamist movements and parties. Several of those same parties have even participated in training and technical assistance programs funded by the United States Agency for International Development (USAID) and the National Endowment for Democracy (NED).[58]

There are still many in the security and political establishment who believe that funding "gradualist Islamists" will help to undermine violent Islamists. Emile Nakhleh, for example, proposes engagement with those who are designated as being unthreatening through utilizing "soft power" and strengthening cultural links to the West.[59]

As we have already seen, this position demonstrates a failure to understand that all Islamists have the same non-negotiable goal of establishing Islamic states across the world under shari'a. Furthermore, on a practical level, there would be some difficulty in categorizing any given individual or group, as the divide between "gradualist" and violent Islamists is often quite blurred. "Gradualist Islamists" help to radicalize Islamic communities, which leads to a greater terrorist threat. Engaging with the Islamists could also have the unintended consequence of undermining those Muslims who are seeking to reform Islam in a way that will make it truly compatible with modern values. Nakhleh himself proposes the empowerment of modernist Muslim reformers to confront radicalism.[60] It would, however, be tragic if this excellent policy were to be nullified by simultaneous engagement with Islamists.

It is essential not to underestimate the potency of Islamism, an ideological movement that moves easily from one context to another, nor to underestimate the length of the struggle that is likely to be needed against it.

Engaging With My Enemy's Enemy

There is an Arab saying that has become common parlance in the English-speaking world: "My enemy's enemy is my friend." But this approach can lead to some unexpected and undesirable alliances.

An "accidental" engagement with Islamists is currently taking place in the context of the civil war in Syria and, just prior to that, occurred in Libya, at least since the UK's involvement in overthrowing the Gaddafi regime. UK Prime Minister David Cameron and his administration now face the same problems as does the U.S. Having hailed ideology, together with individuals and institutions, as a primary plank from which to fight AQ and religious terrorism (albeit denoted as violent extremism), his administration now finds itself on the side of the Muslim Brotherhood of the Gulf States and potentially also the allies of AQ in Syria. This situation has arisen because the UK and U.S. appear to have decided that Syrian President Bashar al-Assad is their enemy, due to his brutal suppression of civilian demonstrations. They are therefore offering support of various kinds to Assad's enemy, the Free Syrian Army (FSA). But the Free Syrian Army has a galaxy of associated militias, most of which are Islamist, and some of which are closely linked to AQ. When the U.S. administration proscribed the strongly Islamist Syrian militia al Nusra, the FSA actually came out in support of al Nusra, which makes the U.S. and the FSA strange bedfellows.

An increasing number of Muslims from Europe, the U.S. and Canada are going to fight in theaters such as Libya and Syria. Were these European Muslims to turn up in Pakistan and Afghanistan they would be arrested, but arriving in Libya and now increasingly in Syria, they are frequently hailed in the West as freedom fighters and modern-day heroes. The individuals concerned see themselves as participating in wars of liberation and, fighting alongside terrorist organizations, they are learning techniques such as sniping, construction of IEDs, assassination, among others, that may easily be applied in their home country on their return.

A Muslim youth leader in Birmingham, UK, has stated that Prime Minister Cameron is helping the process of radicalization because these young Muslim men see the British government as backing the rebel forces in Syria and Libya. If that is indeed the case, then one may judge the British government to be complicit in their radicalization, with all the potential dangers that Western societies such as the UK and the U.S. will face in the future. For if these young men are heroes of a new jihad, how are they to be condemned if they practice in their home countries what they learned abroad? Are we repeating the same mistake of Afghanistan in 1979-89? There the US, the UK and their allies supported, funded and trained radical jihadis against the Soviets. Once the jihadis had managed to free Afghanistan from the Soviets, they turned violently against their Western mentors.

Implications

It is recognized that since 9/11 much thought, money and effort have been put into attempts both to defeat Islamist terrorism and to address the ideology that drives it. Some have claimed that AQ has been defeated and the "War on Terror" has been won. I believe, however, that these claims are premature and that we must be careful not to engage in wishful thinking.

Unless ideology and theology are clearly recognized as key drivers for Islamist radicalism, the prospect of being able to contain, let alone reduce, its impact is not hopeful. For example, in the context of the current Syrian conflict, Steven Heydemann, a senior adviser at the United States Institute of Peace, which works with the State Department, acknowledged in 2013 that the current momentum in Syria towards radicalism could be hard to reverse. The challenge, he said, is to end the conflict before "the opportunity to create a system of governance not based on militant Islamic law is lost".[61]

Can Islamist radicalism be defeated? Heydemann has expressed serious doubts about whether this can be achieved in the Syrian context, and many others are reluctantly coming to a similar conclusion about the question in general. If this pessimism is justified, as it may well be, there are serious consequences for Muslim countries as well as for the West. An ideology can be defeated only by a superior ideology. Yet what does the U.S. and its allies have to offer in terms of ideology? As the Italian Chief of Defense Staff, General Camporini, asked in his keynote address at a NATO conference[62] in Rome, "For what do our soldiers fight? We have no ideology."

Perhaps the single biggest failure of the West now is that the ideology, based on Judeo-Christian values that once underpinned their societies is no more. Contemporary Western societies seem to be based on nothing more substantial than pleasure and self-interest, postmodernism having apparently succeeded in deconstructing all absolute moral values. While a secular structure for society can be a valuable safeguard of many freedoms, secularism has now taken such control in the West that it has become the master, not the servant, of society. At the very point in time when Islamist radicalism and political Islam are gaining ground rapidly, secularism has to a great extent replaced faith in the West, the faith that was formerly the foundation of Western societies.

The current position of the Muslim Brotherhood, the first modern Islamist movement, is very instructive. In Egypt, moderate Muslims, secularists, and Christians have successfully joined forces to apply pressure against the Brotherhood in its country of origin, where the new government is leading the attack on the Brotherhood's ideology and doctrines. In Qatar, by contrast, the Brotherhood is flourishing and has established a new international headquarters there. Although Qatar is active with Saudi Arabia and the U.S. in striving to combat terrorism, its government is failing to tackle the ideology from which the terrorism stems. It is not sufficient for the West to engage kinetically with Muslim allies against terrorists if at the same time those Muslim allies are allowed to propagate an ideology that could in the end destroy the West.

The irony is that even if the West had a suitable ideology to offer in place of Islamism, they would still be severely hampered in dealing with Islamist ideologies because of those very principles that characterize democratic societies. In such societies, the law does not permit individuals and organizations to be banned merely for what they believe, only for breaking the law. It means, therefore, that extremists can continue to propagate their message (carefully avoiding open incitement to violence), knowing that little can be done to stop them. Furthermore, if banned, such organizations would simply change their form and name or go underground, making it harder to keep track of them and to monitor their activities. It would also considerably hinder any negotiations between governments and Islamists if their organizations were considered illegal. Furthermore, at the governmental level it is appropriate that governments deal with governments bilaterally, whatever their ideology.

A Way Forward

I would like to suggest four courses of action.

1. **Learn from the lessons of history**. The Islam of today most closely resembles European Christianity at the time of the Reformation, where religious doctrine, or theology, drove the many wars – sectarian, within states and between states – for over a hundred years. Separation of state and religion was the solution to this disaster, aimed at limiting the violence engendered by religious fanaticism's desire to impose its doctrines by force on those deemed heretical. Of course, politics, economics, class and self-interest also played significant roles, camouflaged in religious idiom.

2. **Refrain from facilitating the dissemination of Islamist theology and ideology**. Amongst the major disseminators are the U.S.'s allies, Saudi Arabia and Qatar. Continued support for these two nations simply enables them to continue freely with their global programs to promote the ideology that lies behind Islamist violence.

3. **Make proactive efforts to deconstruct this ideology**. The most effective way to do this is likely to be by funding appropriate Muslim scholars and by enabling their liberal interpretations of Islamic theology to be disseminated widely to the Muslim community worldwide. American cooperation in such projects should be discreet, as an overt American government input would hinder the acceptance of the Muslim scholars' work.

4. **Disable the institutions and individuals who propound the ideology**, by whatever means are possible, including the banning of organizations, closure of institutions, preventative arrests and censorship of social media. Seek to prevent them from functioning effectively and achieving their aims.

Dennis Ignatius, a retired Malaysian diplomat, has written about the threat posed to South-East Asian nations by Wahhabism, the official religion of Saudi Arabia, which he argues is now being "aggressively exported". Ignatius describes Wahhabism as "an exceptionally virulent, narrow and militant interpretation of Islam".[63] He advises that South-East Asian governments give urgent consideration to the following steps, in addition to security measures, against extremist groups and their ideology:

1. Begin an honest conversation with the Saudis about the damage that Wahhabism is doing to their societies.
2. Work with the international community to identify and dismantle the entire infrastructure of extremism (the institutions, the organizations and groups, the schools and madrasas, the funding, the dissemination of extremist literature).
3. Reaffirm commitment to pluralism and democracy and aggressively incorporate its values into the political, educational, social and legal fabric of society.[64]

These too are courses which Western governments should consider if Islamic extremism is to be effectively confronted.

And finally ...

Islamic societies are based primarily on faith and obedience to Allah's law. America's dealings with Islam appear to be hampered by America's respect for faith. America has had no hesitation in tackling nonreligious ideologies such as communism, which shaped societies as diverse as the Soviet Union and North Korea. But the U.S. holds back respectfully from reacting in the same way to an ideology that is derived from a theology. The U.S. should not sacrifice its historic principle of freedom to conform with the principles of allies such as Saudi Arabia and Qatar. Still less should the U.S. do anything to further the propagation of these principles or the way of life derived from them. Rather, the U.S. should insist that Saudi Arabia and Qatar adapt to American principles.

An ideology that is derived from a religion should not be treated as a no-go area for American policy-makers. Indeed, the U.S. is uniquely able to help 21st century Islam cut off its Islamist accretions, by sharing with Muslims the lessons that America herself has learned in the last 400 years about finding theological support for horrifying injustice and violence. "Learn from us," is a message of humility, not of pride, if the full message runs, "We've been there; we got it wrong; we've put it right; learn from our mistakes."

Notes

1 President Discusses War on Terror at National Endowment for Democracy, Ronald Reagan Building and International Trade Center, Washington, D.C., 6 October 2005.

2 White House, National Security Strategy, May 2010 (emphasis added), *White House*, http://www.whitehouse.gov/sites/default/files/rss_viewer/national_security_strategy.pdf (viewed 20 September 2013).

3 "Prime Minister Blair's Speech", *New York Times*, 16 July 2005.

4 Samuel T. Huntington, *The Clash of Civilizations and the Remaking of World Order*. New York: Simon & Shuster, 1996.

5 Michael Scheuer, *Through our Enemies' Eyes: Osama bin Laden, Radical Islam, and the Future of America*. Dulles: Potomac Books, 2006, p. 281.

6 Henry A. Crumpton, *The Art of Intelligence: Lessons from a Life in the CIA's Clandestine Service*. Dulles: Penguin Books, 2012, p. 172.

7 Crumpton, *The Art of Intelligence*, p. 184.

8 Emile A. Nakhleh, *A Necessary Engagement: Reinventing America's Relations with the Muslim World*. Princeton and Oxford: Princeton University Press , 2009.

9 Nakhleh, *A Necessary Engagement*, p. 17.

10 Nakhleh, *A Necessary Engagement*, p. 2 and *passim*.

11 Ozan Ormeci, "Assessing Current Developments in Turkey", 27 August 2013, http://danielpipes.org/13322/turkey-developments (viewed 20 September 2013).

12 "The 9/11 Commission Report", Final Report of the National Commission on Terrorist Attacks Upon the United States, National Commission on Terrorist Attacks Upon the United States, 21 August 2004, http://govinfo.library.unt.edu/911/report/911Report_Exec.htm (viewed 20 September 2013).

13 Walid Phares, *The War of Ideas: Jihadism Against Democracy*. New York: Palgrave Macmillan, 2007, p. xx.

14 "Rumsfeld: U.S. Losing War of Ideas", *CBS News*, 27 March 2006, http://www.cbsnews.com/2100-224_162-1442811.html (viewed 20 September 2013).

15 William Fisher, "Karen Hughes' New Job: Make Muslims Love Bush", *Albion Monitor*, 15 March 2005.

16 Robert R. Reilly, "Public Diplomacy in an Age of Global Terrorism", in Katharine C. Gorka and Patrick Sookhdeo (eds.), *Fighting the Ideological War: Winning Strategies from Communism to Islamism*. McLean, VA: Isaac Publishing, 2012, p. 151. See also Fisher, "Karen Hughes' New Job".

17 Quoted in *CNN Security Blog*, 1 August 2012.

18 Nasr Hamid Abu Zayd, "The Mythological Dimension of Universal Violence", in Jochen Hippler (ed.), *War, Repression, Terrorism, Political Violence and Civilisation in Western and Muslim Societies*. Stuttgart: Institute for Foreign Cultural Relations (IFA), September 2006 (emphasis added).

19 Abdallah 'Azzam, *Join the Caravan*. London: Azzam Publications, 1996, p. 30.

20 Sayyid Qutb, "Social Justice in Islam", in W. Shepard (ed.), *Sayyid Qutb and Islamic Activism*. Leiden: Brill, 1996, p. 277.

21 Source: Faraj, Muhammad 'Abd al-Salam, Al-Faridah al-Gha'ibah [The Neglected Duty]. English translation in Jansen, Johannes J. G. *The Neglected Duty: The Creed of Sadat's Assassins and Islamic Resurgence in the Middle East*. New York: Macmillan, 1986, pp. 169-175.

22 See: Robert W. Hefner, "September 11 and the Struggle for Islam", in Craig Calhoun, Paul Price, and Ashley Timmer (eds.), *Understanding September 11*, Project coordinated by the Social Science Research Council. New York: The New Press, 2002, pp. 41-52. For a more liberal view see also: *Contextualising Islam in Britain: Exploratory Perspectives*. University of Cambridge in Association with the Universities of Exeter and Westminster, Centre of Islamic Studies: Cambridge, October 2009.

23 Muhammad 'Abd al-Salam Faraj, *The Neglected Duty, (Al Farida Al Ghaiba)*, English translation in Johannes J.G. Jansen, *The Neglected Duty: The Creed of Sadat's Assassins and Islamic Resurgence in the Middle East*. New York: Macmillan, 1986, p. 200.

24 Al-Banna, Hasan, *Five Tracts of Hassan al-Banna (1906-1949): A Selection from the Majmuat Rasail al-Imam al-Shahid*. Berkeley, CA: University of California Press, 1978, pp. 15-17, 89.

25 Sayyid Qutb, *Milestones, (Ma'alem Fil Tariq)*, English Translation. Indianapolis: American Trust Publications, 1990, pp. 30, 67-69, 107-108. See also Ronald Nettler, "A Modern Islamic Confession of Faith and Conception of Religion: Sayyid Qutb's Introduction to the Tafsir, Fi Zilal Al-Qur'an", *British Journal of Middle Eastern Studies*, 21: 1, 1994.

26 Ali Shari'ati, *Martyrdom: Arise And Bear Witness*. Teheran: Ministry of Islamic Guidance, 1981, pp. 20-21.

27 Ali Shari'ati, *What Is To Be Done*. Houston: IRIS, 1986, p. 1; Shari'ati, *Martyrdom: Arise and Bear Witness*, 1981, p. 78.

28 Alison Pargeter, *The Muslim Brotherhood: from Opposition to Power*. London: Saqi Books, revised edition 2013, pp. 186-187.

29 Sayyid Qutb, *Milestones*. Indianapolis: American Trust Publications, 1990, pp. 94-96; Sayyid Qutb, "Social Justice in Islam" in Shepard, W. (ed), *Sayyid Qutb and Islamic Activism: A Translation and Critical Analysis of 'Social Justice in Islam'*. Leiden: E.J. Brill, 1996, pp. 284-288.

30 Nakhleh, *A Necessary Engagement*, pp. 41-43.

31 Ali Soufan, "How Al Qaeda Made Its Comeback", *Wall Street Journal*, 7 August 2013.

32 Soufan, "How Al Qaeda Made Its Comeback".

33 Soufan, "How Al Qaeda Made Its Comeback".

34 Ali Soufan, *The Black Banners: Inside the Hunt for Al Qaeda*. London: Allen Lane, 2011.

35 Khalil an-Anani, "The Myth of Excluding Moderate Islamists in the Arab World", The Saban Center for Middle East Policy at the Brookings Institution, Working Paper 4, March 2010, p. iii.

36 Quoted in J. Michael Waller (ed.), *The Public Diplomacy Reader*. Washington DC: The Institute of World Politics Press, 2007, p. 379.

37 "Countering International Terrorism: The United Kingdom's Strategy", July 2006, www.official-documents.gov.uk/document/cm68/6888/6888.pdf (viewed 20 September 2013).

38 "Prevent Strategy", Presented to Parliament by the Secretary of State for the Home Department by Command of Her Majesty, June 2011. https://www.gov.uk/government/uploads/system/uploads/attachment_data/file/97976/prevent-strategy-review.pdf (viewed 20 November 2013).

39 "Channel: Protecting vulnerable people from being drawn into terrorism: A guide for local partnerships", October 2012, https://www.gov.uk/government/uploads/system/uploads/attachment_data/file/118194/channel-guidance.pdf (viewed 16 April 2015).

40 Dina Temple-Raston, "New Terrorism Adviser Takes a 'Broad Tent' Approach", *NPR*, 24 January 2011, http://www.npr.org/2011/01/24/133125267/new-terrorism-adviser-takes-a-broad-tent-approach (viewed 20 November 2013); "The White House Official Who Brought CAIR To England; Former College Professor Architect Of U.S. Counter Extremism Strategy", *The Global Muslim Brotherhood Daily Watch*, 28 May 2013, http://www.globalmbwatch.com/2013/05/28/white-house-official-brought-cair-england-college-professor-architect-counter-extremism-strategy/ (viewed 20 November 2013).

41 Lieutenant General David H. Petraeus, "U.S. Army, Counter Insurgency, FM 3-24", December 2006.

42 David J. Kilcullen, "Three Pillars of Counterinsurgency", Remarks delivered at the U.S. Government Counterinsurgency Conference, Washington D.C., 28 September 2006.

43 Alan Judd, "Mission Accomplished", *The Spectator*, 12 May 2012, p. 37.

44 Quoted in C. Glenn Ayers and James R. Orbock, "Sourcing Perception Warriors", *NDU Press* 49, Second Quarter 2008.

45 Stephen Ulph highlights an example of the importance attached by Muslims to Islamic history and how this can guide their actions today. The fifteenth Islamic century opened on 20 November 1979, and it was no coincidence that this was the day on which Juhayman al-Utaybi, who called himself "Renewer of the Century," chose to storm the Mosque at Mecca. As a *mujaddid* (restorer) he rejected any form of modernity, including a technology, for being incompatible with the original Islam he sought to re-establish. (Stephen Ulph, "Boko Haram," Desk Study 2.2.B Ideological Contextualization, 2013, footnote 14.)

46 The Messianic Shi'a doctrine of Mahdism predicts the return of the 12th Shi'a Imam (the Hidden Imam, who disappeared in Iraq in 874 AD) at the end of time as the saviour who will set up the final Muslim kingdom of righteousness. Since Khomeini, the leaders of Islamic Iran believe that they are actively preparing the way for his second appearance.

47 Ambassador John Christopher Stevens was killed in an attack on the U.S. consulate in Benghazi, Libya. The attack began on 11 September 2012, and the ambassador was pronounced dead early in the morning on 12 September. The attack was carried out by heavily armed Islamist militants.

48 Personal communication by confidential source to the author, 14 February 2013.

49 C.J. Chivers and Eric Schmitt, "Arms Shipments Seen From Sudan to Syria Rebels", *New York Times*, 12 August 2013.

50 Robert Fisk, "Does Obama Know He's Fighting on al-Qa'ida's Side?" *The Independent*, 27 August 2013.

51 "A New Beginning," speech by President Barack Obama, Cairo University, 4 June 2009.

52 Jim Guirard, "General James Mattis – Attacking the al Qaeda 'Narrative'", *SmallWarsJournal.com*, 7 August 2007.

53 Transcript of discussion "A New Approach for Safeguarding Americans", *Center for Strategic and International Studies*, 6 August 2009, http://csis.org/files/attachments/090806_brennan_transcript.pdf (viewed 20 September 2013).

54 Quoted in Jerry Gordon, "Coughlin on Major Hasan, Islamic Jihad threat, and Official Myopia", New English Review, 24 November 2009, http://www.newenglishreview.org/blog_direct_link.cfm/blog_id/24360/ (accessed 17 April 2015).

55 Martin E. Dempsey, "Memorandum for Chiefs of the Military Services, Commanders of the Combatant Commands, Chief, National Guard Bureau, Subject: Review of Military Education and Training Curriculum, CM-0098-12", 24 April 2012.

56 Ryan Mauro, "Islamists Demand Counterterrorism Training Censor Ideology", *Frontpage Magazine*, 13 December 2011 (viewed 13 December 2011).

57 Andrew Marshall, "Terror 'blowback' burns CIA", *The Independent*, 1 November 1998, http://www.independent.co.uk/news/terror-blowback-burns-cia-1182087.html (accessed 17 April 2015).

58 Peter Mandaville, "The Unexceptional Islamists", *Foreign Policy*, 24 July 2012, http://mideast.foreignpolicy.com/posts/2012/07/24/the_unexceptional_islamists (viewed 20 September 2013).

59 Nakhle, *A Necessary Engagement*, pp. 125-139.

60 Nakhle, *A Necessary Engagement*, p. 135.

61 Ben Hubbard, "Islamist Rebels Create Dilemma on Syria Policy", *New York Times*, 27 April 2013, http://www.nytimes.com/2013/04/28/world/middleeast/islamist-rebels-gains-in-syria-create-dilemma-for-us.html?pagewanted=all&_r=0 (viewed 20 September 2013).

62 "Exploring Military Dimensions in Countering Ideological Support for Terrorism", George C. Marshall European Center for Security Studies and CASD conference, Rome, 12-14 May 2008.

63 Dennis Ignatius, "The Wahhabi threat to Southeast Asia", *The Malaysian Insider*, 30 March 2015.

64 Ignatius, "The Wahhabi threat to Southeast Asia".

2

INFORMATION OPERATIONS:
SUCCESSES AND FAILURES

Robert R. Reilly

From my experiences in the Cold War and since 9/11, I have formulated a few brief principles for the conduct of wars of ideas. First, do not go into a war of ideas unless you understand the ideas you are at war with. Second, do not go into a war of ideas unless you have an idea. Third, wars of ideas are conducted by people who think; people who do not think are influenced by those who do. Try to reach the people who think.

Successful information operations show understanding of the target audience, have the right message in the right format to reach that audience, and have the means to deliver the message through the media used by the audience. Miss any of these links and you have a failed information operation. You can have the medium but not the message, or you can have the message but not the medium, or you can be without both.

It is been generally acknowledged that we have been in the new war of ideas at least since 2001. *The National Strategy for Combating Terrorism* (2006) stated that "in the long run, winning the War on Terror means winning the battle of ideas".[1] Until recently, this emphasis was reflected in every United States government strategy document, including the *National Defense Strategy of the United States of America* (2005), which calls for "countering ideological support for terrorism".

This emphasis, however, has not produced results in practice. In fact, the U.S. side has failed to show up for the war of ideas. Strategic communication or public diplomacy, the purpose of which is to win such wars, is the single weakest area of U.S. government performance since 9/11. By almost every index, the U.S. is not doing well. Some say it has already lost. After a six-month journey through the Muslim world in 2006, Akbar Ahmed, the chairman of Islamic Studies at American University, said, "I felt like a warrior in the midst of the fray who knew the odds were against him but never quite realized that his side had already lost the war."[2] In a threat assessment issued in September 2013, the Bipartisan Policy Center's Homeland Security Project, chaired by former 9/11 Commission chiefs Thomas Kean and Lee Hamilton, stated that "even though core Al Qaeda may be in decline, 'al Qaeda-ism,' the movement's ideology, continues to resonate and attract new adherents".[3] In fact, al-Qaeda is present in some 16 areas around the globe, according to the report, twice the number of five years ago. On September 28, 2013, *The Economist* reported that "From Somalia to Syria, al-Qaeda franchises and jihadist fellow travelers now control more territory, and can call on more fighters than at any time since Osama bin Laden created the organization 25 years ago."

How can this be? Why is the U.S. not winning?

My job here is not so much to answer this question as it is to reflect upon some practical experiences from the past that may shed light on what we have done that has worked, on what has not worked, and on an overall view of what we have failed to do altogether. Yes, we need a new strategy against al-Qaeda and the Muslim Brotherhood, but we cannot charge ahead unless we have something to charge ahead with.

I have no interest in being autobiographical, but since I have been asked to address the subject of "Information Operations: Successes and Failures," I am invariably drawn to some operations in which I have been personally involved. I am using the term "information operations" in a broad sense to include all the activities of public diplomacy undertaken in a war of ideas. There were several huge failures and some tiny successes. I have not spoken of some of these experiences before; they are almost too painful to relate. I recount them now only in the hope that the lessons from them can be learned and related to the current conflicts in which we are involved. Sometimes the mission was right but the execution was wrong. Sometimes the mission itself was misconceived. At other times there was not even a mission to execute, just a void.

Voice of America

I will not dwell at great length on my experiences at the Voice of America (VOA), but I must admit that when I served as its director in 2001 to 2002, I looked forward to VOA's serving as important a role in the new war as it had in 1942 when it began its broadcasts to Germany. Because of VOA's unique reach into other lands via shortwave, terrestrial and satellite broadcasts, delivering news and information in the languages of its 120 million listeners and featuring careful explications of U.S. policy on key issues, I thought that this would be VOA's finest hour: the hour in which the Arabic service, which was broadcasting 12 hours a day of features, interviews and editorials, would be particularly important. Imagine my amazement when the Broadcasting Board of Governors (BBG), an independent entity that has executive authority over VOA, eliminated the Arabic service and substituted for it a pop music station called Radio Sawa, with two short news breaks in the hour. It carried a mélange of Arab and American music, including Britney Spears, Jay Lo and Eminem. The lyrics in the songs of some of the American singers had to be doctored so as not to offend an Arab Muslim audience.

Soon thereafter, I had the occasion to visit with one of Saudi Arabia's most important princes. I asked him, without prejudice, what he thought of Radio Sawa. He responded, "It's not good; it's not bad. It's just what it is." He then said,

My father, King Faisal, loved the Voice of America and used to listen to it faithfully. He would often go into the desert, and in order not to miss his favorite programs, whose broadcast times he had memorized, he would bring a shortwave radio with him. I, too, used to listen to the Voice of America. Of course, I don't listen to Radio Sawa.

Who cares if the king listens? Our Arabic radio broadcasting's reorientation to youth lost it not just an influential audience but, one might say, the key one. Yes, Radio Sawa gained a considerable youth audience, but to what effect? Senior Jordanian journalist Jamil Nimri told me, "Radio Sawa is fun, but it's irrelevant."

Perhaps the best way to grasp the strategic misalignment of VOA's broadcasting resources by the BBG is to engage in an imaginative exercise: if we were setting up a broadcasting service for the U.S. Government from scratch today, what would we do? We would probably want to focus on the ten most important countries and language-groups in the world: in our own southern hemisphere, Brazil; in Eurasia, certainly Russia, and then China to the south, India to the southwest, and then swinging around to the Middle East, certainly the Arab world with its more than 300 million people.

Our mission would be to tell these countries and audiences who we are, what we are doing, and why: say, out of "a decent respect to the opinions of mankind," as the Declaration of Independence puts it. If we want the world to be reasonable, we had better give it our reasons. We might, in other words, create the Voice of America, whose purpose, by government charter, is to do these very things.

Now, if an outside observer looked at what has happened to the VOA over the past 12 years, he might notice a pattern, that broadcasting to these largest, most important countries of the world has been eliminated: Portuguese to Brazil gone, Hindi to India eliminated, Arabic to the Arab world ended and replaced by Radio Sawa's pop music, Russian gone, except for the Internet, and the Chinese services imperiled by the BBG's attempted elimination of all but their internet presences (which are blocked). In 2011, Congress wisely stopped the BBG from doing this. In its Financial Year 2013 budget, the BBG again proposed eliminating the Cantonese Service.

The pattern is clear but the purpose is not. Why have we done this to ourselves? The excuse 14 years ago or more was that history had ended in the sense that the model of a democratic, constitutional, free-market political order stood undisputed in its moral authority. But 13 years ago, at the expense of 3,000 American lives, we found out that was not true. Why, then, are we continuing the pattern?

Economic considerations might be one explanation, but they cannot account for more than a decade of this behavior, or for the enormous amount of money that has been poured into Radio Sawa. The elimination of Chinese VOA radio and TV, broadcasting in Mandarin and Cantonese, would save $8 million but lose an audience of more than 6 million (according to the BBG's own figures).

Do we no longer need to explain ourselves to the world? Do we no longer need to give it our reasons? Be sure that others are willing to give reasons for us, as China, Russia and Qatar (with its Al-Jazeera TV in both Arabic and English) are doing with their aggressive broadcasting and biting criticism of U.S. policies.

This brings me to the most likely explanation for the elimination of VOA's services to the most important countries in the world: a lost sense of mission. This loss began with the end of the U.S. Information Agency in 1999, when U.S. government broadcasting was placed under the BBG. As the BBG consists of eight part-time CEOs, it is no wonder that confusion ensued. Ancient Rome had trouble with two proconsuls. Imagine if it had had eight. Very importantly, most BBG members have been highly accomplished individuals who made their fortunes in private-sector media. They, therefore, have sought to replicate this success according to commercial criteria. This meant large youth audiences and abandoning markets in which such audiences could not be attracted. Who listens became less important than how many listened or to what.

The new, diminished mission became news: not the full service radio that VOA offered, which also presented and explained US policies, but news. Play music for 40 minutes or more per hour on Radio Sawa if you must, so long as they listen to the news. After all, said the BBG chief of staff in 2008, "It is not in our mandate to influence."[4]

The BBG chairman at the time, Walter Isaacson, said in a 2011 Alhurra TV broadcast that "we just want to get good news, reliable news, and credible information out." (Do not other people offer the news?) Reliable news was always a part of U.S. broadcasting, but the mission has never been reduced to just that. When the Dalai Lama called the VOA Tibet service "the bread of the Tibetan people," and when Aun San Suu Kyi called the Burmese service "the hope of the Burmese people," they were not just talking about the "news". Hope is a theological virtue; it is not engendered by news alone. *The Declaration of Independence* was not a news bulletin.

The US has enduring interests in the world. We need to explain ourselves in the most persuasive way we can, and by the most effective means, particularly to those peoples and countries whose future is going to affect ours most. Destroying the VOA is not the way to do this. We need to begin again to think through to whom we should be broadcasting, about what, and with what. This needs to be done within the U.S. government in a command structure related to our national security, and not by an independent, part-time board, which can, and has, so easily confused its commercial experience with our national purposes.

Failure to do this will be paid, I am afraid, in American lives. Better to win the war of ideas than have to win a war. That's simple economics.

It is also essential to any lasting victory. Judge Hamoud al-Hitar in Yemen said, "If you study terrorism in the world, you will see that it has an intellectual theory behind it. And any kind of intellectual idea can be defeated by intellect."[5] However, the language of the intellect is ideas, not pop music. The war of ideas cannot be fought by a battle of the bands. Its objective is to reach people who think, who, as mentioned before, influence those who do not.

Afghanistan

On the other hand, VOA and the BBG did get something right, at least at the start, concerning Afghanistan. (I should also say that the BBG, much to its credit, did major work in upgrading VOA's broadcast infrastructure from shortwave to medium wave in the Middle East.) Radio was, and continues to be, the primary means through which people in Afghanistan get their information. In late 2001, I met with the Afghan Minister of Information, Dr. Makhdoom Raheen. He explained to me the problem that the new government was facing. It had no means by which to reach its own people. It simply did not possess the broadcasting infrastructure to do so. In the meantime, Afghanistan was being bifurcated by foreign broadcasting from Iran in Farsi on the one side and by broadcasting from Pakistan in Pashtu on the other.

The minister proposed that we would provide the Afghan government with medium-wave transmitters powerful enough for it to reach the majority of the Afghan people, and in exchange, the Afghan government would provide us with the site and license for our own transmitters to do the same. Since this project would cost more than $10 million, VOA had to go shopping for the money. Because of the tremendous work of Andrew Baird at VOA and of Brig. General Simon P. Worden in the unfairly maligned (by the national Press in 2002) Office of Strategic Influence at the Defense Department, and with the help of Secretary of Defense Donald Rumsfeld, the funds were provided and this vital project was completed. At the same time, the BBG proposed merging the Pashtu and Dari services of VOA with those of RFL/RFE into one continuous 24/7 stream of a new Afghan national radio. This, too, was accomplished with alacrity by all parties involved. The VOA side of the broadcasting was directed by the immensely capable Ali Jalali, who went on to become Minister of the Interior in Afghanistan in 2003.

Almost ten years later, however, it was revealed that something was clearly amiss with the content of US public diplomacy efforts in Afghanistan. The International Council on Security and Development (ICOS) located in Kandahar found in its field research that 92% of Afghan male respondents

(1,000 men) in the crucial southern provinces of Helmand and Kandahar were unaware of the events of 9/11. At the same time, ICOS discovered that when its representatives showed a photo of planes hitting the Twin Towers and the Pentagon on 9/11, and explained the event to 500 interviewees in Panjshir and Parwan provinces, 59% subsequently said that "it justified the international presence in Afghanistan."[6] How could it be that after nearly a decade of war we had failed to explain the principal reason for our presence in Afghanistan to its people? This would be very much like prosecuting World War II without mentioning Pearl Harbor. When our grievances are explained, the Afghan people are able to understand them even through their own tribal mores. Leaving this matter unexplained, however, places them in the default position of supposing foreign troops are in their country to attack Islam and to steal their land.

Another egregious error has been in not engaging at the religious level in Afghanistan. Since Afghans identify themselves first and above all as Muslims, whoever provides the interpretation of daily events through Islamic eyes wins the audience's allegiance. The Taliban have been very effective in practically monopolizing the religious network of mosques, mullahs and madrasahs. "They've co-opted the religious narrative for the last several years," said Rear Adm. Greg Smith, NATO's communications chief in Afghanistan in 2010. "They've used that narrative locally very effectively."[7] If you are involved in a conflict which is in large part religious, failing to address it in religious terms concedes to the enemy (in the words of Robert Andrews) a "theological safe haven",[8] which is far more important than any physical safe havens they may enjoy.

In Yemen, Judge al-Hitar engaged in Qur'anic duels with captured al-Qaeda members, undermining their religious legitimacy to the point that they would pledge to abandon violent jihad. The Taliban are very vulnerable on the issue of religious legitimacy and, long ago, should have been broadly challenged in terms of it. The British *Prospect* magazine reported on an effective example of how this can work:

> The Voice of America's Radio Deewa, broadcasting in Pashto to the badlands of the Pakistan-Afghan frontier, has shown how much potential there is here: in the past two years, the number of pro-Taliban callers to popular daily phone-in programmes in the region has declined after their views were very publicly and successfully challenged on air. Many

Islamic militants have a sketchy knowledge of their religion, and their views often do not stand up to serious scrutiny.[9]

In a captured document, al-Qaeda declared that its greatest vulnerability is the "loss of the justice of our cause".[10] This is also true of the Taliban. As Mullah Omar wrote in *The Islamic Emirate* magazine back in December 2001, "We know that taking a Muslim's life is a cause of defeat." On these grounds alone, the Taliban should have been defeated as they are the cause of three times more civilian casualties than the ISAF forces have caused. Yet, strangely enough, this issue was purposely neglected, because it was thought that publicizing Taliban atrocities would expose the weakness of the Afghan government and ISAF forces and give the Taliban a propaganda victory. To his credit, General Petraeus reversed this shortsighted policy. The new US Army Counterinsurgency Field Manual (December 2006) encourages US forces to "exploit inconsistencies in the insurgents' message as well as their excessive use of force or intimidation". Petraeus knew from Iraq that publicly exposing and broadly publicizing the al-Qaeda torture houses and executions helped turn the Sunni population against them.

Iraq

This brings us to the subject of Iraq. Operation Iraqi Freedom had two primary purposes. The first was to end the first Gulf war and finally bring Iraq into compliance with the terms of the ceasefire agreement of 1991, which Saddam Hussein had been in violation of for the prior dozen years. The second was to use the opportunity of his overthrow to sponsor a new constitutional regime in Baghdad that could serve as a model to transform the Middle East from authoritarian to democratic rule, thus, it was thought, draining the ideological swamp that had spawned al-Qaeda and other radical Islamist groups.

Needless to say, this was an ambitious agenda, as there had been, perhaps with the exception of Lebanon, no history of democratic rule native to Arab countries. How would the US communicate its purpose in Iraq and encourage its democratic transformation? Iraq was a one-party totalitarian regime with state-controlled media. Under Saddam, owning a satellite phone had been a capital offense. Possessing a satellite dish was a crime. Overnight, that regime and its media would disappear. What would appear the next day?

As I was working in the Pentagon in late 2002, I began exploring which part of the US government was going to answer this question in regard to

Iraqi media. It turned out that no-one was preparing a replacement for Iraq's state media. It seemed an ideal opportunity to help create a model of free media in that country that would not only serve the immediate purposes of the Coalition but would also have a broader salutary influence throughout the Middle East.

As it happened, when retired Lt. Gen. Jay Garner arrived to fill out his paperwork for the position of director of the new Office for Reconstruction and Humanitarian Assistance (ORHA), he did so in the Policy Office of Near East and South Asian Affairs, in which I was serving at the time. This gave me the opportunity to hand him a short paper in which my colleagues and I proposed the creation of an Iraqi Media Network. We proposed the following analogy: what if the people of North Korea went to bed one night after another evening of state television and radio singing the praises of the Great Leader and awoke the next morning to find the government gone and the airways filled with South Korean broadcasts? Obviously, the effect would be electrifying and profound. Could we aim to do something similar in Iraq?

Gen. Garner immediately embraced the idea and went to the National Security Council and the Office of Management and Budget in the White House to obtain support. One problem was money. Even without contemplating the replacement of any of the Iraqi broadcasting infrastructure, which we knew might be destroyed in the invasion, the annual personnel and programming costs to start a national television and radio station and newspaper would easily reach one hundred million dollars. The other problem was that there was no equivalent in Arabic to South Korean broadcasting material: quite the opposite, as Al Jazeera and other Arabic state-controlled media illustrated. In other words, we would have to start from scratch. To launch 24/7 TV and radio stations successfully with original programming material would take at least a year or two of preparation.

Gen. Garner was able to pry loose around $3 million to start the IMN project in January 2003. This allowed me to leave for Europe to begin recruiting Iraqi expatriate journalists to come with us and to help develop programming ideas. This proved to be extremely difficult, because the best Iraqi journalists were already employed and we were not in a position to offer them even annual contracts.

When this extremely modest effort began, we did not know how long we had to prepare. As it turned out, we were deployed in March to Kuwait to await the commencement of Operation Iraqi Freedom. At that point, I knew that the IMN project would be a failure: too little time, not enough Iraqi talent, no prepared programming, almost no equipment and pathetically little money. Nonetheless, the effort had to be made. When the invasion began, we awaited apprehensively to see if the Iraqi Ministry of Information would survive. Within it were all the broadcasting resources and infrastructure we needed. Unfortunately, it was destroyed, if I recall correctly, on the last day of precision bombing. My heart sank when I saw the building split in two. When the modest IMN effort arrived in Baghdad, there was no broadcasting infrastructure left. There was not a single functioning television studio or camera; there were perhaps two intact radio studios; and not one rotary press for newspaper printing remained operational. Of course, for the most part, there was no electricity either. When the television station was up and running, the tiny IMN TV news team was able to produce only 15 to 20 minutes of programming per day. The rest of the schedule was filled out with pirated tapes from Uday Hussein's defunct Youth TV channel.

We did not have money to buy programming. IMN member Siyamend Othman offered an ingenious proposal to fill the huge gap. He negotiated a plan with an American Middle Eastern businessman to fill the TV airwaves, 24/7, with programming in exchange for a monopoly on advertising rights for a period of six months. The programming, which we would select from the archives of MBC, would be uplinked from Dubai and downlinked in Iraqi studios. IMN would retain editorial control over everything, including the advertising. When I sought approval at United States Department of Defense (DOD) to proceed with this plan, I was told that it was too early to introduce commercial considerations into our broadcasting. Yet there was no offer of funds to buy the programming or to provide any alternative means of obtaining it.

Another attempt was made to present the plan, this time to Ambassador Paul Bremer, the Administrator of the Coalition Provisional Authority, who immediately dismissed it and said he never wanted to hear about it again. Gen. Jay Garner, who had already been replaced by Ambassador Bremer, was in the meeting at which this happened. I remarked to him that we had just lost the war of ideas and appealed for his help. He suggested that we try again in a week. Unfortunately, a week from then, he was no longer there.

We had tried to get Iraqi Media Network's radio station off to a start while still in Kuwait, by downlinking to an AM transmitter just over the Iraqi border that, we were told, might reach as far north as south of Baghdad at night, when transmission was best. With fewer than a half-dozen experienced Iraqi on-air talents operating from borrowed studios, it was very difficult to fill the airwaves. The first broadcast in mid-April announced,

Welcome to the Iraqi Media Network, the voice of the new Iraq. We are the first free, independent media broadcasting to you from inside the country in more than three decades. After so many years of lies and propaganda, we take as our first and most sacred obligation to tell you the truth. Not only were our bodies imprisoned during the reign of Saddam, but our minds as well. The truth will set our minds free so that we may live as a free people, as God intended. ... We will bring you news and information vital to the recovery of our country as we work together, through this difficult period of transition, to create a democratic, tolerant and prosperous country. We will keep you informed of the intent and activities of the coalition forces and of the civic administration that is now beginning its activities. We will tell you about the issues most directly affecting the safety, health, and other humanitarian matters.

That, in any case, was the idea with which we began.

One successful and particularly powerful program, hosted by IMN member Shameem Rassam, was *At Last, I Speak*, which gave at least some of the survivors and families of victims of Saddam's atrocities a chance to tell their stories. This was novel for an Arab country: to have torture victims broadcast in the country in which they had been tortured. The stories were very moving. The guests would often break down when trying to relate their experiences. When I asked IMN cameraman and TV director Farid Putres what happened during his nearly four years of imprisonment in the 1990s, he laughed, shrugged his shoulders, and said, "It was normal." However, when the time came to tape his story for broadcast, he was barely able to get through it. The underground cells, the beatings, the sounds of executions at night were not "normal". Another program featured Sheikh Hussein Al-Shami, who was sentenced to death but escaped in 1978. His wife and five brothers were imprisoned at that time, and he has had no word from them since. His 25-year-old son, Ali, has not seen his mother since he was six months old. The frightening thing about this story is that it, too, was typical.

General Najib Salehi, with whom I lived for two months, fled with his family from Iraq to Jordan. One day, he received a videocassette in the mail. Unwittingly, he put it in the player with his family watching in the living room. To his horror, it was a film of his niece being gang raped by the Mukhabarat: Saddam's retaliation for the general's defection.

Other films were surfacing in Baghdad as a result of the looting of jails. Saddam had torture and mutilation sessions filmed so that he could be sure his orders were carried out. The Iraqi Media Network obtained a tape of physicians cutting off the hands of merchants who were caught pricing gold in dollars after Saddam had forbidden it. Several of them died of the complications; several fled Iraq; the others survived in Baghdad and were subsequently located by IMN journalist Don North, about whom more will be told below.

Only one part of the Iraqi Media Network began completely smoothly and successfully (at least in terms of production and content, if not distribution), and that was the national newspaper, *Sumer*. *Sumer* was meant to represent the face of a new Iraq, with Arab, Kurdish, Chaldean, Assyrian, Turcoman, Christian and even Jewish contributors. This was the vehicle through which we wished to attract the intelligentsia of Iraq and in which we wished to see published the Iraqi equivalent of the *Federalist Papers*. The senior Iraqi journalist, Hasan al Alawi, responsible for its production, did a brilliant job. Since there were no rotary presses in Baghdad, the paper had to be printed in Kuwait and shipped into Iraq. In order to secure the printing contract, Mr. Alawi gave his personal financial guarantee.

However, a rival newspaper, *al-Sabah*, had been started in Baghdad, with local talent, by an IMN contractor who had been explicitly told by me not to launch one. Two papers were too expensive to sustain. *Al-Sabah* was printed on sheet-fed presses and was journalistically a clearly inferior product to *Sumer*. Nonetheless, the Coalition Provisional Authority decided in its favor and ordered the shutdown of *Sumer*. When I attempted to plead on its behalf, I was told that Iraq did not need its own version of the *Wall Street Journal* at this point in time, but only a broadsheet to announce weapons turn-in checkpoints. Kanan Makiya, one of the leading Iraqi expatriate intellectuals, tried to appeal directly to Ambassador Bremer on the behalf of *Sumer*, but to no avail. Mr. Alawi, who had placed his trust in the United States, was left holding the bag for more than a hundred thousand dollars due to the Kuwaiti printing contract he had had to sign on our behalf.

Before the United States or Coalition could broadcast from within Iraq, Iran had already blanketed the country with two 24/7 TV channels. A survey by Radio Free Europe/Radio Liberty found that the vast majority of radio and TV broadcasts heard in Iraq originated in Iran. When the media vacuum in Iraq resulting from the failure of IMN became too obvious to ignore, a large contract for $96 million to run and expand IMN was given to the

Harris/LBC/Al Fawares group. It too failed. Al-Iraqiya, the TV station begun by IMN, eventually turned into another Arab state media organ, except this time a strongly Shi'a one. The opportunity was lost.

NB

The lesson here would be: do not plan a military strategy without a communication strategy that is integral to it, or you may squander your entire effort. One may ask why preparations did not begin sooner. Who was at fault for that? Why was not the entire Office for Reconstruction and Humanitarian Assistance project begun well before December 2012? The answer is, in part, political. The Bush administration had to present itself as open to solutions to the Iraqi problem short of war. Therefore, it could not afford to prepare openly for war in a way that made it seem that the war was a foregone conclusion. While that may have been a political necessity, it exacted a high price, the magnitude of which became clear only with the occupation of the country that we had come to liberate.

After this macro failure, I would now like to focus on some micro failures but also some micro successes.

After returning from Iraq in June 2003, I worked with the Spirit of America Foundation and its CEO, Jim Hake, an energetic and successful entrepreneur, to support an Iraqi Federalist Papers project. We wanted to commission a group of Iraqi intellectuals to write papers on how the new Iraqi constitution ought to look in order to prevent a recurrence of the nightmare through which the Iraqi people had lived under the Ba'ath Party and to secure a democratic constitutional order. We worked up a budget for the commissioning of the papers, printing them, placing them in important newspapers throughout the country and distributing them in mosques, as well as engaging their authors in radio and television discussions. We needed only a little more than $1 million. To lead the project, we recruited an Iraqi scholar who subsequently became the executive assistant to the president of Iraq. Unfortunately, we could not find the money either inside or outside of the government. Therefore, there were no Iraqi Federalist Papers. When I was at an interagency meeting on Iraq, I asked the head of Agency for International Development's programs in Iraq why he had not funded such a project. His dismaying response was, "We were not tasked with it." It was such an obvious thing to do, with no one in authority to give the order to get it done.

There was, however, one project that did get done. The Iraq Memory Foundation (IMF) approached the Defense Department with a proposal to make Steven Spielberg-like documentaries on the victims of Saddam's regime across a broad spectrum of Iraqi society in an interview format. These long interviews would then be edited down for ten, ten-minute television spots on Iraqi TV. Enough funds were found to begin this project. IMF then proposed a more ambitious project: a one-hour television program that would incorporate the shorter interviews but also have other segments on the legacy of Saddam's regime and how to overcome it, not only politically and legally, but psychologically and morally as well. The discussion part of the program would also include topics such as the debate over the new constitution and human rights issues. This program helped support the ideas behind constitutional structures that would prevent the recurrence of such crimes and further discredited the Ba'athist revanchists, fostered reconciliation and put the trials of Saddam and others into a larger context. It also provided a strong antidote to the Saddam nostalgia that was beginning to surface owing to the disorder following his downfall.

This program, titled *Light* or *Overcoming the Legacy of Evil,* was produced in Baghdad with such fine production values that some members of the audience thought it must have been made outside of the country. In any case, it drew a large audience when it began appearing on al-Iraqiya TV. During Ramadan, when TV viewership is highest in the Arab Muslim world, Prime Minister Maliki ordered al-Iraqiya to play the program daily. Al-Iraqiya reported that *Overcoming the Legacy of Evil* was its second most popular program, coming only after *Terrorism in the Hands of Justice,* a program in which captured terrorists were interviewed. This project cost only a little more than $1 million per year. The funds were provided by both the Defense and State Departments. It was one of the most cost-effective and worthwhile public diplomacy programs that the US quietly sponsored. One can contrast it with the Coalition television PSAs made in London that cost eight times the annual IMF budget to produce and broadcast *one* five to ten-minute spot.

Once back from Iraq, I also concentrated on collecting the films of Saddam's atrocities, mostly made by his own regime. While in Iraq, we were given the films of nine Iraqis having their right hands cut off in Abu Ghraib prison hospital and then having their foreheads scarified with an X. This was in punishment for these merchants having either possessed or priced their goods in dollars, which for a short period of time Saddam had forbidden. Don North, a very experienced journalist and original IMN team member, took it upon himself to track down the survivors. He then made a one-hour documentary about them, called *Remembering Saddam.*

To his enormous credit, North also sought help for them. By special order of the Secretary of Defense, DOD eventually flew the Iraqis out of the country to Germany on military aircraft. From that point on, private donors took care of their airfare, lodging and medical care, which included corrective surgery and the provision of prosthetic devices, at a cost of $50,000 each. Their new prosthetic right hands allowed them to tie their shoes, to pick up pens, and to write. After their surgery in Houston, they were brought to Washington by the American Foreign Policy Council, which served as their local host and sponsor. The US Department of State's Bureau of Educational and Cultural Affairs provided program support and language interpretation for the men's visit to Washington. When they visited with the Senate majority leader, Senator Bill Frist, who was also a transplant surgeon, he asked them to give a demonstration of their prosthetic hands. One of them picked up a pen and wrote a message. He handed it to Senator Frist, who teared up when he read it. The message said, "Thank you forever."

A series of coordinated events and actions were planned to convey the powerful message that the presence of the Iraqi amputees provided. First of all, the Defense Department bought the rights to broadcast *Remembering Saddam* for the Middle East. The film was supplied to Al Hurrah TV, the Arabic language TV channel started by the BBG. It was shown on May 24, 2004, in Iraq, throughout the Middle East and in Europe. The morning of May 25, the *Washington Post* ran a front-page story on the Iraqi amputees. Thanks to Tim Goeglein in the Office of Public Liaison in the White House, a meeting with President Bush was arranged for the seven Iraqis, the surgeon who performed the *gratis* operations on their right hands, Dr. Joe Agris, and Don North on May 25. *Remembering Saddam* had already been seen in Iraq by the time the international newscasts reported on the President's meeting with the seven men. It was a very effective one-two punch. First, the Iraqis saw the documentary about the men and their treatment under Saddam, ending with their departure for the United States. The next day, they saw the very same men with new prosthetic hands in the office of the President of the United States. The message was clear: America was intent upon helping the very people whom Saddam Hussein had harmed. Since the Abu Ghraib scandal of the U.S. mistreatment of Iraqi prisoners was still in full bloom, this message was particularly needed. North went on to make a second documentary, *A Show of Hands*, highlighting the medical treatment the Iraqi amputees received in Houston, their meeting with the President, and the dramatic conclusion when they met and embraced a U.S. Marine who had also lost his right hand through injuries in Iraq. An Arabic version was completed and broadcast on Al Hurrah.

Other attempts to convey this message had to be undertaken privately or through Congress because the Defense Department public affairs office declined to sponsor them. By the time the Iraqis arrived in Washington, my colleagues and I had completed a gruesome DVD made out of Saddam's atrocity films, titled *The Victims of Saddam's Regime*. The images of the executions, tortures, and beatings were every bit as searing as the material in the Holocaust Museum. The palpable presence of evil in them was almost overpowering. I requested that the public affairs office in the Pentagon provide a stage on which we could present the seven Iraqi amputees with the film. The Iraqis were eager to speak about the Abu Ghraib scandal perpetrated by some American troops' mistreatment of Iraqi prisoners. They had repeatedly said to us in private, "Yes, this was a bad thing to happen, but you are punishing the people who did it. Look at our hands. The people in Abu Ghraib who did this to us were promoted by Saddam Hussein." They wanted to say this publicly. It was a vitally important message. Nonetheless, the public affairs office declined to do what we asked. An excuse was made that since the Iraqis could speak very little English a press event with translation would not play well.

The frustrated Iraqis learned that there was going to be an antiwar demonstration in front of Donald Rumsfeld's home. Somehow, with their very limited English, they found their own way on the Metro to the location. Rumsfeld was overseas at the time, but there, in front of his house, were the Iraqis defending the United States in a way the United States itself refused to do.

Therefore, Herman Pirchner and the American Foreign Policy Council stepped in to sponsor a press conference at the Press Club. Contrary to the DOD public affairs office's expectations, it was very well attended by the press and was carried live on C-SPAN, where it can still be seen in the archives. In fact, the combination of the stories of the White House meeting and the press conference made national news throughout the United States, in addition to the TV and print press coverage abroad.

While DOD declined to host a showing of *The Victims of Saddam's Regime*, Senators Rick Santorum, Joseph Lieberman and Jeff Sessions sponsored a press conference in the Capitol to present the seven Iraqis and show excerpts from the film. In fact, this was the first occasion for the Iraqis to see parts of this documentary, which included footage of their hand amputations. Senator Santorum explained the source of the film footage and encouraged the journalists present to contact the Pentagon public affairs office if they had any questions concerning it. Even though the most explicit parts of the film excerpts were edited out, the small but full room of journalists was left in a state of shock after the showing. No one spoke. They silently filed out of the room.

I waited for the stories to break from the news conference. There were none. How could this be? Only later, when approached by a friendly source within the Pentagon, did I learn that, when journalists had called the public affairs office to verify the film, the public affairs office had disavowed it. This happened despite the fact that Senator Santorum, before the press conference, had called the Assistant Secretary of Legislative Affairs in the Pentagon to tell him of the showing and to request that the Defense Department vouch for the authenticity of the material. Apparently, the Assistant Secretary assured Senator Santorum that this would be taken care of. Obviously, it was not.

Why did this happen? It happened because the entire effort regarding the Iraqi amputees had been undertaken by various individuals in different parts of the government and the private sector ad hoc, without any overall executive branch institutional sponsorship. It was a one-off. In fact, some of the best parts of it happened despite opposition. For instance, the relevant staff members of the National Security Council, who were first approached with the idea of the meeting with the President, were emphatically against it and expressed annoyance that it had taken place by going around them through the Office of Public Liaison. While the relevant part of DOD in the Middle East that was tasked with collecting Iraqi material was at first cooperative in providing the video material of Saddam's atrocities, it later ceased cooperating. Nonetheless, someone in that office saw the merit of what we were attempting to do and personally carried some of the material from the Middle East and passed it off to me in a paper bag at a Trader Joe's one night in a Washington suburb. Why was this seemingly semi-clandestine behavior necessary? Again, the answer is because there was no official institutional sponsorship of the effort.

Although the DOD public affairs office did not want to have anything to do with *The Victims of Saddam's Regime*, Senator Santorum ensured that every member of Congress received a DVD copy with a 'dear colleague' letter. Nonetheless, its impact was muted because it did not have the sponsorship of the institution that produced it. That impact could have been considerable in a number of ways. To explore its potential, I asked an officer who had recently returned from service in Al Anbar province to watch it. When I asked for his reaction, he said that every member of the US military deployed to Iraq should see it. I asked why. He responded,

> When you're in a combat zone, you tend to develop a callous attitude that not ten of these Iraqis is worth one American life. After seeing this, you realize what these people have been through. It develops sympathy and understanding. Next, you think: we put a stop to this? Then we have done something really fine.

I tried to pass on to the Pentagon his suggestion that it be made available to deploying troops, but it went nowhere.

I used the film on a number of occasions in addressing bipartisan foreign policy groups across the United States, but I never showed it, except to a group of European parliamentarians. I would flip open a portable DVD player on the speaker's podium and briefly tell the audience what it contained. I would explain that they were a pushbutton away from looking into the face of evil. Never once, after introducing the subject matter of the film, did the topic of weapons of mass destruction ever arise. *The Victims of Saddam's Regime* could have been used overseas in this way and would have been a very powerful public diplomacy tool.

Conclusion

The single biggest failing on the US side in the war of ideas is that there is no institution tasked with and responsible for the conduct of it, only individual, sporadic initiatives. This is the legacy of the elimination of the U.S. Information Agency after the end of the Cold War. Therefore, whatever efforts are undertaken, like those described above, are done piecemeal and ad hoc. This is a product of both organizational dysfunction and intellectual confusion. There are a number of very experienced Americans who know how to conduct the war of ideas in the Islamic world and elsewhere. They need a place to work from and funds to work with. Neither is currently available.

If we are to have a new strategy against al-Qaeda and the Muslim Brotherhood, we must first understand their claims to moral legitimacy and be prepared to undermine them. There is a theological and spiritual battle underway. We must be prepared to fight it in those terms. If not, as mentioned before, we will concede to our opponent an impregnable "theological safe haven" from which they cannot be dislodged.

What practical suggestions do I have for now? The first thing we should do is stop doing what we are doing because it is not working. It may even be counterproductive. It is not keyed to the essential effort of establishing our own moral legitimacy and undermining that of our enemy. Any activity that we are undertaking in the realm of public diplomacy that is not addressing one of those two missions, either directly or indirectly, is superfluous and possibly harmful. We must begin again from the ground up because this problem is not going away.

Notes

1   http://georgewbush-whitehouse.archives.gov/nsc/nsct/2006/sectionIII.html (viewed 24 May 2015).

2   Cited in Tony Blankley, "Journey into Islam," http://www.realclearpolitics.com/, 20 June 2007.

3   Cited in Devlin Barrett, "Diffuse Terror Groups Said to Be a Threat to U.S.," *The Wall Street Journal*, 9 September 2013.

4   As stated to the author by conference participant Yigal Carmon, October 20, 2008.

5   Cited in James Brandon, "Koranic Duels Ease Terror," *The Christian Science Monitor*, 4 February 2005, http://www.csmonitor.com/2005/0204/p01s04-wome.html (viewed 24 May 2015).

6   Norine MacDonald, "Afghanistan: the Relationship Gap", The International Council on Security and Development, July 2010, http://www.icosgroup.net/2010/report/afghanistan-relationship-gap/ (viewed 24 May 2015).

7   Ernesto Londoño, "Taliban steps up propaganda war," *The Washington Post*, 2 October 2010, A7.

8   Robert Andrews, conversation with the author, 2009.

9   Gordon Adams "Could the media save Afghanistan?" *Prospect*, 172, July 2010.

10 Captured al-Qaeda letter to Ayman al-Zawahiri, Iraq, 2005.

3

THE MUSLIM BROTHERHOOD: DOCTRINE, STRATEGY, OPERATIONS AND VULNERABILITIES

J. Michael Waller

Introduction

The Muslim Brotherhood is an Egypt-based global political movement founded in 1928, and rooted in the idea that it should be the political vanguard of Islamic transformation of an individual's ordinary life and of political society. Known in Arabic as *Ikhwan*, the brotherhood is organized under a political leader and a clerical spiritual leader, and a Shura Council. The Brotherhood's strategic goal is to re-establish the Caliphate, a totalitarian theocratic imperial regime, for the purposes of maintaining political power and expanding it worldwide. The Ikhwan's ultimate objective is to lead the Caliphate to place the entire world under Islamic totalitarian rule. By definition, the Muslim Brotherhood seeks the eventual overthrow of the Constitution of the United States. This chapter focuses on a U.S. approach based on the premise of an external and internal attack on its Constitution, but other countries may draw parallels for their own systems of government. Depending on the circumstances, the Brotherhood's tactics range from direct support for terrorism to working legally within political, legal and cultural sections of society.

Strategic Culture

The Muslim Brotherhood has never diverged from its mission of serving as the vanguard to re-establish the Caliphate as a totalitarian Islamic regime, and to expand the Caliphate globally to impose political control over all of humanity – Muslim and non-Muslim – worldwide. During its development in the 1930s, the Brotherhood stressed its view of "Islam as a total system, complete unto itself, and the final arbiter of life in all its categories," and "applicable to all times and to all places".[1] That view grew from the confines of Egypt to encompass all Islamic believers, and ultimately, to all of humanity worldwide. After concentrating on social, cultural and spiritual matters, the Brotherhood began its "political" operations in the late 1930s, and in so doing, moved beyond Egypt to aid Palestinian Arabs. Founder Hasan al-Banna officially noted the Brotherhood's political role in 1938, after political work had already begun, marking what he called "the beginning of their involvement in the external and internal political struggle". By 1939, al-Banna defined the Brotherhood itself as a "political organization," which it has been ever since. The Brotherhood profited politically from the ambiguity of the totalist essence of Islam, with al-Banna telling his followers, "If you are told you are political, answer that Islam makes no such distinction."[2]

The Ikhwan's strategic culture has been shaped by decades of operating underground or in semi-clandestinity. The organization's members did indeed live up to their formal name as a Society of Muslim Brothers. Faced with inevitable clashes with authority in Egypt, al-Banna stressed the need for secrecy and deception – even among friends and allies – as the organization grew in the 1930s. As Mitchell recounted in his scholarly study during that decade,

> But if the secret apparatus as such had not yet been set up, emphasis was laid on secrecy as to the purpose of existing formations. In a remarkable statement, made in 1938 but published only after the revolution in 1952, Banna, informing a questioning youth of the 'revolutionary' nature of the organization in matters of both 'reform' and 'liberation,' reminded him that in the face of 'the law,' it was a mistake to be candid, and that secrecy was necessary in the beginning of any movement to maintain its solvency and assure its survival.[3]

Secrecy became institutionalized with the creation during World War II of a secret apparatus along with "a more minute, flexible, controllable, and natural form of organization," a system known as "families," that operated openly. These "families" came to dominate the inner relationships that linked the Brotherhood together.[4]

The Ikhwan's periodic tactics of violence and political assassination, followed by government crackdowns that resulted in the executions of small groups of its members who became revered as martyrs, hardened the organization. While the Brotherhood welcomes people of different mindsets as long as they move closer to, and submit themselves under, its own doctrine, it does not tolerate significant doctrinal dissent among its actual members. The Muslim Brotherhood's strategic culture is governed by:

- its absolutist religious doctrine that subsumes all of one's life into "total" submission;
- its totalitarian political doctrine to operationalize its theocratic beliefs for waging political conflict and exerting political domination and control;
- its unlimited global objective to dominate and control humanity;
- its practical experience as a clandestine, underground, secretive, conspiratorial organization;
- its belief that the ends generally justify the means, and that all forms of violence are permissible in order to achieve and maintain those ends;
- its recognition that it cannot achieve its doctrinaire strategic goals with doctrinaire tactics, and therefore that it must expand its influence among its strategic enemies through infiltration, co-optation, inclusion, intimidation, information dominance, denial and deception;
- its recognition that violence must be waged when necessary and condemned when necessary, but is never rejected outright as a tool of political warfare, even where violence cannot be construed doctrinally as a last resort;
- its belief and experience that violence is often unnecessary, undesirable, or counterproductive, and that some of its best gains are made through political, economic, legal, social and cultural means;
- its experience that it must calibrate its tactics as circumstances require for it to further its expansionist strategic goals;
- its core belief that everyone, Muslim and non-Muslim, who resists its doctrine or refuses to submit to its domination, is a strategic enemy.

The Muslim Brotherhood operates overtly when possible, and covertly where it is banned, repressed, or suffers from a negative reputation. In all of its areas of operation, the Brotherhood expands its capabilities and presence through front organizations and through independent organizations that it has penetrated for the purpose of control or influence. Brotherhood fronts include charitable foundations; political parties; professional and labor associations and guilds; children's and youth organizations; student associations; athletic and social clubs; publishing houses and media organizations. Brotherhood Fronts also include nonprofit-making institutions that own networks of mosques, and which train and credentialize clerics and laity, legal support groups, political action and activist groups, and terrorist organizations.

As the vanguard of a global political and spiritual movement, the Brotherhood seeks to dominate the totality of individuals' lives as the ultimate totalitarian revolutionary organization.

For tactical purposes toward its strategic end goal, the Brotherhood uses a combination of violence and nonviolence as methods of conflict. Even where it is not exercising violence, the Brotherhood raises money and material support for terrorist organizations elsewhere, and provides political pressure and legal assistance to individuals and organizations accused or arrested for terrorism-related crimes. It has inspired a range of terrorist spinoffs, including Islamic Jihad groups, Hamas and al-Qaeda. It also incites others to violence, using its authority to appear to quell that violence should the actions prove counterproductive. Addressing different audiences in different languages, and engaging in flexible and often contradictory tactics as the situations warrant, the nature of the Muslim Brotherhood can confuse the outside observer – a purposeful defensive mechanism to keep its opponents off guard.

Organizational Evolution

The Muslim Brotherhood began as a religiously inspired political movement in 1928 to re-establish the totality of Islamic life on the individual Egyptian. As it evolved over the next decade, it developed the goal of establishing the Islamic Caliphate in Egypt as a replacement for Kemal Ataturk's abolition of the Caliphate in Turkey after the collapse of the Ottoman Empire following World War I. Originally Egypt-centric, the Brotherhood's initial mid-term goal was to take over the Egyptian government and establish the Caliphate in an Arab, as opposed to non-Arab, regime.

The compelling threats that the Brotherhood, by its doctrine, posed towards successive Egyptian governments, and the Brotherhood's acts of political violence and assassination, caused those governments to repress the Ikhwan (Brotherhood) and its members. The Brotherhood remained intact and cohesive by becoming an underground organization, learning clandestine tradecraft in an already conspiratorially-minded culture. The hardships of functioning as an underground movement hardened the Brotherhood's members and helped unite them. Meanwhile, as an underground organization, the Brotherhood was able to operate overtly by joining established political, social, business and cultural organizations, taking control of those it could and influencing the voices of those it could not control. In addition, it established its networks of front organizations to perform charitable, cultural, religious, political, economic, professional, and social work. By such means, the Brotherhood was able to establish a devoted following while minimizing the likelihood of being repressed. Over time, especially after the fall of the Nasser regime, the Brotherhood was able to operate less clandestinely through its fronts and affiliated organizations.

This type of existence allowed the Brotherhood to mask its presence officially and legally as the Muslim Brotherhood, even if it did not seek completely to conceal its hand; and to project an image of "many voices, one message" through arrays of entities that, on the surface, do not appear connected with one another. In this way, the Brotherhood was able to portray a less extreme and more mainstream image of itself – without compromising its doctrine, principles or strategy – by creating or stimulating other voices to provide the echo chamber effect that magnified its message.

By the 1970s, with the rise of Palestinian nationalist and Islamist violence in the Middle East, the Brotherhood supported and became more engaged in organized, transnational violence. Some Brotherhood figures in Egypt, Saudi Arabia, the Palestinian diaspora and elsewhere formed or led terrorist organizations that either became controlled Brotherhood fronts or assets; or spinoffs independent of the Ikhwan but still sharing the same strategic goals.

By the 1980s, the Brotherhood had become an internationalist movement and established organizational presences worldwide, including the United States, through national sub-units or chapters, and through national chapters of its international fronts, or nation- or continent-specific fronts and controlled affiliates. Organizationally and functionally, the Muslim Brotherhood can be likened to an Islamist Comintern.[5]

Internationally, the Muslim Brotherhood is guided by its central Shura Council, whose members operate disproportionately from Qatar, with national sections in selected countries, including the United States. Where there are no Muslims native to those countries who are properly indoctrinated and sufficiently trusted to be in the Ikhwan, the Brotherhood sends its own third-country nationals to reside in given countries as agents of influence. Those agents then lead a Brotherhood chapter or subunit for that country, and preside over setting up new national chapters of existing transnational Brotherhood organizations, new local or national front organizations catering to various constituencies or serving specific functions, and taking over the leadership of existing Muslim organizations not under Brotherhood control.

The pattern is similar to almost any international revolutionary movement, regardless of ideology. The best-known practitioners, the Soviets and their network of controlled Communist Parties, pioneered many of the tactics. However, socialists, labor unions, cultural organizations, and even churches and religious movements have organized and grown in similar fashion.

The Muslim Brotherhood views its political and organizational development to be carried out in distinct stages, described below.

Violence

Historically, the Muslim Brotherhood has a lengthy record of using terrorism, political assassination and other forms of violence to achieve its goals. Its leading theoreticians, including founder Husein al-Banna and theoretician Sayyid Qutb, have provided ideological and moral justifications for deadly violence on a large scale in pursuit of the Ikhwan's strategic goals, including the ideological worldview of al-Qaeda.

In recent decades, the Brotherhood's support for violence has varied, depending on the geographic area or on its own staged development. The Muslim Brotherhood's Egyptian terrorist affiliate, the Egyptian Islamic Jihad alternated between violence and lack of violence for tactical reasons. It is unclear whether the Egyptian Islamic Jihad is a splinter from the Brotherhood or is actually a covertly controlled organization, the "bad cop" that can make the Ikhwan look like the "good cop". EIJ spiritual leader Omar Abdel Rahman, commonly known as the Blind Sheik, sent word from his prison cell in the United States for the EIJ to lift its "cease fire," at which point the EIJ resumed its terrorism. Rahman is serving a life sentence for his plots in the 1990s to bomb the Holland Tunnel, Lincoln Tunnel, and United Nations headquarters in New York, and for his role in the 1993 bombing of the World Trade Center in which six people were killed and more than a thousand injured.

Whether the EIJ is a breakaway group, as the Brotherhood and its sympathizers claim in English – and as many credible independent experts also conclude – or remains part of the Brotherhood enterprise, remains unclear. What is clear is that as of 2012, the Brotherhood leadership openly called for Rahman's release. After his election as the first known Muslim Brotherhood leader to become chief of state of a sovereign country, Mohammed Morsi of Egypt announced he would pressure the United States to free Rahman and unspecified "detainees". Morsi made the comment in one of his first public statements as president-elect in June 2012. Surveying tens of thousands of supporters at Cairo's Tahrir Square, Morsi diverged from his scripted comments to acknowledge the placards and banners: "I see signs for Omar Abdel Rahman and detainees' pictures," Morsi told the gathering. "It is my duty and I will make all efforts to have them free, including Omar Abdel Rahman."

In reporting Morsi's speech, the *New York Times* commented that the unscripted statement "runs sharply counter to assiduous efforts over many years by Brotherhood leaders to convince the West that their group advocates only peaceful reform and does not condone violence".[6]

Morsi's and the Brotherhood's public ambivalence about violence surfaced again in their initial responses to the planned September 11, 2011 attacks on the United States Embassy in Cairo, and on the American consulate in Benghazi, Libya, in which the United States ambassador and members of his personal security detail were murdered. Initially, both Morsi and the Ikhwan were reticent to condemn the violence. Indeed, the Muslim Brotherhood had publicly endorsed the violent protests and sought to expand the expressions of anti-American outrage by calling for Egypt-wide protests for the following Friday.

Only a "backlash from Washington" caused the Brotherhood as an organization, and Morsi as president, to soften their public position. The President of the United States had to intervene personally in a 20 minute phone conversation with Morsi before Morsi would issue a statement of unequivocal denunciation of the violence.[7] Yet the Brotherhood maintained its bifurcated line. In its English-language statements – including a letter in the *New York Times*, tweets on Twitter, and statements on its official website, Ikhwanweb.net – the Brotherhood and its affiliates sounded resolutely against the violence and expressed sincere-sounding condolences. By contrast, its Arabic-language statements to its own audiences remained firm. A U.S Embassy official in Cairo thanked the Brotherhood in a Twitter conversation for its English-language condolences but added, "By the way, have you checked out your own Arabic feeds? I hope you know we read those too."[8]

It remains difficult if not impossible to gauge specifically where and when the Brotherhood tacitly supports terrorist violence, and where that violence is perpetrated by breakaway individuals or groups without Ikhwan support. The Brotherhood's opportunistic approach to conflict, and its support for violence in some places at some targets, but not in others, its simultaneous support via front groups for Islamist terrorists on the one hand, and for FBI counterterrorism efforts on the other; and its opposite statements to different audiences in Arabic and English can be confusing to the outside observer. Therefore, one must presume that the most authoritative Brotherhood statements are those that it issues to its own audiences in Arabic, and that its English-language statements are designed for deceptive purposes against the United States and others.

This presumption is validated both by Muslim Brotherhood doctrine and operational practice. Scholar William Gawthrop describes the Qur'anic doctrine of *taqiyya*:

> Concealing or disguising one's beliefs, convictions, ideas, feelings, opinions, and/or strategies at a time of imminent danger, whether now or later in time, [is permissible] to save oneself from physical and/or mental injury. *Taqiyya* has been used by Muslims since the 7th century to confuse and split 'the enemy'. One result is the ability to maintain two messages, one to the faithful while obfuscation and denial is sent – and accepted – to the non-Muslim audience.[9]

We find the manifestation of Garthrop's description of *taqiyya* in the transcript of a Hamas meeting in Philadelphia, secretly recorded by the FBI, concerning the deceptive work of a Hamas spinoff and Muslim Brotherhood front, the Council on Islamic-American Relations (CAIR). The transcript was provided as evidence in the 2004 *United States v Holy Land Foundation et al.* terrorism financing case. Hamas operative Omar Ahmad is quoted as saying in private to his colleagues:

> I believe that our problem is that we stopped working underground. We will recognize the source of any message which comes out of us. I mean, if a message is publicized, we will know . . ., the media person

among us will recognize that you send two messages: one to the Americans and one to the Muslims. If they found out who said that – even four years later – it will cause a discredit to the Foundation as far as the Muslims are concerned as they say, "Look, he used to tell us about Islam and that is a cause and stuff while he, at the same time, is shooting elsewhere."[10]

Cooperation with U.S. and allied authorities does not necessarily mean that a Muslim Brother is against terrorism. High-profile cases exist of the same Muslim Brotherhood operatives in cooperative relationship with the U.S. military and providing material support for terrorism.[11] The apparent dichotomy, upon examination, is actually consistent in the eyes of the Brotherhood, as both seemingly divergent actions in reality are working toward the same goal. Seldom, if ever, is the cooperation with U.S. authorities decisive against Islamist terrorists, with concessions coming from American officials and institutions, and not from the Ikhwan itself. Most of the "cooperation" comes in the form of subject-matter expertise and advice that advance the Ikhwan's frame of reference on the federal investigator or intelligence analyst. This propagandistic expertise is also provided with demands for "inclusion" within the U.S. defense and security community. Discussion of Brotherhood support for extremists and terrorists is discouraged, and usually dismissed as ignorant conspiracy theories or motivated by racism and bigotry – a conversation-killer in present American society that discourages professional independent inquiry and enforces groupthink.

Medium and Long-Term Strategic Goals

The Muslim Brotherhood's medium-term goals are to survive and grow as a viable vanguard movement of the Islamic faithful worldwide, to unify what it calls "observant Muslims," and to serve as the leading political, social and doctrinal vehicle in the world for Islam in general. A reaffirmation of its long-term strategic goals, in the words of an internal 1991 memorandum to the Muslim Brotherhood Shura Council, is to establish "the global Islamic state wherever it is".[12]

Balance Between Religious and Political Objectives

The Muslim Brotherhood has long grappled with the difficulties of public acceptance of its politicization of a profound religious faith that is deeply entrenched, if not always observed, in Islamic societies. Half a century ago, scholar Manfred Holpern concluded:

> When traditional Islam reacts by transforming itself into a religio-political totalitarian party (like the Muslim Brotherhood), it can safely be challenged as a novel ideology rather than as a hallowed way of life. There will still be battles, but this particular war is over in the great majority of Middle Eastern states.[13]

While the latter sentence may have been true at the time, with dictatorships repressing the Muslim Brotherhood and executing or scattering its main operatives, the "war" had begun again by the early 1970s with the rise of terrorism based on the ideologies of Brotherhood leaders in Egyptian prisons. The generally non-violent Islamist alternative to terrorism therefore became a more popular way of expressing discontent, aiding a global expansion of the Muslim Brotherhood that blossomed in the 1990s. That expansion received new energy with the rise of al-Qaeda and the September 11, 2001 attacks that made the Muslim Brotherhood look "moderate" in comparison, and intensified a decade later with the Arab Spring, where the Ikhwan succeeded where al-Qaeda could not by gaining political power in a sovereign state.

Meanwhile, the Muslim Brotherhood as we shall see below, avoided being challenged into irrelevance by broadening its appeal and superficially moderating its appearance, without altering its strategic goals. Rather than becoming the temporary novel ideology that it appeared to be fifty years ago, it has recast itself as the guarantor of a hallowed way of life as it focused its violence on common enemies (Israel, secular dictators and Ba'athism), and chose the socio-political route to power of "civilization jihad".

Since its beginnings, the religion of Islam has manifested itself as a political ideology for temporal purposes. A. A. A. Fyzee wrote in his contribution to the late Harold Lasswell's compendium on the interplay of religion and politics:

> Islam is a religion which teaches spiritual values and proposes social reform; it is not a political revolution in its essence. It is only when its ethical and social rules come into conflict with the political structure of the state that the impact becomes significant and begins to affect political conduct. It may therefore be asserted that primarily Islam is not a revolution in Political Theory, but has always had an influence

on the political conduct of the state. Where, however, Religion and Politics clash, it appears that in the hands of the statesman religion is made subservient to political ends.[14]

Fyzee said that in Islam's early days, during the life of Mohammed, Arab tribal culture and the Persian dynastic system had to reconcile their political practice with Islamic theology. He continued,

> The institution of the Caliphate is one of the most important results of the influence of religion on politics. After the death of the Prophet [sic], it was necessary to create machinery for the enforcement of the laws of Islam, and a direct result was the creation of the Caliph. He was the successor to the Prophet; he was to be an independent ruler and not a mere satrap; it was he who maintained the unity of Islam and enforced obedience to Islam.[15]

Over the centuries, the idea of the Caliphate weakened as multiple leaders claimed that they were the true caliph, along with the rise of sectarianism within Islam. Turkish leader Kamal Ataturk's abolition of the Caliphate in 1924 finished off the Caliphate as a ruling political institution, leading to the founding of the Muslim Brotherhood four years later whose express purpose would be to bring the Caliphate back. According to Fyzee,

> The abolition of the Caliphate in 1924 constitutes one of the most important phases of Muslim history. It changed the character of the Turkish State; it decapitated the body politic of Islam and rendered it headless; and it ushered in a new phase of Islamic law unknown to previous doctrine and ancient practice.[16]

Brotherhood founder al-Banna stressed then, as his successors do today, that the Ikhwan is the leading organization to rebuild and maintain ideological unity and to enforce obedience to that ideology.

Applicability of Distinctions

Doctrinally, the Brotherhood makes no distinctions between religion and politics. The United States and other secular societies are the ones stymied by such distinctions, particularly the U.S. with its Constitutional prohibition of a government-established religion and its Supreme Court-defined "separation of church and state".[17] In the fundamentally held belief of many Muslims, and of the Brotherhood in particular, there is absolutely no corresponding "separation of mosque and state". Consequently, the U.S. has limited its ability to understand and respond to the Ikhwan and other Islamists through the limits of its own worldview. This Western secular distinction simply does not apply to the Brotherhood – but the Brotherhood exploits this peculiar American-inspired handicap in order to stymie any policies that might hinder the Ikhwan's progress.

Egyptian President Morsi explained the distinctions – and overlap – in a September 2012 interview with the *New York Times*. "I grew up with the Muslim Brotherhood," he said. "I learned my principles in the Muslim brotherhood. I learned how to love my country with the Muslim Brotherhood. I learned politics with the Muslim Brotherhood. I was a leader of the Muslim Brotherhood."[18]

The Muslim Brotherhood does make a practical distinction between Islam in its theological and cultural forms, and "Islamism" as a political manifestation of the same. Therefore, the U.S. and its allies – including its Muslim friends and allies worldwide – can exploit this distinction by attacking the politicized force of "Islamism" without attacking the religious beliefs and cultural values of those professing Islam. At present, the U.S. is not making such a distinction, to the Brotherhood's benefit.

The Muslim Brotherhood's Enemies, and How It Understands Them

The Muslim Brotherhood understands its enemies to be all who refuse to submit to the totality of Islam as defined by the Ikhwan, including faithful Muslims. It does not treat individuals as enemies if they have not yet refused to submit, reasoning that they can be converted, or at least, persuaded or pressured to submit.

Means of Warfare: Violent

A survey of its more than 80 year history shows the Muslim Brotherhood as flexible with its use of violence, using it when repressed or for specific tactical purposes toward its strategic goal. Oftentimes the Brotherhood would wage violence in one area through controlled sections under different names, while its networks in other areas would publicly frown on terrorism (or make excuses for it) as they worked within civil society through charities, mosques, Islamic centers, the legal system, and the political process.

Use of political violence is a pragmatic matter, not a philosophical one. In its first decades of existence, the Brotherhood conducted political assassinations in Egypt, permitting the authorities to repress it and imprison and even execute its members. The Brotherhood assassinated or attempted to murder a series of Egyptian leaders, although there is debate about whether the assassination of Anwar Sadat, conceived and carried out by known Brotherhood members, was centrally authorized or controlled, or was carried out by a splinter group. The fact that the Brotherhood failed to condemn the attack and discipline the Islamist extremist movement through its own brutal enforcement methods indicates that the assassination was indeed supported, if not directed, by the Brotherhood leadership. And so we must assume that the Brotherhood's pattern of tacit support for political murder, like its tacit support for Islamist terrorism, is indeed rooted in active sympathy or approval, even if we cannot easily prove active support in practice.

Over the past 25 to 30 years or so, the Brotherhood became more refined and sophisticated, learning from the successes and failures of other revolutionary movements, as well as from their own. What is striking is how closely the Brotherhood's flexible use of violence or lack of violence parallels the experiences of left-wing extremist movements, as if at some point elements of the Ikhwan received political warfare and insurgent training from the same masters.

A well-documented contemporary case study of Muslim Brotherhood organized violence can be seen in the Islamic Resistance Movement, better known as the Palestinian terrorist group Hamas. Hamas is an armed Palestinian unit of the Muslim Brotherhood. It was formed by the Brotherhood, is led by Brotherhood members, and receives political, doctrinal, financial, material, and propaganda support from the Brotherhood and its known front organizations. According to an exhaustive study by Matthew Leavitt, despite a "critical philosophical distinction" between Hamas and the Brotherhood" about whether a Muslim must first follow the "true path" of Islam before waging violent jihad,

Hamas never fully broke from the Brotherhood. Hamas is not a splinter group; rather, it *is* the Palestinian branch of the Muslim Brotherhood, but with an explicitly violent agenda. [Hamas leader] Khaled Mishal acknowledges that "inside, we had several names: the

Islamic Movement [Hamas]; Muslim Brotherhood, Islamic Front, the (Islamic) Youth Center and the Islamic Bloc. It was one organization with different names."[19]

The inventing of the Hamas name in 1987 provided a front group or proxy for the Muslim Brotherhood in illegal and violent operations against Israel. "In so doing," Leavitt writes, "Hamas sought to safeguard the legal status of the Muslim Brotherhood, its parent organization. Despite its divergence from the priorities of the Brotherhood, Hamas has always existed as a dependent of the Brotherhood hierarchy."[20]

Means of Warfare: Political/Ideological/Psychological

In Egypt where it was repressed for decades as an official organization, the Muslim Brotherhood flourished as an underground movement, united by its guiding doctrine and the fellowship forged by constant persecution. As a result, it became proficient at operating clandestinely yet out in the open at the same time. Its trademark techniques were to create front organizations through which its operators could work publicly while not appearing to be with the Brotherhood, and to infiltrate and take over independent organizations. Brotherhood operatives participated in other social institutions that they could not dominate or control, in order to network and to gain influence.

These fronts and controlled organizations, as well as independent organizations in which Brotherhood operatives participated, spanned the breadth and depth of Egyptian civil society: business, organized labor, culture, religious charities and social clubs. According to a recent study,

> These positions enabled them to build their stature at a time when avenues for more direct political participation were often blocked. Such activity also helped the group expand its outreach networks, through which it gained popular support by providing social services and increasing its recruitment efforts.[21]

The Egyptian Muslim Brotherhood is guided by both political and spiritual leadership from the top, but also by consensus of its constituent elements in the form of a shura or council. The rapid population of sensitive posts in the Mohammad Morsi government of Egypt means that, for the Brotherhood, having longtime members in top posts ensures that its leaders have all been vetted over the course of decades for their willingness to comply with the internal shura committee's decisions. This does not mean that internal divisions are impossible, but the tight, time-tested circle in which decisions are made makes this highly unlikely. As a result, the Brotherhood maintains a unity of purpose that other Egyptian political groups have yet to achieve.[22]

Gaining power democratically did not moderate the Brotherhood's positions. The ouster of Mubarak early in 2011 during the "Arab Spring" was followed about a year later with electoral victories that gave the Brotherhood control of both houses of parliament and the committee responsible for writing Egypt's new constitution. In June 2012, Brotherhood leader Morsi was elected president. Morsi quickly took control of the most powerful Egyptian government ministries by appointing Ikhwan members to key posts, purged the senior officer corps of the military, decreed total executive and legislative powers, and took control of the authorship of the new constitution. He also began a campaign of intimidation and repression of news organizations that criticized his leadership or the Brotherhood in general. These actions were predictable to anyone familiar with the Brotherhood's guiding doctrine as a vanguard party that would coalesce others and repress opponents while moving toward its strategic goal.

Techniques from Within: "Civilization Jihad"

From its decades of experience as an underground organization in Egypt, and its negative image in the Western democracies, the Gulf states and elsewhere, the Muslim Brotherhood placed great emphasis on stealth, as its use of front organizations indicates. Violence, physical force, and other illegal actions in those countries would hinder the Brotherhood's ability to build political cadres and influence populations and decision makers; indeed, as had long been the case in Egypt, they would result in restrictions, repression, arrests and public opprobrium.

This practical tactic is what divides the Muslim Brotherhood from its even more extremist offshoots like al-Qaeda: for the time being, with specific exceptions such as Israel and targeted regimes like Libya under the former regime of Muammar Qaddafi and the secular Ba'athist Assad regime in Syria, direct acts of violence are generally forbidden, as they will provoke reactions that will hinder the movement from its strategic goals.[23]

The Muslim Brotherhood nevertheless views its generally legal activities through front groups and proxies as a type of ideological warfare. This is true both in Israel and Israeli-occupied areas as well as, say, Egypt, Kuwait or the United States. Participating in the democratic process – even winning national elections – does not moderate the Brotherhood's extremism; political action is simply a different instrument of the Brotherhood way of war.[24] The Brotherhood's term for waging warfare within legal, political, social and general cultural norms of the target civilization is "civilization jihad".[25]

We know about "civilization jihad" not from the Brotherhood's political subversion overseas, but from its operations in the United States. The circumstances that led to the discovery of the inner workings of "civilization jihad" show the dual nature of the organization's purpose, and the dangers of being seen as too close to those practicing violence. In August 2004, an alert policeman on the Chesapeake Bay Bridge near Annapolis, Maryland, noticed an SUV containing a couple and their three children, with the woman making videos of the four mile-long steel suspension bridge's structural details. Another officer pulled over the SUV, driven by Ismail Selim Elbarasse, and saw his wife attempting to hide the video camera. A routine computer check revealed that Elbarasse was wanted in Chicago on a federal material witness warrant relating to his involvement in funding a terrorist organization. The FBI then raided Elbarasse's home in Annandale, Virginia, and discovered a sub-basement that contained the archives of the North American Muslim Brotherhood.[26]

Elbarasse was an assistant to Mousa Mohammed Abu Marzook, a Muslim Brother who was deputy head of the political wing of the Islamic Resistance Movement, better known as Hamas. In Article Two of its 1988 founding charter, known as the Covenant, Hamas defined itself thus: "The Islamic Resistance Movement is one of the wings of Moslem Brotherhood in Palestine. Moslem Brotherhood Movement is a universal organization which constitutes the largest Islamic movement in modern times."[27]

Federal prosecutors introduced the documents as evidence, which the Brotherhood did not contest, in the 2004-2008 Holy Land Foundation terrorism financing trials in Texas. A federal judge released the evidence after all defendants were convicted and sentenced to prison, which is how the Brotherhood's internal documents became available for research.[28] This is how we learned about the Muslim Brotherhood's "civilizational jihad" strategy.

In 1987, the Shura Council of the Muslim Brotherhood approved and adopted what one of its members, Mohamed Akram (a.k.a. Mohamed

Aldouni) referred to as a "long term plan" to penetrate Western societies via stealthy means – while attacking Israel's occupation of Gaza through violence. Akram authored a document titled "An Explanatory Memorandum on the General Strategic Goal for the Muslim Brotherhood in North America" four years later, and appended what he called "A list of our organizations and the organizations of our friends," which, as a result of the FBI raid, is how we know definitively what the Muslim Brotherhood considered to be its U.S. fronts and controlled organizations two decades ago.[29]

Akram's Explanatory Memorandum for the Shura Council references the Brotherhood's strategic goals for a "global Islamic state". The movement toward that global Islamic state is to be "led by the Muslim Brotherhood which adopts Muslims' causes domestically and internationally," to expand the base of compliant Muslims, and to be the lead agent in "unifying and directing Muslims' efforts" under Brotherhood control. That movement, Akram stated, would be in support of "the global Islamic state, wherever it is".

The Brotherhood-led movement would become "a part of the homeland" of the host country, "'stable' in its land, 'rooted' in the spirits and minds of its people, 'enabled' in the [life] of its society and has firmly-established 'organizations' on which the Islamic structure is built and with which testimony of civilization is achieved," according to the document. The "grand mission," Akram affirmed, is a "'Civilization Jihadist' responsibility, which lies on the shoulders of Muslims and – on top of them – the Muslim Brotherhood in this country."[30]

"Civilization jihad" is carried out through the following "keys and tools":[31]

1. **"Adopting the concept of settlement and understanding its practical meanings"** to assist with the migration to and "settlement" of Muslims in other countries, including the United States and Canada, and integrating them into society *for the purposes of organizing and directing all aspects of their lives.*

2. **"Making a fundamental shift in our thinking and mentality in order to suit the challenges of the settlement mission."** The Brotherhood's shift in thinking was intended to accommodate and co-opt the diversity of Muslims living in North America, consistent with its doctrine to lead all Muslims everywhere. Among other internal changes, the Brotherhood called for:

- "A shift from the partial thinking mentality to the comprehensive thinking mentality." The Ikhwan would become outwardly more inclusive.

- "A shift from the mentality of caution and reservation to the mentality of risk and controlled liberation." Rather than exist in the shadows, the movement would now push political boundaries.

- "A shift from the mentality of the elite Movement to the mentality of the popular Movement." The vanguard would now become a grassroots people's movement.

- "A shift from the mentality of preaching and guidance to the mentality of building and testimony." Rather than lead openly with a rigid ideology that would alienate, the Brotherhood would lead by the example of its actions, to include advocacy, fraternity, charity, and defense of all Muslims, not just its ardent followers.

- "A shift from the single opinion to the multiple opinion mentality." A dictatorial tone in an established democracy would spell only failure; now the Ikhwan would become more accepting of different viewpoints for the purpose of expanding a movement toward its own strategic goals.

- "A shift from the collision mentality to the absorption mentality." Confrontation would now be necessary only to marginalize, discredit or otherwise combat intractable opponents – both Muslim and non-Muslim. The Brotherhood would change its own way of thinking to be more inclusive of others (again, both Muslim and non-Muslim) for the purpose of absorbing them under its vanguard.

- "A shift from the principles mentality to the programs mentality." The Brotherhood would establish itself as the leader through actions of political and legal action, charity and service, and defense of all Muslims in a country where they formed but a small minority.

- "A shift from the abstract ideas mentality to the true organizations mentality (This is the core point and the essence of the memorandum)." To accomplish all of the above, the Brotherhood would have to master political and social organization for the purpose of turning its doctrine into action.

3. **"Understanding the historical stages which the Islamic Ikhwani activism went through in this country."** Here, the Muslim Brotherhood operative lists eight distinct stages of the Ikhwan's development:

- "The stage of searching for self and determining the identity."
- "The stage of inner build-up and tightening the organization."
- "The stage of mosques and Islamic centers."
- "The stage of building the Islamic organizations – the first phase."
- "The stage of building the Islamic schools – the first phase."
- "The stage of thinking about the overt Islamic Movement – the first phase."
- "The stage of openness to other Islamic Movements and attempting to reach a formula for dealing with them – the first phase."
- "The stage of reviving and establishing the Islamic organizations – the second phase."

4. **"Understanding the role of the Muslim Brother in North America."** Key number four is extremely important, as it states clearly that the Muslim Brotherhood's purpose is to subvert and sabotage free societies, and specifically the United States, from within. "Civilization jihad" would use American institutions as instruments of their own self-destruction. The memorandum explained to the Shura Council: "The process of settlement is a 'Civilization-Jihadist Process' with all the word means. The Ikhwan must understand that their work in America is a kind of grand Jihad in eliminating and destroying Western civilization from within and "sabotaging" its miserable house by their hands and the hands of the believers so that it is eliminated and God's religion is made victorious over all other religions. Without this level of understanding, we are not up to this challenge and have not prepared ourselves for jihad yet. It is a Muslim's destiny to perform jihad and work wherever he is and wherever he lands until the final hour comes, and there is no escape from the destiny except for those who chose to slack. But, would the slackers and the Mujahedeen be equal?"

5. **"Understanding that we cannot perform the mission by ourselves or away from people."** The Muslim Brotherhood saw itself as far too small to do its work alone, and recognized the need to build coalitions for it to lead and control. The writer explained to the Shura Council, "Without their [Muslims'] capabilities, human, financial and scientific resources, the Ikhwan will not be able to carry out this mission alone or away from people . . . As for the role of the Ikhwan, it is the initiative, planning, leadership, raising the banner and pushing people in that direction. They are then to work to employ, direct and unify Muslims' efforts and powers for

this process. In order to do that, we must possess a mastery of the art of 'coalitions,' the art of 'absorption' and the principles of 'cooperation.'"[32]

6. **"The necessity of achieving a union and balanced gradual merger between private work and public work."**

7. **"The conviction that the success of the settlement of Islam and its Movement in this country is a success to the global Islamic Movement and a true support for the sought-after state, God willing."** In key number 7, the Muslim Brotherhood strategist in the U.S. took issue with the notion that organizing and leading the relatively small Muslim community in the United States would divert from progress toward establishing a global caliphate. To the contrary, he argued, the plan was crucial for creation of a new caliphate. In his words,

> There is a conviction – with which this memorandum disagrees – that our focus in attempting to settle Islam in this country will lead to negligence in our duty towards the global Islamic Movement in supporting its project to establish the state. We believe that the reply is in two segments: One – The success of the Movement in America in establishing an observant Islamic base with power and effectiveness will be the best support and aid to the global Movement project. And the second – is the global Movement has not succeeded yet in 'distributing roles' to its branches, stating what is . . . needed from them as one of the participants or contributors to the project to establish the global Islamic state. The day this happens, the children of the American Ikhwani branch will have far-reaching impact and positions that make their ancestors proud.[33]

8. **"Absorbing Muslims and winning them with all of their factions and colors in America and Canada for the settlement project, and making it their cause, future and the basis of their Islamic life in this part of the world."**

Dominance of the Muslim Narrative

The Brotherhood's guidance of all Muslims toward this political goal required it to dominate or co-opt as many Muslim groups and leaders as possible, and to discredit or otherwise marginalize its opponents. Targets would not merely be non-Muslim critics, but fellow Muslims, including and especially Muslims with distinguished academic, theological or cultural authority.

The first and most important Brotherhood instrument to gather Muslims from the United States and Canada, and to influence and assess them as the vanguard of the "civilizational jihad", is a front called the Islamic Society of North America (ISNA), now based in Plainfield, Indiana. Listed first among the 29 groups that Akram informed the Muslim Brotherhood Shura Council were either fronts of, or dominated by, the Ikwhan in North America, ISNA sponsored annual conventions in the 1990s to begin unification of the Islamist movement under Brotherhood control. ISNA encouraged Muslims of different ideological persuasions to debate and discuss the issues. In the end, ISNA would expel and ban the non-compliant. Other Brotherhood front groups would then take the lead in marginalizing and rendering those Muslims resistant to Brotherhood domination, through a campaign of public denunciation, ostracism and humiliation.

Marginalization of Independent Muslims and Domination of the Narrative

Where it cannot succeed in unifying a Muslim leader of faction under its umbrella, either through persuasion or enforced obedience, the Brotherhood opts – in democratic societies, at least – to silence the non-subservient through political and social means. It employs its superior political organization and ideological discipline to marginalize and diminish its targets through public ostracism, intimidation, and humiliation.

Even in democratic societies, the Muslim Brotherhood operates in a similar clandestine fashion. To obscure its own presence while magnifying an illusion that mainstream Muslims from all walks of life share its views, the Brotherhood works through networks of front organizations and groups under its financial or political dominance or control. Those organizations claim to represent large Muslim constituencies, when in reality few have any significant membership at all – although they managed to expand their bases of support over the years by serving as public advocates and providing fraternal organizations, charitable services, and doctrinal and political training.

The groups, in turn, form ad hoc coalitions to project the image of a large, broad-based, diverse coalition of independent organizations representative of the Muslim mainstream, much as non-Muslim radical groups and clandestine organizations did during the Cold War to inflate the appearance of their small numbers.[34] The tactic is common to revolutionary movements with comparatively few members, which Saul Alinsky summarizes in his *Rules for Radicals*:

1) *deceptions*

> If your organization is small in numbers ... conceal the members in the dark but raise a din and clamor that will make the listener believe that your organization numbers many more than it does.[35]

The Brotherhood-dominated coalitions then launch political attacks on individual targets, isolating them for ostracism, and making them seem out of the mainstream and not worthy of attention. Alinsky describes how to do it: "Pick the target, freeze it, personalize it, polarize it." He stresses again: "the opposition must be singled out as the target and 'frozen.'"[36] The point is to make the target look vulnerable to discourage sympathizers, and to make the target feel vulnerable to discourage resistance. It does not matter, for the moment, if that target has allies. According to Alinsky, "One of the criteria in picking your target is the target's vulnerability . . . When you 'freeze the target,' you disregard . . . for the moment, all the others to blame."[37]

In this line of attack, the target must be a person, not a thing, group or idea: "it must be a personification, not something general and abstract," according to Alinsky. "With this focus comes a polarization ... all issues must be polarized if action is to follow."[38] Follow-on action includes vilification of the target. If he is to be neutralized in the public eye, he can be conceded no redeeming qualities. In Alinsky's words,

> Can you imagine in the arena of conflict charging that so-and-so is a racist bastard and then diluting the impact of the attack with qualifying remarks such as 'He is a good churchgoing man, generous to charity, and a good husband'? This becomes political idiocy.[39]

We find the Alinsky tactical template in the Muslim Brotherhood's attempts to present a false image of the size and diversity of its following, and to minimize, ostracize, and destroy the credibility of its opposition. The key is to project political authority and strength for oneself, while diminishing the most credible of critics.

For an operational example of the Muslim Brotherhood at work in this fashion, we need not rely on foreign occurrences translated from other languages, but can view the tradecraft close to home. By the 1990s, the Muslim Brotherhood – generally not free to operate politically in most Muslim-majority countries – had established a network of U.S.-based front organizations and affiliates to project the appearance of strength well beyond its numbers, and, indeed, to imply that the front groups were representative of the American Muslim mainstream. The network provided a myriad of seemingly independent voices sharing the same message, a manufactured echo chamber effect that made its individual targets seem that much smaller. They claimed to represent Muslim students, Muslim communities, Muslim social scientists, Muslim scientists and engineers, Muslim physicians, Muslim teachers, Muslim businessmen, Muslim youth and Muslim attorneys.

Our specific example took place at the Loy Henderson Auditorium at the State Department in Washington, DC, on January 7, 1999. The event was a State Department Open Forum of about 250 government officials and invited guests to discuss "The Evolution of Extremism".[40] This was a defining period for Washington decision makers to understand "Islamism" and "Islamic extremism," as the Clinton Administration was just beginning to grapple with the threat from al-Qaeda. Until that point, more mainstream Muslim figures would refer to extremism behind closed doors and seldom with specifics, both out of deference to fellow Muslims in the presence of nonMuslims, and out of fear of retaliation from extremists.

At the State Department forum, Shaykh Mohammed Hisham Kabbani of Detroit, the spiritual leader of Sufi Muslims in the United States, rose with a strong message of caution. Shaykh Kabbani knew how the extremists, including the Muslim Brotherhood, operated in his native Lebanon, where his family dominated the muftiate for more than a century. A theologian who was nonpolitical and by nature nonconfrontational, Shaykh Kabbani spoke in general terms whose meaning was unmistakable to certain Islamists in the audience.

He told the gathering that some Muslim groups in the U.S. were taking money they were raising for humanitarian aid, and using it "to buy weapons to fight in the name of Islam" – a reference to the Holy Land Foundation of Texas and other organizations, including the Islamic Society of North America (ISNA). Noting the state of generally low-budget mosques in America, Shaykh Kabbani said that "extremism has spread to 80 percent of the Muslims in the U.S," adding that of the more than 2,000 mosques in the country, "80 percent of them are being run by extremist ideologies" – a reference to the North American Islamic Trust (NAIT), which owned the deeds or helped pay the mortgages and leases for those mosques, and ISNA, which provided the Islamist doctrinal literature and trained and certified Islamist clerics. The shaykh warned of penetration of American universities by Islamist extremists – a reference to the Muslim Students Association (MSA), which the Muslim Brotherhood considers as its own appendage.

Americans needed to understand the different tenets of Islam much better than they did, the shaykh continued, saying, "extremism can be solved if the West better understands Islam and builds bridges between the U.S. and Islam". The problem, he added, was that "those advising the U.S. government are extremists themselves" – a reference to the American Muslim Council (AMC), the Council on American-Islamic Relations (CAIR), and ISNA. "You are not hearing the moderates among Muslims," he told the government functionaries present. "You are hearing the extremists among Muslims."[41]

That could not stand. Kabbani would not identify individuals and groups in public (though he would in private), and his Muslim Brotherhood-related critics knew it; the shaykh's followers had been in bitter confrontations with the Islamists for years, with reports of "ugly scenes" at the Islamic Society of North America (ISNA) conventions in 1994, 1996, 1997 and 1998, after which the Islamists spread rumors that the shaykh was a "Zionist agent" receiving "Zionist funding," and they barred the Sufis from participating.[42] Now, in front of the U.S. government officials, the Islamists challenged him to provide proof. As a theologian, naming personalities was not his way. He was not a politician. Immediately, an AMC organizer challenged Shaykh Kabbani. After the event, an ostensibly ad hoc group of Muslim organizations sent out a joint news release to attack and anathematize the cleric. They claimed to represent a majority of American Muslims. Pointedly depriving the clergyman of his clerical title, the news release stated:

> Mr. Kabbani has put the entire American Muslim community under unjustified suspicion. In effect, Mr. Kabbani is telling government officials that the majority of American Muslims pose a danger to our society. Additionally, Islamophobic individuals and groups may use these statements as an excuse to commit hate crimes against Muslims.[43]

The groups then made a final cut to humiliate the shaykh in the eyes of other Muslims as they again spoke as the self-appointed representatives of the "American Muslim community". The release continued:

Deceptiveness

We therefore ask Mr. Kabbani to promptly and publicly retract his statements, to apologize to the American Muslim community, and to exert his utmost effort to undo the damage these statements have done. The issue is not that of a mere difference of opinion within an American religious community, but involves the irresponsible act of providing false information to government officials. This false information can jeopardize the safety and well-being of our community and hurt America itself by damaging its values of inclusiveness, fairness and liberty.[44]

None of the signatories of the news release expressed any concern about any Muslim in the United States who might be aiding and abetting terrorism of Islamist extremism. They were concerned only with delegitimizing the sole Muslim of stature who dared raise the issue to others, and defending themselves against possible investigation or harassment.

Federal investigations and terrorism trials would later prove that Shaykh Kabbani was correct. But that would not happen for several years. Shaykh Kabbani had been frozen, isolated and vilified in front of scores of U.S. government officials who knew little about the many apparently different voices castigating him. One observer of the conflict noted the successful tactics employed against the Shaykh:

> Whatever Shaykh Kabbani's original intention . . . the spectacle of a lone American Muslim leader expressing strong political views in the name of 'nearly all Muslims' may have the shock effect of forcing the majority of national U.S. Muslim leaders to agree on a comprehensive political platform to start speaking for themselves.[45]

That is precisely what ultimately occurred. Those groups that were not under the sway of the Muslim Brotherhood felt compelled to sign on. The Brotherhood fronts ended up as invited White House guests under presidents Bill Clinton and George W. Bush, with Shaykh Kabbani effectively being banned until 2003 – long enough for the fronts to become credentialized and accepted as mainstream Muslims in America.

But were they in fact? Let's look at the groups that signed the news release to denounce Shaykh Kabbani for his concerns about extremism:

- The **American Muslim Council** (AMC), led by Muslim Brotherhood operative Abdurahman Alamoudi, collapsed a few years later after

Alamoudi was seen on video proclaiming his support for Hamas and Hizbullah, and after his executive director refused to denounce al-Qaeda by name. Alamoudi was apprehended in Britain in 2003 and turned over to the United States on charges of illegally transporting more than $300,000 in cash from Libyan leader Muammar Gaddafi's Jihad Fund, either to assassinate Saudi Arabia's Crown Prince (now King) Abdullah, or to fund insurgents to kill American soldiers in Iraq.

- The **American Muslim Political Coordination Council** (AMPCC);
- The **American Muslim Alliance** (AMA), chaired by Agha Saeed, reportedly a former head of the Communist Party of Pakistan, who later built an alliance with the Islamists. He sought to buy influence with the successful Senate campaign of a prominent politician. The present U.S. Secretary of State, during her 2000 Senate campaign, returned $50,000 in campaign donations raised by the AMA, citing AMA's support for terrorism.[46]
- The **Council on American Islamic Relations** (CAIR) was founded in 1994 as a Muslim Brotherhood front.
- The **Muslim Public Affairs Council** (MPAC), cofounded in 1988 in California by Hassan Hathout, an Egyptian native who credits Muslim Brotherhood founder Hassan al Banna as his teacher and as the person "who most influenced my life".[47]
- The **Islamic Circle of North America** (ICNA), which a federal court found to be a Muslim Brotherhood front or controlled organization in the 2008 Holy Land Foundation terrorism financing case.[48]
- The **Muslim Students Association** of the USA and Canada (MSA), which a federal court found to be a Muslim Brotherhood front or controlled organization in the 2008 Holy Land Foundation terrorism financing case.
- The **Islamic Society of North America** (ISNA), which apparently did not sign the news release but did ban the Shaykh and his people from its conventions, was revealed in internal Muslim Brotherhood documents to be a Brotherhood front. ISNA provided ideological materials and training to 1,100 of the country's estimated 1,500 mosques. A federal court found ISNA to be a Muslim Brotherhood front or controlled organization in the 2008 Holy Land Foundation case. The federal judge revealed that ISNA was an "unindicted co-conspirator" in the terrorism funding case. The timeline shows that ISNA was involved in funding terrorism at

precisely the time that Shaykh Kabbani voiced concerns about Islamic charities raising money for violence in the name of Islam.[49]

As for Shaykh Kabbani, neither he nor the Sufi Muslims were able to have a serious impact on how nonMuslims in the U.S. could measure Islamist extremism. After the 9/11 attacks, he wistfully told the *Detroit News*, "I'm sad because when I spoke up in 1999, they didn't listen. And to the extent that the extremists are everywhere – in the administration, on Capitol Hill – they didn't do their homework."[50]

Alliances (tactical and strategic)

The Muslim Brotherhood has built a constellation of alliances of varying degrees and durations, with a diverse variety of organizations based in different countries. Most of these alliances appear to be of an opportunity-based, tactical nature. Others do not appear on the surface to be alliances at all, but the evidence suggests tangible and even strong relationships.

NB

Historically, the Brotherhood made whatever tactical alliances it could. It briefly aligned itself with Nazi Germany during World War II, against both the British, who had ruled Egypt, and the Soviets, whose communist, atheist ideology ran diametrically opposite the Ikhwan's Islamist dogma. In 1950, to purge Egypt of British influence, the Muslim Brotherhood joined political forces with the Egyptian Communist Party. Neither group was sufficiently strong; both had to set aside ideology and work with one another. According to Ginat,

> Communist activity became possible when the state of emergency came to an end, at the beginning of 1950. The communists started a new political approach when they realized that their aims could not be achieved without increasing cooperation with the main opposition groups; this became the communists' short-term aim and first priority, and they were ready to sacrifice some basic elements of their ideology for its realization.[51]

Left-wing secular parties, with Communist support, formed the Democratic Popular Front in August 1951. The Muslim Brotherhood did not formally join, but actively collaborated. Salah al-Ashwami, a Muslim Brotherhood leader, explained, "at the present time the Brotherhood does not find any real objections which would prevent the Brotherhood from establishing a common front with the Communists against our common enemies, the imperialists".[52]

MB During the Cold War, with Gamel Abdel Nasser's secular regime in an alliance with the Soviet Union, the Brotherhood may have covertly worked with the United States, though that well publicized contention does not appear to be supported by the facts.[53] When Anwar Sadat overthrew Nasser, aligned Egypt with Washington, made peace with Israel, and continued repressing the Brotherhood, the Brotherhood shifted again and may have worked covertly with the Soviet Union – which the Ikhwan saw as a long-term threat because of Moscow's strong backing for secular Ba'athist and atheist Marxist regimes.

As is typical with most banned political movements, as the Muslim Brotherhood was in Egypt until 2012 and remains in many countries, the Ikhwan takes allies where it can find them, while at the same time – seemingly paradoxically but in fact quite logically – preparing to break with or even attack them.

The Brotherhood can maintain these shifting and often conflicting alliances by maintaining a series of front organizations, both transnational and national, around the world. The Brotherhood's main point of contact with many of its tactical allies is therefore indirectly through its fronts and other controlled organizations, and through its agents who operate those fronts.

Ties to Al-Qaeda

Given that the Muslim Brotherhood provided the ideological origins of al-Qaeda, that present al-Qaeda leader Ayman Al-Zawahiri and other terrorists got their start in the Ikhwan, and that the Brotherhood and al-Qaeda share the same strategic goals, it would appear that the two could become united by a commonality of purpose. "For salafists, the Muslim Brotherhood is a cornerstone organization. They articulated the original philosophy on which all subsequent Salafi-Jihadist activism is based. The writings of Sayyid Qutb are the intellectual and theological underpinnings behind organizations like Egypt's Islamic Jihad, a group headed by al-Zawahiri that ultimately merged with al-Qaeda," according to Lydia Khalil.[54] The Brotherhood's infiltration and election route in Egypt and elsewhere frustrated al-Qaeda and its terrorism strategy. Al-Zawahiri's bitter denunciations of the Muslim

Brotherhood in Egypt during the late Mubarak years were over tactics, not goals; the terrorist chief saw the Brotherhood as diluting its ideological purity and making itself subservient to the Mubarak regime and its patron, the United States.[55]

Even so, U.S. authorities report that they have found hard operational links between at least one top Muslim Brotherhood operative and al-Qaeda. In 2005, the U.S. Department of the Treasury described the 2003 arrest of Abdurahman Alamoudi, one of the principal Brotherhood political operatives in the United States, as "a severe blow to Al Qaeda, as Alamoudi had a close relationship with Al Qaida and raised money for Al Qaida in the United States".[56]

NB Ties to Other Religions

The Ikhwan builds relations with other religious organizations or individual figures, but only insofar as the others do not criticize the Brotherhood or its agenda. Its expulsion of the Sufis and its non-inclusiveness of Shi'a Muslims from its supposedly inclusive networks shows the limits of its cooperation. Even so, the Brotherhood has used "interreligious dialogue" and "understanding" as ways of building relations with other faiths, as long as they are not criticized. In calibrating its arguments before American audiences, for example, Muslim Brotherhood operatives show nuance and sophistication about the many different tendencies of Christianity.

For example, this writer has personally observed a senior Ikhwan operative, Louay Safi of ISNA, stress to predominantly Southern Baptist and non-denominational Christian evangelical audiences in the U.S. military that "Muslims are Christians who observe Jewish law." That argument supposedly makes the Muslim Brotherhood acceptable to Bible Christians by making Islam appear to be Biblical and even Christian. Meanwhile, before Catholic audiences, that same Ikhwan operative would attempt to link Islamic values with Roman Catholic social doctrine, and even become ensconced at Georgetown University's Prince Alwaleed Bin Talal Center for Muslim-Christian Understanding in Washington, D.C.[57] Brotherhood residents at places like Georgetown would then gradually convince the students, staff and faculty of the Catholic school to refer to Muhammad as "Prophet," with a capital "P," while one is challenged to find Georgetown officials casually calling Jesus Christ by his proper title of "Messiah" or "Savior".

Ties to Marxists

For decades, Muslim Brotherhood fronts have joined broad coalitions with radical secular organizations, including Marxists and those whose social values are regarded as *haram* and subject to severe punishment under the Ikhwan's own doctrine. Early popular front activity with the Egyptian Communist Party in 1950 was noted above. In the 1980s, for example, Muslim Student Association chapters across North America joined into popular front coalitions with avowed Marxist-Leninist organizations and in support of such causes. Brotherhood organizations and members have satisfactorily joined forces with avowed Marxists, radical feminists and others in solidarity coalitions and legal cases. An example is the "blind sheik" Omar Abdel Rahman, whose longtime lawyer and collaborator, Lynne Stewart, is an avowed Marxist and radical feminist.

In an interview with the *Marxist Monthly Review*, Stewart chided her fellow radicals and defended both Rahman personally and Islamist extremism in general, with this ideological justification:

> I think that we, as persons who are committed to the liberation of oppressed people, should fasten on the need for self-determination, and allow people who are under the heel of a corrupt and terrifying Egypt—where thousands of people are in prison, and torture and executions are, according to Amnesty International and Middle East Watch, commonplace—to do what they need to do to throw off that oppression. To denigrate them [Islamists] as rightwing, I don't think is proper. My own sense is that, were the Islamists to be empowered, there would be movements within their own countries, such as occurs in Iran, to liberate.[58]

Ties to the United States Government

Through its fronts, the Muslim Brotherhood has worked extensively with the U.S. government to promote its ideological goals. Alamoudi was instrumental in working with the Department of Defense to start the Muslim chaplain program within the military, and to induce DoD to name ISNA, the Brotherhood front group, as a certifying entity for U.S. military chaplains. ISNA, CAIR and others provide training and subject matter expertise to the FBI, CIA, Department of Defense, Department of Homeland Security, Department of Justice, and other agencies.

Elected officials of both parties have welcomed Muslim Brotherhood figures as advisors, fundraisers, and even as special guests in Congress and at the White House. Leaders of Muslim Brotherhood front organizations frequently make accusations of racial or religious bigotry or threaten to cease cooperation with government agencies if they deem those agencies' actions to be "offensive". This writer can provide extensive specific details, but the subject is beyond the scope of this paper. The U.S. government does not appear to have a means of properly vetting Muslim experts, or evaluating the potential for undue Muslim Brotherhood influence on the perceptions, attitudes and understandings of U.S. intelligence, diplomatic, law enforcement and military personnel. Indeed, there is reason for concern that professionals in public service and independent subject-matter experts have been professionally penalized for raising legitimate concerns about Muslim Brotherhood penetration of the U.S. military and other entities.

Key Vulnerabilities of the Muslim Brotherhood

While the Muslim Brotherhood is well disciplined, well organized, well-funded, and finally in control of a state, it has key vulnerabilities that, if properly exploited, could become its undoing. The vulnerabilities are principally of a doctrinal, ideological or political nature, thus to exploit them, an opponent would need the human resources and the will to identify and exacerbate them in a thoughtful political warfare campaign.

Let us survey some of the principal vulnerabilities that an opponent could exploit if it so chose. The following partial list is merely illustrative, and does not purport to be complete:

- A totalitarian political ideology that naturally breeds suspicion, fear, opposition and animosity.
- A transnational, expansionist ideological doctrine that requires it to attack, infiltrate, dominate and even control the governments of other countries. This ideology constitutes a "threat doctrine" in the U.S. understanding of the term.
- A militant, organized aggressiveness that creates widespread resentment and fear which, if properly harnessed, could turn tables against the Brotherhood.

- A militant, organized aggressiveness that exploits the slightest political openings in undemocratic regimes, thus placing governments on the alert to crack down hard.

- A known proclivity toward violence if it is repressed or does not get its way; this known proclivity invites others to defend themselves with violence.

- A global strategic vision of ideological and political dominance worldwide, including the United States, by definition making it a conspiracy to subvert or overthrow the Constitution of the United States. As such, all U.S. government officials who swear an oath to uphold and defend the Constitution "against all enemies, foreign and domestic," are statutorily bound to be vigilant against the Muslim Brotherhood and its fronts.

- A resurgence of premodern doctrine and compulsory lifestyle during a time of accelerated modernization, diversified communication, and increased social expectations and demands that would be expected to undermine the austere and stifling social conditions that the Brotherhood seeks to impose.

- A totalitarian politicization of a cherished way of life by millions of people who choose to live out that lifestyle in ways counter to the politicized dogma being imposed.

- A well-networked, identifiable global network that is easy to track, disrupt and, if necessary, destroy.

- A decades-old trail of mortal enemies, mainly among fellow Muslims, who have scores to settle.

- Sufficient connections with specially designated terrorists and wanted terrorists to warrant action against it as an organization, and against its constituent elements and organizations.

- A sufficient quantity and diversity of enemies or presumed enemies, in the forms of governments and regimes that it has either identified for overthrow, or who are in fear of a Muslim Brotherhood overthrow.

- Lifestyles of certain of its leaders that, if exposed, would discredit their moral and ideological authority, demoralize their followers, and cause them to be punished under their own harsh code.

- Finally, the Muslim Brotherhood has offered itself as a source of hope and change, with the benefit of having no track record of actually ruling and administering a country. While an asset in many ways to help it take power with a degree of popular support – no track record allows it to attack the track record of the political establishment – that lack of experience is a significant vulnerability: The Ikhwan must show rapid, tangible progress in a short period of time lest it lose public confidence and with it, political authority and prestige.

Therefore, a determined opponent can stunt the Brotherhood's success at governing by devising a strategy to undermine its effectiveness. That strategy would include bilateral assistance; multilateral lending; military and security support; public diplomacy to magnify the voice of any domestic political opposition and to provide training in political organization; diplomatic and security policies to pressure other governments (such as Qatar and Saudi Arabia) not to subsidize an Ikhwan-led regime; aggressive intelligence collection for the purposes of waging a sustained, long-term political warfare offensive against the Brotherhood, its leaders, and their supporters.

How the 'Arab Spring' Has Affected the Muslim Brotherhood

Events in both the Middle East and the United States emboldened and energized the Muslim Brotherhood well before the Arab Spring. Reasonable people can differ on the approximate times and circumstances of the Brotherhood's rejuvenation, but the aftermath of the September 11, 2001 terrorist attacks on the United States is a good estimate of the time when the Brotherhood's fortunes began to shift. That aftermath validated the Muslim Brotherhood's outwardly unviolent general strategy. With the U.S. leadership's uncompromising post-9/11 view that one was "with us or with the terrorists," the Ikhwan, like a number of Muslim heads of state who played a double game with both terrorists and the United States, saw that it had everything to lose by embracing violence, and everything to gain by recasting itself and its members as "moderate Muslims".

By that time, the Muslim Brotherhood had established a presence inside the United States that afforded it access to American decision-makers. That initial presence was relatively small within the fragmented and largely disorganized Islamic demographic in the U.S. However, as the most organized group within a disorganized community, the Brotherhood had the political advantage. In the 1990s, having taken over existing organizations and building front groups of its own, the Brotherhood reached out successfully to significant nonMuslim figures in both major American political parties, and even gained access to, and recognition from, the White House.

One might even say that the events leading up to the U.S.-directed ouster of Saddam Hussein and his Ba'athist regime in 2003 emboldened the Ikhwan, well before the Arab Spring. While the Brotherhood was not well organized in Iraq, it viewed the secular and decidedly antiBrotherhood Ba'athist party as a mortal enemy. Its agents in the United States were supportive of Operation Iraqi Freedom. U.S. officials, classifying Saddam Hussein's regime as a state sponsor of terrorism and fixed in their "with us or with the terrorists" view, gratefully accepted subject-matter expertise, ideological instruction, analytical assistance, and other forms of knowledge-related help from Muslim Brotherhood agents and fronts. With the toppling of Saddam Hussein, one of the Brotherhood's primary immediate targets was gone.

The end of Saddam Hussein and the total (and arguably counterproductive) deBa'athification of Iraq left the only other Ba'athist government, the Assad regime in Syria, to be dealt with. Though generally secular and hostile to Islamization domestically, the Syrian regime was a strong ally of the Shi'a Islamist regime in Iran, likewise not a strategic partner of the Muslim Brotherhood.

The Arab Spring proved to be the political payoff for the Muslim Brotherhood's "civilization jihad" tactic. The Ikhwan had had scant hopes of gaining power in any Arab country until the toppling of the Tunisian, Libyan and Egyptian regimes. Few Arab countries have viable, organized political opposition movements apart from the Muslim Brotherhood that are ready or able to govern. Consequently, the ouster of status quo Arab regimes – friend or foe – means that the Muslim Brotherhood is among the best organized to exploit any instability or political vacuum – or, as the liberalization in Kuwait shows, any opening up of a political system. While it is generally not large enough outside Egypt to control a government outright, it is organized and regimented enough to dominate the proper levers of power, and to make at least tactical alliances with elements of the armed force, police, security and intelligence services, and the bureaucracy.

This political development could have profound effects on U.S. security relationships in the Middle East. "The Muslim Brotherhood, the force that has emerged from the Arab Spring, [is] plotting regime change in the Gulf," Dubai police chief Dhahi Khalfan stated publicly in March, 2012. "My sources say that the next step is to make the Gulf ruling families powerless. This will begin with Kuwait in 2013 and end in 2016 with other countries."

Khalfane said he warned all six Gulf monarchies – Bahrain, Kuwait, Oman, Qatar, Saudi Arabia and his own UAE – against the Muslim Brotherhood.[59]

Four months later, after the Muslim Brotherhood's takeover of the Egyptian government, the Dubai police chief warned the Brotherhood against using social media to destabilize Gulf Cooperation Council (GCC) governments.[60] In an appearance marking Ramadan, Lt. Gen. Dahi Khalfan explicitly referenced what he called an "international plot" based in "North Africa" to overthrow the governments of the wealthy UAE and its neighbors. The purpose, he said, was financial: To take control of their vast wealth. "This is preplanned to take over our fortunes," the police chief said. "The bigger our sovereign wealth funds and the more money we put in the banks of Western countries, the bigger the plot to take over our countries," he added, fingering "the Brothers" as a main culprit.[61]

The Muslim Brotherhood in Kuwait responded loudly and harshly – in ways similar to their repeated smack-downs of critics in the United States. They singled out the UAE's Khalfan for opprobrium, accusing him of "offending" and "insulting" the "Kuwaiti people". They then held the Kuwaiti prime minister, a member of the royal family, personally responsible for the UAE general's remarks, hinting that the prime minister's silence was a sign of weakness – a major slap at the personal honor of the chief of government. In a dig at the prime minister's honor and an attempt to cause rifts between Kuwait and the UAE, an Islamist Kuwaiti member of parliament stated publicly, "Kuwait's Prime Minister bears the responsibility for [Lieutenant General Dhahi] Al-Khalfan's offensive remarks for failing to protect the dignity of citizens described by Al-Khalfan as street thugs."

Police chief Khalfan was undaunted, raising the Brotherhood's ire through five consecutive days of attacks via Twitter, and saying that the GCC would have to expel Kuwait if a Muslim Brother became prime minister. Another Islamist politician tweeted back that the Dubai general's "insults to the Kuwaiti people, their MPs, families and tribes are unacceptable". A former dean of the Faculty of Sharia at Kuwait University raised the issue even higher, holding the entire UAE government responsible for the views of the police chief of one of the emirates: "for the insults Al-Khalfan made" against the theology professor's family.[62]

We see from this exchange a pattern typical of the Muslim Brotherhood's political attacks, be they in Arab countries or the United States, or among Muslims or between Muslims and nonMuslims:

N B

- The Brotherhood infiltrates political institutions through "civilization jihad";
- A courageous authority figure raises objections and warnings against rising extremism through the political process, and against the Muslim Brotherhood specifically;
- That authority figure is singled out for personal attack;
- The Brotherhood knows that the warnings are aimed narrowly against it, but claims that entire social groups or entire peoples are "insulted" and "offended," and speaks out in defense of the much larger groups;
- If the critic does not submit, the Brotherhood raises the stakes by holding the critic's superiors personally accountable for the "insults" and "offenses";
- If silent opponents of the Brotherhood do not side with the Ikhwan and criticize the offender, those opponents will be castigated as weaklings and stooges of he who offends the entire nation;
- If the situation is not resolved to the Brotherhood's satisfaction, the Brotherhood tries to break the unity of its opponents and drive wedges between them, with the goal of causing one or more parties to break and to isolate, marginalize and discredit the single courageous authority figure who first raised the objections.

As one would expect in a triumphant revolutionary situation, the toppling of the Qaddafi and Mubarak governments caused the Brotherhood to shed much of its traditional caution. Its leaders began to reveal connections and objectives they had previously left unsaid or even denied.

The Egyptian Muslim Brotherhood's spiritual leader, Yusuf al-Qaradawi, issued a fatwa on al Jazeera in early 2011 to demand Qaddafi's death.[63] The Brotherhood then ran a Libyan front group, the Justice and Construction Party, to compete in the democratic procedures to follow.

In Egypt, the Brotherhood wasted little time in implementing the political and ideological agenda that its critics had long accused it of harboring. We discussed the rapidity of Brotherhood political consolidation after Morsi's presidential victory in 2012, but those efforts appeared well planned out. More revealing are the words and actions that were not carefully planned. In one of his first postelection acts toward the United States, Morsi noted well-wishers bearing large portraits of imprisoned terrorist Omar Abdel Rahman, the "blind sheik" serving a life sentence in federal prison for his role as spiritual leader of the 1993 bombing of the World Trade Center in New York. The president-elect pledged to push for Rahman's release, along with the release of unspecified "detainees". Morsi then paid a visit to the Islamic Republic of Iran before his visit to Washington – while U.S. officials were negotiating with his government to provide billions of dollars more in aid – to attend the Non-Aligned Movement summit, even though most member heads of state declined to attend.

Assessment of US Response to the Muslim Brotherhood

Diplomatically, the United States generally held the Muslim Brotherhood at arm's length, mainly due to its strategic relationship with the long-ruling Mubarak government of Egypt, but with the unfolding of the Arab Spring, the U.S. saw the Brotherhood in more benign and cooperative terms, and indicated little if any public concern about the Brotherhood replacing Mubarak. As of this writing, the Department of State appears to view the Muslim Brotherhood-led government of Egypt as part of the solution to the Syria conflict, with the Voice of America praising Morsi for his role.

As a law enforcement and counterintelligence matter, the FBI and Justice Department at the senior levels do not appear to consider the Muslim Brotherhood to be a problem. To the contrary, the FBI, both at headquarters in Washington and at various field offices, has relied heavily on Muslim Brotherhood front organizations to provide translations, subject matter expertise, training of agents, and policy advice. At lower levels, many agents show that they are well informed about the Brotherhood's operations in the U.S., and it was the FBI that collected some of the most important intelligence released to the public about the subject.

The Department of Homeland Security (DHS) at senior levels has generally paralleled the policies of the FBI leadership, though at the agent level, as with the FBI, there is an awareness that the Brotherhood may present a problem.

The Department of Defense appears torn about how to deal with the Muslim Brotherhood, especially within the ranks of the DoD bureaucracy and the uniformed military. DoD continues to use Muslim Brotherhood front organizations as certifying entities for the military chaplains, and as subject matter experts and trainers. It is not known to have done any internal assessments about the veracity of reports in the press and from think tanks about Brotherhood penetrations, despite the fact that the Treasury Department publicly identified the founder of the Muslim chaplain program as a fundraiser for al-Qaeda, that that individual pled guilty to being part of a plot to assassinate the present king of Saudi Arabia, and that a federal court sentenced that same individual to a 23-year prison term.

As long as the Muslim Brotherhood does not engage directly in terrorism, the U.S. government has been taking a "see no evil" approach. The simplistic, black-and-white focus on an ideologically motivated group's tactics, as opposed to its threat doctrine and strategic goals, has effectively protected the Muslim Brotherhood from significant federal investigations, intelligence collection and analysis, and exclusion from federal installations and officials.

As long as federal authorities do not question the motives of the Muslim Brotherhood or resist its predicable complaints and demands for accommodation, (and indeed, as long as authorities discourage national security professionals from actively posing such questions), the Brotherhood is likely to continue its "cooperation" with the U.S. – at least for as long as the tactic of cooperation is useful in furthering the movement's strategic goals.

Those strategic goals, as enunciated by the Muslim Brotherhood's founder Hassan al Banna more than eight decades ago, by its top theoretician Sayyid Qutb just over four decades ago, and by the organization's global governing Shura Council two decades ago, remain constant. And they remain consistent with the strategic goals of the most notorious terrorist spinoff, al-Qaeda. Those strategic goals center on the establishment of a global caliphate that would place all of humanity, including the United States, under Islamist extremist rule.

Whether or not one considers such an end state to be achievable is not the point. The point is that the Muslim Brotherhood does believe it, and is working toward that end, which by definition would require the overthrow of the Constitution of the United States.

Toward a Different U.S. Approach

The Muslim Brotherhood presents a national security challenge to the United States because of its threat doctrine and its end goal. Like Communism from years past, the Brotherhood embraces an aggressive, expansionist, and totalitarian ideology that requires the destruction of the present world order and of free societies. It envisions itself as a vanguard of a movement that seeks political control over all of humanity. Because it is a transnational organization whose goal is also to subvert or overthrow the Constitution of the United States, the Muslim Brotherhood, strategically speaking, is a foreign and domestic enemy.

Although officeholders and U.S. military personnel take oaths to defend the Constitution of the United States "against all enemies, foreign and domestic," the understanding of that oath is often unclear. The U.S. military has no official definition of the term "enemy".[64]

That said, the United States could conceivably benefit from certain tactical relations with the Muslim Brotherhood and its fronts, once it recognizes the Brotherhood as a strategic enemy and is wary of the Brotherhood's tactics and tradecraft. Thus any tactical relationship would be solely for the purpose of using the Muslim Brotherhood in a larger set of divisive operations against Islamist radicals. Shorn of their ideology, such tactics and tradecraft are generally generic to any seasoned practitioner of clandestine intelligence operations, political subversion and psychological warfare. They include:

- Clandestine transnational political organization, including subversion, political infiltration, and secret financing;
- Tradecraft that rivals the tradecraft of established intelligence services;
- Denial and deception concerning the nature of its organization and motives;
- Information dominance – to take control of the narrative among Muslims and among non-Muslims; and to cause the U.S. to alter its own terminology and understanding, and therefore its policies;
- Intimidation of critics, including fellow Muslims, to silence and discredit dissent and promote self-censorship and intellectual submission;
- Co-optation of national institutions and policymakers, with rewards for their cooperation and punishments and castigation for any questioning;
- Infiltration of national institutions, both governmental and nongovernmental, that influence or shape attitudes and public policy;
- Infiltration of law enforcement, security, military and other government services, for the purposes of penetration with agents of influence and internal "fifth column" cadres, and to change the attitudes, perceptions, practices and behaviors of those services;
- Constantly shifting tactical alliances with and among its own Islamist foes;
- Continued operational and doctrinal ties to designated terrorist organizations;
- And so forth.

Therefore, a properly designed U.S. policy toward the Muslim Brotherhood should consider how these tactics can present opportunities for the United States to limit, cripple and ultimately break the Muslim Brotherhood's developing alliances among the world's many Islamist factions and forces. A carefully conceived counteroffensive strategy can peel away, onion-style, the layers forming the Ikhwan's sphere of influence down to the organizational core.[65]

The 2013 ouster of the Ikhwan-led government in Egypt offers many lessons and opportunities. First, it shows that the entire Muslim Brotherhood is vulnerable to a serious counteroffensive against it. Second, it proves that a Muslim Brotherhood regime can be ousted easily, as long as it has not had the chance to consolidate political control over the armed forces, police, and security intelligence services. Third, it shows that, even if the Ikhwan takes power with popular support against a repressive regime, that support is fleeting once the Brotherhood starts imposing its own repressive agenda on the population, and therefore an attempt to oust such a regime can be greeted with popular support and legitimacy. The ouster of the Morsi regime also shows that U.S. policy, with its focus on "countering violent extremism" and on building "democracy" while ignoring threat doctrine, is strategically counterproductive, as it facilitates the Ikhwan and similar movements while undermining friends and allies.

Some of the opportunities emerging from the Ikhwan ouster in Egypt can spring from the priceless documents, computer drives, and other media seized by the authorities. This information is believed to include invaluable intelligence on the internal workings and networks of the Muslim Brotherhood in an important country, and globally. The printed and electronic documentation should be indexed, translated into English for more universal use where practical, and used to expose and uproot the Ikhwan worldwide, help peel away the disgruntled and disillusioned to serve as defectors or defectors-in-place, and serve as resources for the employment of divisive operations inside the Ikhwan and among its financial and political sponsors abroad. Of special value are the identities of individuals and institutions in other countries that have aided the Ikhwan and its networks. Authorities should release as much as possible for the public record for journalists, private activist groups, and others to learn about Muslim Brotherhood methods and internal workings, operational and support networks, and other aspects as an aid in monitoring and defeating the Ikhwan worldwide. The information can be used to discredit Ikhwan supporters and enablers, educate the public and policymakers, and expose and shame those who had hidden behind the Ikhwan's own secrecy and the outside world's veil of denial.

The bottom line is that the Muslim Brotherhood can be defeated through a concerted campaign of ideological warfare that attacks the root of the Brotherhood's raison d'etre, the internal corruption and doctrinally very unsound sexual practices that its members perform with, or at least in the presence of, one another; and the psychological brutality that enforces its orthodoxy on entire families and clans. No willing collaborator – including and especially regimes and individuals in places like Qatar and elsewhere that finance the Ikhwan – should be spared shame and embarrassment unless they are willing to turn against their cause. Once the very fiber of the Ikhwan is discredited, with enough peer pressure and persistence, determined opponents can quite possibly force elements of the Brotherhood to turn against one another with almost the same gusto of certain American and other Western figures who turn against their own societies out of deference to the Ikhwan.

Notes

1 See Richard P. Mitchell, *The Society of the Muslim Brothers*. Oxford University Press, 1969, 1993, p. 14.

2 Mitchell, *The Society of the Muslim Brothers*, pp. 15-16.

3 Mitchell, *The Society of the Muslim Brothers*, p. 31.

4 Mitchell, *The Society of the Muslim Brothers*, pp. 32-33.

5 The Communist International (Comintern) was founded under the state sponsorship of the Russian Soviet Federated Socialist Republic in 1919, with the Bolsheviks' Communist Party as the vanguard. Other movements of the early 20th century sought to emulate the Comintern in terms of its structure and function. The Muslim Brotherhood achieved its international networks without the benefit of direct state sponsorship, though the Brotherhood has received substantial funding from the rulers of sovereign states as varied as Libya, Qatar and Saudi Arabia, even though the support did not come in the form of state control.

6 David D. Kirkpatrick, "Egypt's New Leader Takes Oath, Promising to Work for Release of Jailed Terrorist", *New York Times*, 29 June 2012, http://www.nytimes.com/2012/06/30/world/middleeast/morsi-promises-to-work-for-release-of-omar-abdel-rahman.html?pagewanted=all (viewed 26 August 2014).

7 David D. Kirkpatrick, Alan Cowell and Rick Gladstone, "Embassy of U.S. and Allies Under Siege in Muslim World", *New York Times*, 14 September 2012, http://www.nytimes.com/2012/09/15/world/middleeast/anti-american-protests-over-film-enter-4th-day.html?pagewanted=all (viewed 26 August 2014).

8 @USEmbassyCairo Twitter conversation with @ikhwanweb, 12 September 2012. "U.S. Embassy in Cairo Gets in Twitter Spat with Muslim Brotherhood", *CBS/Associated Press*, 13 September 2012, http://www.cbsnews.com/8301-202_162-57512519/u.s-embassy-in-cairo-gets-in-twitter-spat-with-muslim-brotherhood/ See: https://twitter.com/USEmbassyCairo (viewed 26 August 2014).

9 William Gawthrop, "Islam's Tools of Penetration", *CIFA Working Brief*, 19 April 2007. Quoted in William G. Boykin and Harry Edward Soyster et al. (eds.), *Shariah – The Threat to America: An Exercise in Competitive Analysis, Report of Team 'B'II*. Washington: Center for Security Policy, 2010, pp. 98-102.

10 *Shariah – The Threat to America*, p. 155.

11 Cases in point: Muslim Brotherhood organizer Abdurahman Alamoudi, who worked with the Pentagon successfully to establish a Muslim chaplain corps and to have a Brotherhood front, the Islamic Society of North America (ISNA), certified as a vetting entity for chaplains, publicly declared his support for Hamas and Hizbullah, and is presently serving a 23-year federal prison sentence for providing material support to al-Qaeda. Fellow Brotherhood agent Louay Safi of ISNA became a pre-deployment trainer for the U.S. Army, even though he was actively engaged in assisting the Palestinian Islamic Jihad and a federal court identified his organization as a material supporter of terrorists.

12 "An Explanatory Memorandum on the General Strategic Goal for the Brotherhood in North America", 22 May 1991, p. 18, *Investigative Project*, http://www.investigative project.org/documents/misc/20.pdf (viewed 24 September 2014).

13 Manfred Holpern quoted in John O. Voll, "Foreword", in Richard P. Mitchell, *The Society of the Muslim Brothers*. Oxford: Oxford University Press, 1993, p. x.

14 A. A. A. Fyzee, "The Impact of Islam upon Political Conduct in Recent Times (A Brief Survey)", in Harold D. Lasswell and Harlan Cleveland (eds.), *The Ethic of Power: The Interplay of Religion, Philosophy, and Politics*. New York: Harper & Brothers, 1962, p. 113.

15 Fyzee, "The Impact of Islam", p. 113.

16 Fyzee, "The Impact of Islam", p. 115.

17 That Supreme Court-defined separation itself is a misnomer, in that, as a pronouncement of federal government doctrine, it presumes the supremacy of a Christian "church" above all other houses of worship, and therefore separates neither.

18 David D. Kirkpatrick and Steven Erlanger, "Egypt's New Leader Spells Out Terms for U.S.-Arab Ties", *New York Times*, 22 September 2012.

19 Matthew Leavitt, *Hamas: Politics, Charity, and Terrorism in the Service of Jihad*. New Haven: Yale University Press, 2006, p 30.

20 Leavitt, *Hamas*, p. 30.

21 Eric Trager, Katie Kiraly, Cooper Klose, and Eliot Calhoun, "Who's Who In Egypt's Muslim Brotherhood", *Washington Institute for Near East Policy*, September 2012, http://www.washingtoninstitute.org/policy-analysis/view/whos-who-in-the-muslim-brotherhood (viewed 24 September 2014).

22 Trager, "Who's Who In Egypt's Muslim Brotherhood".

23 The Brotherhood considered raising and channeling funds in support of Hamas, the Palestinian Islamic Jihad and other terrorist organizations to be an unviolent jihad activity. However, the practice in the United States exposed the Brotherhood and its fronts to unprecedented scrutiny and exposure. During the 2004-2008 *United States v Holy Land Foundation et al.* trials, federal prosecutors presented evidence unearthed by the FBI in the Annandale, Virginia raid, that exposed key details of the Brotherhood's clandestine operations in the United States. The court identified more than two dozen U.S.-based groups to be Muslim Brotherhood fronts and controlled organizations, identified several Brotherhood operatives by name, and determined several individuals and organizations to be unindicted coconspirators in terrorism finance activity.

24 "In other words, while Hamas engages in military, social and political activities alike, the strategic purpose of each of these tactics is the same jihadist principle of destroying Israel under the ideological framework of confronting the perceived enemies of Islam, and Islamizing Palestinian society. It should, therefore, not surprise that even after its sweeping electoral victory in Parliamentary elections Hamas leaders did not soften their rhetoric," Leavitt writes. "Instead of allowing participation in the political process to co-opt them into moderation, Hamas leaders underlined their intention to continue attacking Israel and to make Palestinian society more Islamic." Leavitt, *Hamas*, p. 31.

25 "An Explanatory Memorandum on the General Strategic Goal for the Brotherhood in North America", 22 May 1991, p. 19, *Investigative Project*, http://www.investigative project.org/documents/misc/20.pdf (viewed 24 September 2014).

26 Eric Rich and Jerry Markon, "Va. Man Tied to Hamas Held as Witness: Annandale Resident Detained After Wife Allegedly Filmed Bridge", *Washington Post*, 25 August 2004, http://www.washingtonpost.com/wp-dyn/articles/A28476-2004Aug24.html (viewed 25 September 2014).

27 "Hamas Covenant 1988: The Covenant of the Islamic Resistance Movement", *Yale Law School*, http://avalon.law.yale.edu/20th_century/hamas.asp (viewed 25 September 2014).

28 A facsimile of the actual document in Arabic, as released by the federal court, as well as the full translation into English, are available from the Investigative Project on Terrorism. Mohamed Akram, "An Explanatory Memorandum on the General Strategic Goal for the Brotherhood in North America", 22 May 1991, p. 24, *Investigative Project*, http://www.investigativeproject.org/documents/misc/20.pdf (viewed 24 September 2014).

29 As of 1991, when the document was sent to the Muslim Brotherhood Shura Council, those organizations were: Islamic Society of North America (ISNA), Muslim Students Association (MSA), Muslim Communities Association (MCA), Association of Muslim Social Scientists (AMSS), Association of Muslim Scientists and Engineers (AMSE), Islamic Medical Association (IMA), Islamic Teaching Center (ITC), North American Islamic Trust (NAIT), Foundation for International Development (FID), Islamic Housing Cooperative (IHC), Islamic Centers Division (ICD), American Trust Publications (ATP), Audio-Visual Center (AVC), Islamic Book Service (IBS), Muslim Businessmen Association (MBA), Muslim Youth of North America (MYNA), ISNA Fiqh Committee (IFC), ISNA Political Awareness Committee (IPAC), Islamic Education Department (IED), Muslim Arab Youth Association (MAYA), Malaysian Islamic Study Group

(MISG), Islamic Association for Palestine (IAP), Occupied Land Fund (OLF), Mercy International Association (MIA), Islamic Circle of North America (ICNA), Baitul Mal Inc (BMI), International Institute for Islamic Thought (IIIT), Islamic Formation Center (IFC). See "A list of our organizations and the organizations of our friends," undated but attached to Mohamed Akram's "An Explanatory Memorandum on the General Strategic Goal for the Brotherhood in North America," May 19, 1991. The documents were part of the North American Muslim Brotherhood's archive seized by the FBI in Northern Virginia and used as evidence, uncontested by the defense, for the successful prosecution of five terrorist collaborators in the Holy Land Foundation terrorist financing case in Texas.

30 Mohamed Akram, "An Explanatory Memorandum on the General Strategic Goal for the Brotherhood in North America", 22 May 1991, p. 19, *Investigative Project*, http://www.investigativeproject.org/documents/misc/20.pdf (viewed 24 September 2014).

31 Akram, "An Explanatory Memorandum", p. 19-21.

32 Akram, "An Explanatory Memorandum", p. 21.

33 Akram, "An Explanatory Memorandum", p. 22.

34 For a detailed description of how Soviet-sponsored front organizations operated through networks of Communist Parties to project a broad-based "popular front," as well as tactical shifts between violence and non-violence, see Franz Borkenau, *World Communism: A History of the Communist International*. Ann Arbor: University of Michigan Press, 1962. See especially Chapter XII, "United Front". The Muslim Brotherhood has emulated the popular front political warfare tactic.

35 Saul Alinsky, *Rules for Radicals: A Pragmatic Primer for Realistic Radicals*. New York: Random House, 1971, p. 126.

36 Alinsky, *Rules for Radicals*, p. 130.

37 Alinsky, *Rules for Radicals*, p. 133.

38 Alinsky, *Rules for Radicals*, p. 133.

39 Alinsky, *Rules for Radicals*, p. 134.

40 The writer interviewed Shaykh Kabbani on several occasions in 2002 and 2003, as well as members of his organization, the Islamic Supreme Council of America, who provided specifics. Richard H. Curtiss wrote an account of the incident at the State Department, in which he appeared critical of Shaykh Kabbani and uncritical of the Muslim Brotherhood fronts he quoted in his story. See Richard H. Curtiss, "Dispute Between U.S. Muslim Groups Goes Public", *Washington Report on Middle East Affairs*, April/May 1999, pp. 71, 101, http://www.wrmea.com/backissues/0499/9904071.html (viewed 25 September 2014).

41 Curtiss, "Dispute Between U.S. Muslim Groups Goes Public", p. 101.

42 Dilshad Fakroddin, Report, *The Muslim*, October 1998. Quoted in Curtiss, "Dispute Between U.S. Muslim Groups Goes Public", p. 101.

43 Curtiss, "Dispute Between U.S. Muslim Groups Goes Public", p. 101.

44 Curtiss, "Dispute Between U.S. Muslim Groups Goes Public", p. 101.

45 Curtiss, "Dispute Between U.S. Muslim Groups Goes Public", p. 101.

46 Dean E. Murphy, "Mrs. Clinton Says She Will Return Money Raised by a Muslim Group", *New York Times*, 26 October 2000, http://www.nytimes.com/2000/10/26/nyregion/mrs-clinton-says-she-will-return-money-raised-by-a-muslim-group.html?scp=1&sq= Mrs. Clinton Says She Will Return Money Raised by a Muslim Group&st=cse&pagewanted=1 (viewed 25 September 2014).

47 Hassan Hathout, "The Man Who Influenced My Life", *Voice of Islam*, 25 December 1997, http://www.islamicity.com/voi/transcripts/HassanAB.htm (viewed 25 September 2014).

48 Mohamed Akram "An Explanatory Memorandum on the General Strategic Goal for the Brotherhood in North America", 22 May 1991, p. 32, *Investigative Project*, http://www.investigativeproject.org/documents/misc/20.pdf (viewed 24 September 2014).

49 "United States of America vs. Holy Land Foundation for Relief and Development", p. 8, *Investigative Project*, www.investigativeproject.org/documents/case_docs/423.pdf (viewed 24 September 2014).

50 Diane Katz interviewing Shaykh Mohammed Hisham Kabbani, "Sheik: Moderate U.S. Muslims have become 'the Silent Majority'", *Detroit News*, 11 October 2001, http://groups.yahoo.com/group/al-Zawiya/message/2136?var=1 (viewed 2 September 2002).

51 Rami Ginat, *The Soviet Union and Egypt, 1945-1955*. London: Frank Cass, 1993, p. 39.

52 Salah al-'Ashmawi quoted in Rami Ginat, *The Soviet Union and Egypt, 1945-1955*. London: Frank Cass, 1993, p. 39.

53 *Wall Street Journal* reporter Ian Johnson generated publicity about a supposed relationship between Said Ramadan and the CIA during the Eisenhower Administration, but the declassified material indicates quite the opposite: that the CIA considered the Muslim Brotherhood operative a "reactionary" and "Phalangist," and exceedingly difficult to engage. See Ian Johnson, *A Mosque in Munich: Nazis, the CIA, and the Rise of the Muslim Brotherhood in the West*. Boston: Houghton Mifflin Harcourt, 2010. Also see a detailed rebuttal by John Rosenthal, "America, Germany and the Muslim Brotherhood: The Contested History of a Mosque in Munich," *Hoover Institution Policy Review*, 174, August 2012, http://www.hoover.org/research/america-germany-and-muslim-brotherhood (viewed 25 September 2014).

54 Lydia Khalil, "Al-Qaeda and the Muslim Brotherhood: United by Strategy, Divided by Tactics", Jamestown Foundation *Terrorism Monitor*, 4: 6, 23 March 2006, http://www.jamestown.org/programs/gta/single/?tx_ttnews%5Btt_news%5D=714&tx_ttnews%5BbackPid%5D=181&no_cache=1 (viewed 25 September 2014).

55 Khalil, "Al-Qaeda and the Muslim Brotherhood".

56 Mary Beth Sheridan, "Government Links Activist to Al Qaeda Fundraising", *Washington Post*, 16 July 2005, http://www.washingtonpost.com/wp-dyn/content/article/2005/07/15/AR2005071501696.html (viewed 25 September 2014). Sheridan also noted, "Alamoudi, a founder of the American Muslim Council, played a key role in devel-

oping the Pentagon's Muslim chaplain program, traveled abroad as a speaker on behalf of the State Department and attended meetings at the White House."

57 Louay Safi of the Islamic Society of North America (ISNA), an identified unindicted coconspirator in the 2008 Holy Land Foundation terrorism financing case, as of this writing remains listed on the Georgetown University website as the Common Word Fellow of the Prince Alwaleed Bin Talal Center for Muslim-Christian Understanding. See "Louay Safi", *Georgetown University*, http://acmcu.georgetown.edu/louay-safi (viewed 25 September 2014).

58 Susie Day, "Counter-Intelligent: The Surveillance and Indictment of Lynne Stewart", *Marxist Monthly Review*, 54: 6, November 2002, http://monthlyreview.org/2002/11/01/counter-intelligent (viewed 25 September 2014).

59 Dhahi Khalfane quoted in "Dubai Police Chief: Muslim Brotherhood Wants To Overthrow Gulf Leaders", *Al Bawaba*, 25 March 2012, http://www.albawaba.com/main-headlines/dubai-police-chief-muslim-brotherhood-wants-overthrow-gulf-leaders-418383 (viewed 25 September 2014).

60 Dahi KhalfanTamim quoted in Bassam Za'za, "Dubai Police Chief Warns Muslim Brotherhood over Social Media Use," *Gulf News*, 26 July 2012, http://gulfnews.com/news/gulf/uae/general/dubai-police-chief-warns-muslim-brotherhood-over-social-media-use-1.1053883 (viewed 25 September 2014).

61 "Dubai Police Chief Warns of Muslim Brotherhood, Iran Threat", *Reuters*, 26 July 2012, http://www.reuters.com/article/2012/07/26/us-emirates-police-brotherhood-idUSBRE86P0EG20120726 (viewed 25 September 2014).

62 "Islamist MPs Demand Action Over Dubai Police Chief's 'Insults'", *Kuwait Times*, 29 August 2012, http://news.kuwaittimes.net/2012/08/29/islamist-mps-demand-action-over-dubai-police-chiefs-insults/ (viewed 25 September 2012).

63 "Yusuf al-Qaradawi Issues Fatwa to Kill Gaddafi" (video embed from al Jazeera), *Digital Islam*, 21 February 2011, http://www.digitalislam.eu/article.do?articleId=6243 (viewed 25 September 2014).

64 For example, the *Department of Defense Dictionary of Military and Associated Terms*, As Amended through 15 August 2012, does not have an entry for "enemy". The closest contains the qualifier "enemy combatant," defined as "In general, a person engaged in hostilities against the United States or its coalition partners during an armed conflict." The term "hostilities" or "hostile" is also not defined, with the closest being "hostile act," which the Dictionary states is "An attack or other use of force against the US, US forces, or other designated persons or property". Presumably this would be an attack with kinetic force, blast or some other physically destructive element, not a political, subversive or ideological attack.

65 For a greater discussion of peeling away factions from the hard core, see J. Michael Waller, *Fighting the War of Ideas like a Real War*. Institute of World Politics Press, 2007, pp. 122-124. The passage relates to peeling support from designated terrorist organizations, but the model is applicable to the Muslim Brotherhood.

4

ISLAMIST ACTIVISM THROUGH THE LENS OF SOCIAL SCIENCE

Anna Bekele

SMT and Islamic Activism

There is a path well-trodden by researchers who have applied the findings of social science to the study of Islamic activism. They approach Islamic activism as a social movement. In the words of Goodwin and Jasper social movements represent "conscious, concerted, and sustained efforts by ordinary people to change some aspects of their society by using extrainstitutional means".[1] The term Social Movement Theory (SMT) is applied to a body of research and theories that has gained prominence in recent years among social science scholars. Social Movement Theory (SMT) emerged from the study of collective behaviour. Its focus is the mobilization process – how and why people become involved in collective action.

One of the initial explanations identified contextual predispositions for mobilization in a theory known as Relative Deprivation (RD). This theory has been extremely influential and still is, as poverty or relative poverty is considered to be one of the major mobilizing factors. However, grievances alone do not fully explain the rise of protest movements. Other factors need to be considered. Additional theories emerged in the 70s-80s as possible explanations for mobilization and social activity. Among them are Resource Mobilization or Resource Mobilization Theory (RMT), framing, and political opportunities. These became the dominant themes in the discussion of social movements.[2] Collective action and then collective identity became the prime loci in the study of mobilization. There has also been a growing interest in the role that networks and social structures play in the movements.

As research on social movements is mostly in the form of case studies, scholars tend to emphasize particular components in their research. For instance, Snow et al. bring initial studies together by singling out several key axes in the definition of a social movement: collective action, change-oriented goals, some degree of organization and a degree of temporal continuity.[3] In turn, Diani and Della Porta emphasize the network component of social movements.[4] Diani even defines social movements primarily as "a network of informal interactions between a plurality of individuals, groups and/or organizations".[5] Thus the notion of social movement has appeared to evolve as further theorizing and reflection has been contributed which refers to changing social, political and cultural phenomena.

The following framework is an attempt to bring together the existing studies. A general framework for social movement seems to have four key categories – (1) facilitating factors and conditions, (2) action and dynamics, (3) sociopsychological dimensions, and (4) outcomes. Under each category the table also outlines some of the possible components:

Facilitating Factors/ Conditions	Action and Dynamics	Sociopsychological Dimensions	Outcomes
Context	Structure	Networks	State legislative and political changes
Opportunities	Social Movement Organizations	Framing/ Ideology Discourses	
Constraints	(SMOs)		Personal/ biographical changes
		Collected Identity	
Grievances	Leadership		Social/ cultural changes
		Solidarity/ Commitment	
Resources (RMT)	Associations and Alliances		Social movements influence each other
		Emotions	
	Media/ Public Engagement		Decline
		Rational Choice (RAT)	
	Repertoires (tactics and strategies)		Radical flank effect
	Globalization		
	Transnationalism		

Table 1: A General Framework for Social Movements

Any given social movement has a complex nature, and its multi-dimensional aspects are often interconnected. There is also a temporal dimension; over a period of time a movement may either remain in its informal network form or become institutionalized; or it may go into abeyance or develop a radical flank. Each of the components may offer a very special insight into the nature of a movement. Some components may also exhibit a fluid and variable nature. For instance, media may emerge as a resource (especially traditional media, such as TV or satellite broadcasting), but also can be an element in a mobilization process (especially social media). The latter was very evident during the events of the Arab Spring with mobilization facilitated via *Twitter* and other social media. Another striking example is ISIS (Islamic State in Iraq and Syria, also known as simply Islamic State or IS), and its social media campaign. In certain contexts use of media may demonstrate the availability of political opportunities or, conversely, the lack of them. For example, unlike the Salafis, the Muslim Brotherhood in Egypt used Al Jazeera.

For a long time the study of religious movements, and Islamic movements in particular, remained at the periphery of social movement research. Stephen Vertigans suggests that such neglect was due to the earlier prevailing emphasis on economic issues such as poverty and demands for social justice. It was only with the emergence of the so called New Social Movements (NSM) with their emphasis on cultural dimensions and identity issues in areas such as civil rights, antiwar agitation, and in women's, environmental, ethnic and national movements, that the study of religious movements became integrated into social movement scholarship.[6] In 1984 Snow and Marshall were the trailblazers who applied social movement theory to the study of Islamic activism.[7] Twenty years later Quintan Wiktorowicz edited a further compilation of papers under the title of *Islamic Activism: a Social Movement Theory Approach*. It included studies ranging from research on the Palestinian group Hamas and *Gam'a Islamiyya* in Egypt, to the study of Islamist women's networks in Yemen and Islamic activism in Turkey.[8]

Wiktorowicz is one of the main proponents of SMT in the study of Islamism. He defined "Islamic activism" in a general sense as "the mobilization of contention to support Muslim causes" and "a collective action rooted in Islamic symbols and identities".[9] The key research questions focus essentially on mobilization – how and why Muslims adopt a specific interpretation of Islam, what factors facilitate this process and what are the outcomes? Wiktorowicz's compilation encouraged further application of SMT to the study of Islamic activism. Since then SMT has been increasingly used in the study of radically inclined groups and terrorist groups such al-Qaeda.[10] It was later applied to exploring the development and activities of Islamic groups that refrain from violence and pursue other forms of activism.[11] Wiktorowicz himself entered government service as a counter-radicalization expert, working in senior positions at the White House and within the Intelligence Community. He was influential in promoting partnerships with Muslim communities to counter radicalization on the ground and served as senior advisor to Barak Obama on countering extremism.

The SMT approach has some limitations when employed in the study of Islamic activism. First, there is still no comprehensive and coherent body of theory on social movements. Instead, researchers tend to take a reductive approach to applying SMT when they are studying a movement, for example by focusing on one issue such as Relative Deprivation. There are, however, some attempts to change the situation, i.e. to synthesize and bring together a range of theories and methodological approaches. Secondly, SMT research has typically focused on movements that aim to challenge the state or its policies in Western society, which is essentially democratic. Though there is more research forthcoming on social movements in nondemocratic and repressed societies, this is still a neglected area of study. This neglect at least in part arises from the obvious difficulties of conducting research in countries governed by repressive regimes. Thirdly, initially contention was considered as a distinctive indicator of a social movement. Thus not many scholars considered noncontentious movements, or movements that avoid violence. Emphasis on high-risk activism still seems to prevail in studies of social movements, including studies which focus on Islamic activism. Finally, SMT seems to underestimate the significance of the ideological and spiritual aspects of a religious movement. Framing analysis and the study of discourses appear to be among a few approaches taken to ideology, albeit without any great depth or breadth.

There are also some issues with the terminology, as Islamism and Islamic activism are controversial terms. There is a public and academic debate on the term "Islamism" itself, as some assign it only to the violent forms of activism, while others suggest that a spectrum of Islamic activism can be defined by this term.[12] If forms of Islamic activism are to be located along the spectrum from high risk to risk avoidance, then such Islamic groups as the Fethulla Gülen movement and the Aga Khan Development Network (AKDN) are placed at the risk avoidance end of the spectrum, while al-

Qaeda, ISIS, Boko Haram and others are on the high risk end. Hizb ut-Tahrir and the Muslim Brotherhood seem to be context based and to be more temperate with regard to risk taking. For instance, Hizb ut-Tahrir in Central Asia tries to avoid risk; groups associated with or inspired by the Muslim Brotherhood (MB) in the West also appear to pursue non-violent methods.

Some Insights from SMT

Context (Relative Deprivation)

One of the most persistent claims is that activism is motivated by relative deprivation and socioeconomic disadvantage. In his seminal work *Why Men Rebel* (1970) Ted Gurr argued that people engage in political violence and rebel because of feelings of economic deprivation.[13] His theory remains influential in spite of its short-comings. Hafez bemoans that, "Gurr's theory continues to prevail, explicitly or implicitly, as the leading explanation of Islamist violence and rebellion by area specialists, Islamic study scholars and journalists covering the Muslim world."[14] It has also been an influential theory in the formulation of responses to terrorism, encouraging poverty relief and education as solutions. There have also been variations on deprivation theory. Vertigans, while acknowledging the effect of economic and political exclusions, draws attention to the importance of cultural exclusion.[15] He suggests that the grievances of some Muslims, particularly in the West, can be explained by their sense of cultural marginalization.

Despite Gurr's theory of relative deprivation, the most consistent finding is that movement leaders and core participants are not economically disadvantaged but often middle-class and well-educated. Klueger suggests that terrorist organizations may even prefer to have better educated recruits as they are more interested in politics and may be better suited to carrying out international terrorist acts.[16] Similarly, Atran believes that groups like al-Qaeda and Hamas "spectacularly sacrifice their (and the community's) best and brightest to increase political 'market share' in the competition for popular support".[17] In his analysis of Salafi jihadists, Sageman emphasizes that they are mostly educated individuals from the upper and middle classes. He illustrates that among the pre-9/11 al-Qaeda leadership were bin Laden (a multimillionaire), al-Zawahiri (a surgeon), Mohammad Atef (a police official), Khalid Shaikh Mohhamed/ KSM (an engineer) and Saif al-Adel (an army colonel).[18] In the same vein, the head of ISIS, Abu Bakr al-Baghadi was a former lecturer in Islamic studies and an imam in Baghdad, while a number of other ISIS leaders were former members of Saddam's army (e.g. Abu Muslim al-Turki; Abu Ayman al-Iraqi; Abu Ahmad al-Alwani; Abu Abdurrahman al-Bilawi; Haji Bakr).[19]

A report by the Centre for Social Cohesion (CSC) *Islamist Terrorism: The British Connections* among other things indicates that 31% of individuals convicted of terrorism attended university. The overall conclusion is that, "Analysis of individuals who committed IROs [Islamism Related Offenses] in the UK does not support the assertion made by some that there is a correlation between terrorist activity and low educational achievement and employment status."[20] These findings are in line with Sageman's research.[21] Also, Atran in his list of the "Ten empirical generalizations on terror networks" notes that "A plurality of suicide bombers outside of Iraq… have college education or advanced technical training (except for the Maghreb-European contingent), and are professionals or semiprofessionals (The largest single professional category represented is engineer)."[22] These findings are also consistent with some more general faith surveys that indicate a greater level of religiosity among those in technical/scientific disciplines.[23]

SMOs and Political Opportunities

Social Movements employ a range of resources to attain their political goals. This is the rationale behind Resource Mobilisation Theory (RMT). Resources may be moral, cultural, social, organizational, human, and material.[24] For instance, in order to build a support base, Islamic activists may use mosques, charities, hospitals, educational establishments and Muslim student associations, all of which are essentially social movement organisations (SMOs). Under more restricted circumstances some Islamic groups cannot possibly develop such organisational structures. For instance, Wiktorowicz contrasted the fairly favorable stance of the Jordanian government towards the Muslim Brotherhood with its antagonistic attitude towards the Salafis. The Muslim Brotherhood group was able to run various NGOs throughout the country, in contrast to the Salafi group which was forced to go underground and was able to mobilize only through its informal networks.[25] Context and political opportunities are clearly instrumental in producing either loose networks, that is SMOs with a federative structure, or SMOs with a fairly hierarchical structure. A general opinion is that a more repressive regime or restricted circumstances leave a social movement with informal networks as the only means of mobilization. Al-Qaeda with its nebulous structure is often cited as a conglomeration of networks. Sageman even argues that its current phase may be described as "leaderless jihad".[26]

The Muslim Brotherhood has been particularly effective at spawning its organizations in Europe and the US, often running them as 'front' organizations. According to *An Explanatory Memorandum on the General Strategic Goal for the Group in North America* establishing organizations throughout the country played a key role in the spread of its influence in the United States.[27] Among its main organizations in the United States are the Muslim Student Association (MSA, est. in 1963), the Islamic Society of North America (ISNA, est. in 1982), the Council on American–Islamic Relations (CAIR, est. in 1994), the Muslim American Society (MAS, est. in 1993), and the International Institute of Islamic Thought (IIIT, est. in 1981), among others. They are often founded as nonprofit bodies and some even have a tax-exempt status in the US. They may be classified as "Civil Rights, Advocacy for Specific Groups" in the case of CAIR, as "Educational Institution" in case of IIIT, or as "Religion, Spiritual Development" in the case of ISNA and MAS (according to the NTEE categories). These organizations tend to deny their links to the Muslim Brotherhood, and it is their structural and ideological similarity, financial and organizational links, and loyalty to Yusuf al-Qaradawi, among others, that point to the multiplicity of ties and interconnection between them.

In a similar way Muslim Brotherhood-associated organizations sprang up around the same time in Europe. In the United Kingdom: the Muslim Students Society (est. in 1961) and the Federation of Student Islamic Societies (FOSIS, est. in 1961), the Muslim Association of Britain (est. in 1997) and the Muslim Council of Britain (est. in 1997). In Germany: the Islamic Community of Germany (Islamische Gemeinschaft in Deutschland or IGD, est. in 1958). In France: the Union of Islamic Organisations of France (L'Union des Organisations Islamiques de France or UOIF, est. in 1983). In addition there are prominent umbrella European organizations such as the European Council for Fatwa and Research (ECFR, est. in 1997) and the Federation of Islamic Organizations in Europe (FIOE, est. in 1989). There has been a growing number of regional and supraregional organizations worldwide leaning towards the Muslim Brotherhood ideology and teachings of Yusuf al-Qaradawi. Some of them are nonprofit social organizations or designated charities (e.g. Islamic Relief, Interpal, and Human Appeal International in the UK), or funding bodies (e.g. Europe Trust). Others are educational establishments (e.g. the European Institute of Human Sciences or EIHS in Birmingham, UK), cultural centres (e.g. Islamic Cultural Centre of Ireland) and even the Centre for the Study of Terrorism (CFSOT, est. in 2006). Their proliferation, diversity, and high level of activism have helped the Muslim Brotherhood not only to obfuscate their profile in different countries worldwide, but also to effectively spread their message and influence in many regions.

Networks

The Muslim Brotherhood is an example of a network rather than a single organization. In fact, an alliance of organizations or Interorganizational Network (ION), also a "meta-organization",[28] perhaps appropriately describes the nature of the Muslim Brotherhood in social-scientific terms. Karagiannis' description of transnational Islamist networks fits the Muslim Brotherhood structure equally well,

> Transnational Islamist networks are horizontal structures consisting of multiple entities that interact with each other for the purpose of promoting a political agenda based on Islam. They usually include Islamic charities, NGOs, legal and clandestine groups, Muslim religious leaders and preachers, and individual followers.[29]

Apart from organizational networks, it is also important to consider social and personal networks and their role in the recruiting activists. These networks play a critical role not only in mobilization and in development of the individual's identity, but also in radicalization. There has been a growing body of scholarship on these often intertwined processes. The study of Islamic networks can be traced back to the initial network theories and network analysis.

One of the most prominent proponents of network theory among social scientists is Donatella Della Porta. Her research into a tendency observed among Italian extremists to join causes as "cliques of friends",[30] influenced Sageman's research, and in turn the research of Atran and Vertigan. Atran and Sageman in particular were hoping to debunk a commonly held impression of al-Qaeda's recruitment process. They aspired to demonstrate that it was a bottom-up process which took place through the pre-existing networks, rather than a top-down process. By tracing and analyzing the network connections they were also hoping to overturn a popular concept – the "lone wolf" theory of terrorism. Their findings seem to suggest that in fact most people join jihad as a result of friendship (about 80%) and kinship (about 20%).[31] For instance, Sageman traced the biographies of about 172 terrorists and found that almost two thirds "joined" jihad along with their friend(s), as a "bunch of guys", or some may have already had a friend who was a jihadist.[32] Sageman refers to this network foundation for recruitment by a police term BOG[33] or "bunch of guys" theory, while Atran calls it a "band of friends".[34]

In 2005 Atran and Sageman used social network analysis to test their concept of leaderless resistance. They believed that jihadist groups are moving from a hierarchical organizational model towards a leaderless resistance model (a model initially popularized by Louis Beam). With the help of UCINet (software for analysing social network data)[35] they processed information from a merged database on the jihadists from Southeast Asia and on al-Qaeda associates. The resulting graph certainly seems to indicate that small groups engage in resistance without central co-ordination, while leaders may provide the inspiration for groups and their associates. Atran and Sageman also picked up on the growing role of the Internet in propagating al-Qaeda's ideas. For instance, Global Islamic Media Front (GIMF) took on the role formerly played by Bin Laden.[36]

Atran and Sageman also did further research on the Madrid bombers, retracing their daily lives, family and friendship connections, the school they attended and the cafe where they liked to socialize. In a Western/diaspora context Sageman refers to the dynamic he observed as the "*halal*" theory of terrorism. He describes it as creating a subculture and developing a collective identity over a meal and discussion at a local *halal* restaurant.[37] Furthermore, in his earlier work Sageman notes that the bonds that these, mostly young, people make are of critical importance for understanding terrorism. He argues: "Despite the popular accounts of the 9/11 perpetrators in the press, in-group love rather than out-group hate seems a better explanation of their behavior."[38] According to Sageman such social bonds and in-group love are of greater significance than ideological appeal: "social bonds play a more important role in the emergence of the global Salafi jihad than ideology."[39] Other scholars echo this conclusion. Hegghammer observes similar dynamic forces operating among young people in Saudi Arabia. He observes: "Group dynamics such as peer pressure and intra-group affection seem to have been crucial in the process of radicalization."[40] The British comedy movie *Four Lions* offers a humorous illustration of this process by satirically and farcically depicting would-be terrorists and their bonding in everyday life experiences.

Sageman stresses the fact that the process is a group dynamic. More than that, it is a transformational group dynamic since young people become radicalized through spending time with each other (and also on social media, such as online forums). Sageman believes that actual discussion of radical materials and stories may be more significant in inspiring and radicalizing young people than the extreme nature of the materials in themselves.[41] He also alerts us to the influence of older men on younger ones, i.e. that something suspicious is likely to be going on when men in their forties regularly socialize with twenty year olds.[42] The process also increasingly evidences a transnational group dynamic. In the words of Vertigans, "Across Muslim communities, younger generations are sharing experiences, information and discourse and are collectively contributing to group radicalization or recruitment to existing groups."[43]

Young people are drawn to a radicalized community because of their need to belong and to be accepted. This community becomes their 'family'; and with the growth of the Internet, it is no longer only a physical but also a virtual community. Over time, their beliefs are gradually moulded and reinforced by their friends through collective radicalization. Vertigans has described it as follows: "The dynamics within groups contributed to a growing intensity of belief and practices and led to group solidarity and collective identity transcending individual characteristics."[44] The formative role played by social bonds in the process of radicalization is critical and it is also explored by other scholars. For instance Helfstein argues that, "social process is not simply important but is inseparably intertwined with radicalization".[45]

Atran, Sageman, Vertigans and a number of others argue that radicalization is not a solitary process but a social process – it happens in community. A negative aspect of this approach, however, is that it may downplay the significance of ideology to too great an extent. It could influence some counterterrorism efforts, leading to an exclusive focus on the social and psychological aspects of radicalization. A much more effective strategy would be to combine the two approaches. One needs to give sufficient focus to the importance of networks, but also to understand ideology and its social and political appeal. Ideology does not exist in a vacuum, while bonding experiences and personal networks are not the only significant factors in the process of radicalization. It is important to trace and disrupt radical community networks, but it is equally important to be aware of the ideological narratives that resonate within communities and to determine how one can counter those narratives. In the words of Helfstein:

> The social and ideological aspects become inexorably intertwined through the radicalization and recruitment process, meaning that efforts to address them must consider both in tandem. This is difficult since both ideology and social behavior are difficult and complex on their own, but it is critical in dealing with the problem of violent extremism.[46]

Sadly, the role of ideology has been largely neglected or downplayed in the study of social movements. Framing appears to be the only area of SMT where ideology features to any extent.

Framing

According to Social Movement Theory (SMT), framing is a construction of meaning employed by movement activists: "The process by which organizers 'frame' their issues in a way that resonates with or makes sense to potential recruits and the broader public."[47] Framing embeds ideological and emotional resonances as frames are meant to echo and endorse the convictions, feelings and longings of potential recruits in order to win over their "hearts and minds". Moghadam lists the following frames used by Islamic activists: "Islam is the solution; establish sharia law; end repression; justice for Palestine."[48] Another example is Quiggin's review of al-Qaeda's narrative and the list he produced as a result: "The eight themes that appear on a regular basis in jihadist discourse are: Jihad [struggle], Bayat [pledge], Daru Islam [the House of Islam], Ummah [Muslim community], Takfir [excommunication], Shaheed [martyr], Al-Wala Wal Bara [loyalty for the believers and aversion for the infidels], and Hijrah [emigration]."[49] Those are themes that indeed often emerge in the discourses of other Islamic groups.

The framing process allows a transfer of personal grievances or even perceived grievances to a wider group. Frames have a diagnostic function (what is wrong?), a motivational function (what are the emotional influences?), and a prognostic function (what is the solution?). The latter is heavily influenced by the ideology and interpretation of Islam by a particular Islamic group. For instance, Western conspiracy against Islam is a popular frame. A response to it is exposing this conspiracy and engaging in an open war against the West. The media is important not only as a framing device but also as a powerful tool to intensify the emotional appeal that images may evoke in a future activist. The global reach of media, both traditional and social, has brought dissemination of the message of militant Islam to an entirely new level. Devji argues that, "As a series of global effects the jihad is more a product of media than it is of any local tradition or situation and school or lineage of Muslim authority."[50] Social media in the present times has become a dangerous tool to broadcast propaganda and to attract new recruits.

The Taliban were initially resistant to employing the Internet and have only lately adopted social media and websites. They no longer use only grass-roots methods (e.g. posters) but also posts on *Twitter* and *Facebook*. More importantly, the Taliban have changed their prognostic framing. They now portray NATO as close to defeat, and offer a solution to Hamid Karzai's and then Mohammad Ashraf Ghani's corrupt regimes through bringing about "administrative transparency in all government departments". According to Jelani Zwak, an Afghan political analyst, "They are not only talking about the occupation and civilian casualties. They are acting like an alternative to this government."[51]

However, it was ISIS who really managed to exploit the Internet and new technology to spread its propaganda. It enthusiastically employed interactive media to boast of its achievements, to strike fear in its opponents and to boost its recruitment. Apart from its hyperactive presence on social media and video sharing sites, ISIS also produced slick downloadable reports and its monthly magazine *Dabiq*. It deliberately posts gruesome pictures and videos, demonstrating that its actions match its words.

Early attempts to counter online radicalization have been largely unsuccessful.[52] Sageman was perhaps among the first who warned about the dangers when he wrote in Foreign Policy:

> The world's most dangerous jihadists no longer answer to al Qaeda. The terrorists we should fear most are self-recruited wannabes who find purpose in terror and comrades on the Web. This new generation is even more frightening and unpredictable than its predecessors, but its evolution just may reveal the key to its demise.[53]

Sageman believes that radical Islam is vibrant is as long as it is drawing new recruits. While al-Qaeda may have begun to lose its attractiveness, ISIS and other radical groups seem to brazenly advertise their atrocities and gain new adherents. Islamic organizations like ISIS or al-Shabaab have also been using a combination of online and on the ground recruitment methods, especially since counterterrorism police started taking down some of their online networks.

There is a reason why groups like ISIS and al-Qaeda have been attracting recruits. Vertigans suggests a need to examine the Islamists' discourses (both open and private) in order to understand the appeal of a particular ideology. If one is to evaluate Bin Laden's statements, then even a basic content analysis shows that they are not only belligerent, but also overly religious. In contrast, the appeal of the West to Muslim-majority countries has only a thin veneer of religiosity and does not really resonate with the Muslim public in those places. For instance, one can compare Obama's "A New Beginning" speech delivered in Cairo on 4 June 2009 with Bin Laden's (alleged) "Letter to America" in November 2002. Among other things, Bin Laden not only accuses the West and Saudi Arabia of corruption, but also raises the issue of immorality. This is important and consistent. Vertigans believes that, "Immorality is a common feature within militant rhetoric."[54] Indeed, Islamist groups have frequently and successfully been adopting a higher moral ground position in their discourse.

There are numerous further examples of the failure of Western politicians and policy makers to communicate a message that will resonate with the Muslim audience. Religious vocabulary and concepts are of prime importance in such communications because the message needs to be a disguised political message. According to Sageman, "The interpretation that the global Islamist terrorists adopt is political rather than religious. It is couched in religious vocabulary, which makes it appear to be religious in character."[55] Vertigans reinforces this view by suggesting that religious rhetoric may even be employed to justify violence:

> Framing protest and collective action in strongly religious terms, deferring to a higher power and tapping into highly significant culturally embedded ideas of "holy war" may even lend a stronger legitimacy to ideologically committed violent actions than that available to secular movements.[56]

One needs to understand the meaning behind the message, the nature of the potential audience, and also how and why the message appeals to that audience. One also should search for alternative framing that will resonate with feelings of injustice, grievances, and moral outrage among Muslims. Those Muslims who aspire to achieve reform and transformation within a Muslim community are perhaps best qualified to do this.

Implications

The study of Islamic activism and processes of radicalization should be an interdisciplinary endeavor, drawing not only on religious studies but also social science, political science and social psychology to create a well-rounded and all-encompassing approach. SMT offers a number of opportunities. First, until recently there has been a lack of generalized theory and methodology in the study of Islamism. In turn, SMT helps to analyse people, places and processes; it also looks at the emergence, evolution and decline of movements. It employs not "Who?" but "How?" and "Why?" as guiding questions. SMT offers a workable theoretical framework that helps to identify factors that contribute to mobilization and radicalization. Vertigans calls it "a multilayered framework of explanation".[57] SMT employs a range of methods from ethnographic research to mathematical models, content analysis of news reports and incident-based databases (e.g. Global Terrorism Database/ GTD, RAND Database of Worldwide Terrorism Incidents/ RDWTI).

SMT is systematic; it provides categories and components that may be helpful for organizing and managing information on a movement, and for keeping a track on its development over time. An example of one of the most comprehensive studies of al-Muhajiroun in the UK is that of Wiktorowicz who evaluates the mobilization process and culturing (socializing into the movement) by looking at cognitive openings, religious seeking, the credibility and sacred authority (of leaders) and mobilization tactics, as well as the commitment and solidarity of members/activists.[58] There is a growing body of publications and research on various Islamic movements through the lens of social science, whether it is Gunning's study on Hamas,[59] or Asef Bayat's research on the grassroots movements in the Middle East.[60] Insights from social science were appreciated, especially after Madrid (2004) and London (2005) bombings. Burke relates how by 2005-2006 works by Wiktorowicz, Sageman and Atran became influential among MI5 analysts, while back in 2002-2003 the emphasis was on "sleeper cells", irrational behavior of terrorists and orchestration of atrocities from overseas.[61] Nowadays, intelligence services and governments in the West are regularly briefed by social scientists or employ insights from social science research.[62]

SMT does not treat Islamism as a distinctive body but as any other social movement where activists are subject to similar dilemmas and dynamics. As a result it offers a number of transferrable theories and insights that can help the study of Islamism, mobilization and radicalization. For instance, there are similarities in the structures of social movements; their largely middle-class leadership; the importance of charismatic leaders; and in the critical role played by social networks. Furthermore, one may transfer some of the insights from studies of more "researchable" (i.e. research-available) movements to those that are less accessible to researchers such as al-Qaeda. For instance, Vertigans argues that militant forms of Islam have some commonalities with non-violent discourses – "some of the characteristics and causes associated with militant Islam may be less distinctive than is widely thought".[63]

The ethnographic approach within SMT is particularly helpful for gaining direct knowledge that can facilitate better understanding (e.g. the "talking to the enemy" approach of Scott Atran). It helps to identify some typical dynamics and to offer some plausible explanations. This approach still poses methodological problems, especially with regard to the difficulty of gaining access to clandestine terrorist groups. The results of research from within such groups may produce interesting results and potentially diverge on a number of points from commonly held views. Outcomes can even challenge and debunk some stereotypes. For instance, Sageman argues against relative deprivation as a cause of radicalization. He challenges ideas of brainwashing and indoctrination thus undermining the role of *madrasas*. He deflates the "lone wolf" theory and stresses the importance of networks, promoting a "bunch of guys" theory. He also emphasizes that terrorists are not "experts" on their religion and tend to act in the spirit of camaraderie. Sageman and Atran among others also emphasize that terrorists are not mentally ill, but 'normal' people who lead largely normal routine lives.

For anyone who tries to understand Islamic movements it is critical to follow the operational and ideological connections between different organizations. In the words of Barabasi, one needs to "think networks" in order to understand the world.[64] The Muslim Brotherhood is an example of a highly networked entity. An organization's ideological component is often a tell-tale sign that it may be sympathetic towards the Muslim Brotherhood, or even be a part of a clandestine network. Among these ideological signs are, for example, frequent referencing to Yusuf al-Qaradawi, and promoting the concept of *wasatiyya* or "middle way". There will also a be a persistent attempt to spread Islam throughout all spheres of life, whether through education, NGOs, sports, or politics. This is a direct result of following the doctrine of the comprehensiveness of Islam or *Shumuliyyat al-Islam*, as expounded by the founder of the Muslim Brotherhood, Hassan al-Banna, and re-emphasized by Yusuf al-Qaradawi.[65] Ideological connections are also often intertwined with financial ones. "Following the money" helps to identify those who are promoting a particular ideology, their hidden connections to other interested parties, and even their agenda and motivations. The study of tactical and operational links between groups is also revealing in explaining how networks acquire a particular character. For instance, the alliances that Boko Haram has developed with the AQIM (al-Qaeda in the Islamic Maghreb), and al-Shabaab, in turn facilitated the sharing of experience, tactics, human resources, and material resources, including state-of-the-art weapons. Reportedly these links transformed the Boko Haram organization and made it even more violent and assertive.

Islamic organizations claim to present a viable sociopolitical alternative to failed states or to corrupt authorities. Hizb ut-Tahrir promotes the establishment of a caliphate, while the Gülen Movement pursues the vision of the "golden generation" of Muslims. Boko Haram, judging from its name, takes a vigorous stance against adopting Western ways in Nigeria. Such ways include Western education (known as *boko*, a rough translation from the Hausa language, also a corrupted word for "book"), but also Western civil service structures and endeavors to promote democracy. The organization's central message focuses on Islamization and the prohibition (*haram* in Arabic) of "deviant" Western ways. It also acts aggressively on its grievances against the Nigerian government, and its motivation has been often identified as arising from a sense of victimization and deprivation. However, its religious motivation should not be underplayed, especially since its rhetoric and actions are often explicitly religious. Boko Haram's main targets have not been restricted only to Western agencies (e.g. the UN building) and government and civilian institutions (military barracks, police stations, election polls); but they have also deliberately targeted Christian communities and churches in certain areas. The conflict has not only been about political competition between the predominantly Muslim north and the mainly Christian south, but also about religious differences. Boko Haram has also been mounting attacks on moderate Muslims (for instance, mosques were attacked in the Nigerian city of Maiduguri in 2011 and 2012), reportedly in an attempt to unleash sectarian and ethnic violence in the region. While the means of this group are violent, its vision is actually utopian and unachievable.

There are certain limitations to the SMT approach when applied to Islamist organizations and movements, as SMT tends to underplay the importance of ideology or to focus only on its appeal. This may have a misleading and deceptive effect. For instance, it is possible to take the following finding a bit too far: a potential terrorist may not have a deep and orthodox understanding of Islam, and choose to die not so much for the cause as for his comrades. Such a research finding, which appears to dismiss the highly significant role of ideology in the mind of the terrorist, may lead analysts, policy makers and commentators to make the convenient, even politically correct claim that ISIS and other groups do not reflect true Islam.[66] However, Western observers should not be misled into thinking that the lack of deep knowledge about Islam among some potential recruits somehow negates the attractiveness and transformational power of the message that originally attracted them to a particular movement. In fact, it is the ideology that enhances the intensity of the fellowship among the recruits, making them feel chosen and special, evoking a deep level of commitment among them, and between them and their more ideologically wired and zealous friends. It is also by studying ideology and its application that we may obtain some accurate insights into the way an Islamist organization operates, motivates, and recruits, and into how it propagates its message.

Al-Qaeda, ISIS, Boko Haram and other groups have characteristically justified their actions by going back to Islamic sources and formulating radical interpretations. The ideology of the Muslim Brotherhood is imbued with references to Islamic sources and it is fundamentalist in this sense. Their ideology creates accord and cooperation, offers inspiration and effects a call for action. Furthermore, certain religious components of ideology are often expressed by movements in a coded way through symbols, and one gains deeper insights into the influence of religion on Islamist groups by identifying and engaging at a deeper level with the original sources of ideology to which the symbols refer.[67] The Islamists' message should be analysed not only at content level, but also at connotation and intention levels, and at emotional level. Such an analysis may supply insights that will prove invaluable both to the process of countering their narrative, and to providing an alternative one.

In conclusion, a coherent and comprehensive approach to Islamism must be adopted. Its beliefs and the narrative it promotes need to be studied, its structures and networks analysed, and a thorough understanding developed of its actions, tactics, plans and ultimate goals. Strategists and analysts should not dismiss or underestimate the significance of ideological and religious factors within Islamist movements; on the contrary, such factors should be studied, placed in their historical, social and political contexts, and taken fully into account when policies are formulated.

Notes

1 Jeff Goodwin and James Jasper, "Editors' Introduction", in Jeff Goodwin and James Jasper (eds.), *The Social Movements Reader: Cases and Concepts*. Malden: Blackwell, 2003, p. 3.

2 Doug McAdam et al., "Introduction: Opportunities, Mobilizing Structures, and Framing Processes - Toward a Synthetic, Comparative Perspective on Social Movements", in Doug McAdam et al. (eds.), *Comparative Perspectives on Social Movements: Political Opportunities, Mobilizing Structures, and Cultural Framings*. Cambridge: Cambridge University Press, 1996, pp. 1-20.

3 David Snow et al., "Mapping the Terrain", in David Snow et al. (eds.), *The Blackwell Companion to Social Movements*. Oxford: Blackwell, 2007, p. 6.

4 For instance see: Donatella Della Porta, *Social Movements, Political Violence & the State*. Cambridge University Press, 1995; Mario Diani and Doug McAdam, *Social Movements and Networks: Relational Approaches to Collective Action*. Oxford: Oxford University Press, 2003.

5 Mario Diani, "The Concept of Social Movement", in Vincenzo Ruggiero and Nicola Montagna (eds.), *Social Movements: A Reader*. London: Routledge, 2008, p. 271.

6 Stephen Vertigans, *Militant Islam: A Sociology of Characteristics, Causes and Consequences*. London: Routledge, 2009, p. 36.

7 David Snow and Susan Marshall, "Cultural Imperialism, Social Movements, and the Islamic Revival", in Louis Kriesberg (ed.), *Research in Social Movements, Conflict and Change*, vol.7. Greenwich: JAI Press, 1984, pp. 131-152.

8 Quintan Wiktorowicz (ed.), *Islamic Activism: A Social Movement Theory Approach*. Bloomington: Indiana University Press, 2004.

9 Quintan Wiktorowicz, "Introduction: Islamic Activism and Social Movement Theory", in Quintan Wiktorowicz (ed.), *Islamic Activism: A Social Movement Theory Approach*. Bloomington: Indiana University Press, 2004, p. 2.

10 Examples of research on Islamism and SMT: Azani Eitan, *Hezbollah. The Story of the Party of God: From Revolution to Institutionalization*. New York: Palgrave Macmillan, 2008; Stephen Vertigans, *Terrorism and Societies*. Aldershot: Ashgate, 2008; Sofie Bedford, *Islamic Activism in Azerbaijan: Repression and Mobilization in a Post-Soviet Context*. Stockholm: Sodertorns Hogskola, 2009; Farhad Khosrokhavar, *Inside Jihadism: Understanding Jihadi Movements Worldwide*. London: Paradigm Publishers, 2009; Lukas Strickland, *Approaching Islamic Activism: The Case for Social Movement Theory*. Saarbrücken: VDM Verlag, 2009; Stephen Vertigans, *Militant Islam: A Sociology of Characteristics, Causes and Consequences*. London: Routledge, 2009; Beverley Milton-Edwards and Stephen Farrell, *Hamas: The Islamic Resistance Movement*. Cambridge: Polity Press, 2010.

11 Examples of research on non-contentious forms Islamism and SMT: Mehmet Azani Ergene, *Tradition Witnessing the Modern Age: An Analysis of the Gülen Movement*. Somerset: Tughra, 2008; Helen Ebaugh, *The Gülen Movement: A Sociological Analysis of a Civic Movement Rooted in Moderate Islam*. London: Springer, 2010; Emmanuel Karagiannis, *Political Islam in Central Asia: the Challenge of Hizb ut-Tahrir*. London: Routledge, 2010.

12 Richard Martin and Abbas Barzegar, *Islamism: Contested Perspectives on Political Islam*. Stanford: Stanford University Press, 2010.

13 Ted Gurr, *Why Men Rebel*. Princeton: Princeton University Press, 1970.

14 Mohammed Hafez, *Why Muslims Rebel: Repression and Resistance in the Islamic World*. Boulder: Lynne Rienner, 2003, p. xvii.

15 Vertigans, *Militant Islam*, p. 26.

16 Alan Krueger and Jitka Malecˇkova, "Education, Poverty and Terrorism: Is There a Causal Connection?", *Journal of Economic Perspectives*, 17: 4, Fall 2003, p. 142.

17 Scott Atran, "Global Network Terrorism", *Air University*, http://www.au.af.mil/au/awc/awcgate/whitehouse/atrannsc-042806.pdf (viewed 20 September 2014).

18 Marc Sageman, *Understanding Terror Networks*. Philadelphia: University of Pennsylvania Press, 2004, pp. 30, 76.

19 "Exclusive: Top ISIS Leaders Revealed", *Al Arabiya News*, 13 February 2014, english .alarabiya.net/en/News/2014/02/13/Exclusive-Top-ISIS-leaders-revealed.html (viewed 20 September 2014). "Video: Who are ISIS's Top 20 Leaders?", *Al Arabiya News*, 19 September 2014, english.alarabiya.net/en/News/middle-east/2014/09/19/Meet-ISIS-top-20-leaders.html (viewed 20 September 2014).

20 Robin Simcox et al., *Islamist Terrorism: The British Connections*. London: The Centre for Social Cohesion, 2010, p. vii.

21 Sageman, *Understanding Terror Networks*, p. 76.

22 Scott Atran cited in a report by Arnaud de Borchgrave et al., *Force Multiplier for Intelligence: Collaborative Open Source Networks*. Washington: Center for Strategic and International Studies, 2007, pp. 13-14.

23 For instance see: Rodney Stark and Roger Finke, *Acts of Faith: Explaining the Human Side of Religion*. Berkeley: University of California Press, 2000.

24 Bob Edwards and John McCarthy, "Resources and Social Movement Mobilization", in David Snow et al. (eds.), *The Blackwell Companion to Social Movements*. Oxford: Blackwell, 2007, p. 125-128.

25 Quintan Wiktorowicz, *The Management of Islamic Activism: Salafis, the Muslim Brotherhood, and State Power in Jordan*. New York: State University of New York Press, 2001.

26 Marc Sageman, *Leaderless Jihad: Terror Networks in the Twenty-First Century*. Philadelphia: University of Pennsylvania Press, 2008, p. 125.

27 The document was found during a raid at the mosque in Falls Church, VA in 2004. Mohamed Akram, *An Explanatory Memorandum on the General Strategic Goal for the Group in North America*, 22 May 1991, http://www.investigativeproject.org/documents/misc/20.pdf (viewed 20 September 2014).

28 Susan Hoberecht, et al., "Inter-Organizational Networks", *OD and Sustainability*, 43: 4, 2011, p. 23.

29 Emmanuel Karagiannis, "Transnational Islamist Networks: Western Fighters in Afghanistan, Somalia and Syria", *The International Spectator,* 48: 4, December 2013, p. 119.

30 Donatella Della Porta, "Political Socialization in Left-Wing Underground Organizations: Biographies of Italian and German Militants", in Donatella Della Porta (ed.), *Social Movements and Violence: Participation in Underground Organizations,* vol. 4. Greenwich: JAI Press, 1992, pp. 259-290.

31 Marc Sageman, "Leaderless Jihad: Radicalization in the West", *New America Foundation,* http://www.newamerica.net/files/Microsoft%20PowerPoint%20-%20Sageman.pdf (viewed 20 September 2014).

32 Sageman, *Understanding Terror Networks*, p. 115.

33 Sageman, *Understanding Terror Networks*, p. 101.

34 Scott Atran, " 'Band of Brothers': Civil Society and the Making of a Terrorist", *The International Journal of Not-for-Profit Law,* 10:4, August 2008, *The International Center for Not-for-Profit Law,* http://www.icnl.org/research/journal/vol10iss4/art_3.htm (viewed 20 September 2014).

35 While Atran and Sageman used some simple software such as UCINet, later on government organisations such as the CIA, the Pentagon, and the FBI had more advanced social analysis software such as SNA (Social Network Analysis) by i2, Palantir Government by Palantir, InFlow by OrgNet.com, and Synthesys by Digital Reasoning, among others. There is fierce competition among these software companies. Some even claim to be a step ahead by utilizing both network theory and social psychology for a "dynamic metanetwork analysis" (for instance Organizational Risk Analyzer or ORA). Software for analyzing social networking seems to follow the same basic principle: by feeding the data and then scanning multiple data sources at once, an analyst may discover some important unseen connections. An article in the *Independent* aptly described it as "Terrorist Facebook" – The New Weapon Against Al-Qa'ida" (Steve Connor, "'Terrorist Facebook' – The New Weapon Against Al-Qa'ida", *The Independent,* 19 August 2009). However, this approach also caused some ethical problems. By helping to "connect the dots", SNA augmented the "mosaic philosophy" (also known as the "mosaic theory") of intelligence gathering (extracting seemingly unrelated pieces of information from detainees, including innocent ones). For instance see: John Bohannon, "Investigating Networks: The Dark Side", *Science,* 325: 5939, 24 July 2009, pp. 410-411; "Guest Post by Lawrence Wilkerson: Some Truths About Guantanamo Bay", *Washington Note,* 17 March 2009, http://washington note.com/some_truths_abo/ (viewed 20 September 2014).

36 Islamic State (IS) or ISIS went further in using the Internet as a recruitment tool. Ghastly images and videos on the Internet became part of their propaganda and psychological warfare.

37 Sageman, *Leaderless Jihad,* p. 68.

38 Sageman, *Understanding Terror Networks*, p.156.

39 Sageman, *Understanding Terror Networks*, p. 178.

40 Thomas Hegghammer, "Terrorist Recruitment and Radicalization in Saudi Arabia", *Middle East Policy,* XIII: 4, Winter 2006, p. 50.

41 Sageman, *Leaderless Jihad,* p. 116.

42 Sageman, *Leaderless Jihad,* p. 79. Also, Marc Sageman, "Understanding Terror Networks – The Turn to Political Violence", *HJS Event.* London: House of Commons, 13 July 2010.

43 Vertigans, *Militant Islam,* p. 30.

44 Vertigans, *Militant Islam,* p. 54.

45 Scott Helfstein, *Edges of Radicalization: Ideas, Individuals and Networks in Violent Extremism.* West Point: Combating Terrorism Center, 2012, p. 65.

46 Helfstein, *Edges of Radicalization,* p. 70.

47 Goodwin and Jasper, "Editors' Introduction", p. 6.

48 Valentine Moghadam, *Globalization and Social Movements: Islamism, Feminism, and the Global Justice Movement.* Lanham: Rowman and Littlefield Publishers, 2009, p. 13.

49 Tom Quiggin, "Understanding al-Qaeda's Ideology for Counter-Narrative Work", *Perspectives on Terrorism* 3: 2 (2010), http://www.terrorismanalysts.com/pt/index.php/pot/article/view/67/html (viewed 20 September 2014).

50 Faisal Devji, *Landscapes of the Jihad: Militancy, Morality, Modernity.* London: Hurst, 2005, p. 87.

51 Ernesto Londoño, "U.S. Struggles to Counter Taliban Propaganda", *Washington Post,* 1 October 2010.

52 Tim Stevens and Peter R. Neumann, "Countering Online Radicalisation: A Strategy for Action", *International Centre for the Study of Radicalisation and Political Violence,* 2009, http://icsr.info/wp-content/uploads/2012/10/1236768491ICSROnline RadicalisationReport.pdf (viewed 20 September 2014).

53 Marc Sageman, "The Next Generation of Terror", *Foreign Policy* 165, 2008, pp. 36-42. Marc Sageman, "A Strategy for Fighting International Islamist Terrorists", *The ANNALS of the American Academy of Political and Social Science,* 618: 1, 2008, pp. 223-231.

54 Vertigans, *Militant Islam,* p. 31.

55 Sageman, *Leaderless Jihad,* p. 80.

56 Vertigans, *Militant Islam,* p. 43.

57 Vertigans, *Militant Islam,* p. 163.

58 Quintan Wiktorowicz, *Radical Islam Rising: Muslim Extremism in the West.* Lanham: Rowman, 2005.

59 Jeroen Gunning, *Hamas in Politics: Democracy, Religion, Violence.* London: Hurst, 2008.

60 Asef Bayat, *Life As Politics: How Ordinary People Change the Middle East.* Stanford: Stanford University Press, 2013.

61 Jason Burke, "Talking to the Enemy by Scott Atran – Review", *The Observer,* 24 October 2010.

62 Though according to Scott Atran, government and intelligence service may choose not to act on those briefings from social scientists and anthropologists like himself. Scott Atran, "Talking to the Enemy: Violent Extremism, Sacred Values, and What it Means to Be Human", London School of Economics, 9 November 2010.

63 Vertigans, *Militant Islam*, p. 3.

64 Albert-Laszlo Barabasi, *Linked: How Everything Is Connected to Everything Else and What It Means for Business, Science, and Everyday Life*. New York: Plume, 2003, p. 7.

65 Yusuf al-Qaradawi, *Priorities of the Islamic Movement in the Coming Phase*. Cairo: al-Dar, 1992.

66 For instance, see Mehdi Hasan, "What the Jihadists Who Bought 'Islam For Dummies' on Amazon Tell Us About Radicalisation", *Huffington Post*, 21 August 2014, www.huffing-tonpost.co.uk/mehdi-hasan/jihadist-radicalisation-islam-for-dummies_b_5697160.html?utm_hp_ref=tw (viewed 20 September 2014).

67 An example of this is the black and white ISIS flag. It is deeply and powerfully symbolic for its followers and for many within Muslim communities. The choice of colour, inscription and geometric circle, all make theological, historical and even apocalyptical references. See Ilene Prusher, "What the ISIS Flag Says About the Militant Group", *Time*, 9 September 2014, time.com/3311665/isis-flag-iraq-syria/ (viewed 10 September 2014). For a more detailed explanation of the apocalyptic significance of the black flag in Islamic theology see Ali Soufan and Daniel Freedman, *The Black Banners: Inside the Hunt for Al Qaeda*. London: Allen Lane, 2011.

5

THE IMPORTANCE OF PROGRESSIVE ARAB REFORMERS

Stephen Ulph

It has taken some time for Western analysts to grasp the importance of theology – in the broader, applied sense of Islamic doctrine and law – to the progress of Islamism and its more overt, militant form of jihadism, even though this is hardly news to Arab and Muslim scholars

Yet the centrality of the religious dimension should be immediately obvious from the volume of traffic on projihadist Arabic-language chat forums obsessing about the *fiqh* of jihad, its legal stipulations and conditions. It is clearly an important preoccupation of the readers, and the underlying theme to these anxious discussions seems to be a contest for "authenticity" – Islamic authenticity. It is, to judge from the traffic, the central arena on which the struggle is being fought.

But one might argue that this still has not fully permeated the current analytical culture. How many are there who will grasp how Islamist militants equate religious pluralism to *jahiliyya*, the state of preIslamic ignorance? How many can penetrate the obscure discourse on matters such the *Hadith of Jaththama,*[1] (which details how Muhammad disregarded, for tactical reasons, the injunction against the killing of civilians) or understand why it is that Islamists adduce the name of medieval authorities such as al-Ghazali to justify suicide bombings?[2]

This poor grasp is not helped by the failure of academia to engage fully in the study of Islamic radicalism.[3] The crossover between the religious aspects of the debate (in terms of the textual nature of the argumentation that the jihadists employ) and the implications for security and counterterrorism policy, is something that few institutions as yet appear willing, or equipped, to address.

This is because Islamism does not fit neatly into the catalogue of challenges to democracy that are familiar to Western observers. Its admixture of totalitarian and religious/doctrinal patterns of thought highly complicates the analysis. Meanwhile, the rise of the political philosophy of multiculturalism has rendered reference to cultural starting points to the violence unwelcome.

Yet it is impossible fully to address the challenge of Islamism without a thorough understanding of its ideological starting points, or without a sound grasp of the current dynamics taking place within its own mental universe. The point was emphasized by the Algerian intellectual Mohamed Arkoun:

> We know how political scientists portray fundamentalist movements ... either legitimising their political action against totalitarian, oppressive regimes, or condemning them as violent, fanatical, irrational and opposed to Western rational, democratic values. The theological and spiritual background of religiously inspired movements is rarely mentioned.[4]

Missing, to date, has been what should have been a logical starting point: a determination to take the ideological grounding of extremists seriously, and methodically deconstruct it, instead of relying on a presumed future effectiveness of a security-focused solution to the growing crisis. "It is no use combating these by means of the security forces or even the military," argues the Syrian-French intellectual Hashem Saleh,

> We have to confront them intellectually on the grounds of the Islamic tradition itself. We have to present a new reading in place of the old one, or a new interpretation of Islam in place of the traditional, obscurantist interpretation that is outdated but which nevertheless is still deep-rooted today. For it is this that confers sanctified legitimacy to the voices of extremists and their terrorist bombings which are scything down civilians in a random manner.[5]

More specifically, without such an understanding it is impossible to measure to what degree the Islamists are actually departing from the "orthodox mainstream", or how far they have succeeded in presenting their case as lying within the tradition.

An Unheeded Resource

Western analysts could be forgiven for pleading ignorance, but not for ignoring the pleadings of those who are not so limited in their understanding or hampered by a cultural cringe or (in the case of the United Kingdom) postcolonial guilt. Hashem Saleh has commented on what he sees as the strange marginalization of progressive thinkers:

> The Arab cultural arena is not universally occupied by the obscurantist fundamentalists as the prolific studies dedicated to this in various European languages... would have us believe. Witness the volume of foreign books focusing on the issue of Islamic fundamentalism after the criminal attacks of September 11th. Witness also the giant media corporations and Western satellite programs that can only see fundamentalists everywhere. There are other kinds of renewal in the Arab and indeed the entire Islamic world, but no one speaks of them.[6]

For there are reliable alternative voices, of high intellectual quality and authority, that have embraced the task of combating the Islamist advance, often at high risk to themselves. More importantly, for the sake of an issue such as this that is sabotaged by perceptions, these alternative voices have the virtue of being *culturally bilingual.* This means that, unlike some of our speakers and commentators in the West, Muslim intellectuals are not so reticent to state the obvious: that this is a *religious* issue. It is about Islam. Perhaps not as many perceive this at the moment, but it is very much about Islam, about its legacy and its internal intellectual infrastructures.[7]

It would be useful, then, to highlight the role of progressive Arab Muslim intellectuals as they impact upon the West, and demonstrate how they can help us understand the problem and why their opinions are useful to us in breaking down the wall of reticence that prevents us from fully engaging in the debate.

Perhaps the best demonstration of the clarity this can bring is the definition of the issue of Islamist violence given by the Tunisian intellectual, the late Lafif Lakhdar, as the work of the "Islamic Far Right". That one term solves at a stroke our confusion as to what it is that we are up against. That is, it is not something separate from Islam, some form of contemporary deviant perversion, but more precisely a tendency (and a culturally authentic one at that) that once had fair claim to being the "mainstream," as indeed Islamists claim it is.

How is this possible? To explain this apparent conundrum we should consider the pivotal role played (for good or for ill) by Muslim intellectuals historically. In brief, what aided the virtual triumph of the Islamist claim to represent Islamic authenticity, is their skillful manipulation of the space left by the abdication of Arab and Muslim intellectuals from the task of indigenizing modernity. Arab thinkers of the 19th and the early 20th century *Nahda* ("Resurgence") failed to revisit issues of authority, the state and the individual, issues that had been left unfinished with the medieval closing off of independent jurisprudential reasoning (*ijtihad*). Of particular importance was their neglecting to resolve the debate on "non-divine rule" (*hukm al-taghut*). As Hassan Mneimneh explains:

> The advocates of liberalism, nationalism and leftism in subsequent eras saw no need to focus on this issue... They all relegated religiously derived thought to the status of an atavistic reflex that would soon be swept away by the organic reality of either progress or nation or class. And Islamism in general, and the Muslim Brotherhood in particular, benefited from this omission.[8]

Fascinated by Western achievements in these areas, the Arab educated élite simply imported a foreign conceptual language without indigenizing the underlying issues with reference to the Islamic corpus of inherited law and literature. Abandoned by the leading lights, this Islamic intellectual enterprise languished and simplified, and it was left to lesser minds, such as that of Hasan al-Banna' the founder of the Muslim Brotherhood, to seek the indigenization.

The struggle was, therefore, first and foremost intellectual, before it became a political and subsequently a security struggle. This was highlighted by the *Almuslih* Rome Conference in December 2012,[9] where discussions held between a selection of intellectuals, Arab and Western, concluded that intellectual restructuring would have to precede meaningful reform on the ground. This restructuring, according to Hashem Saleh, one of the participants,

> is where the basic task of the conference and those attending it lies. For a true, future, political Spring must first be preceded by an intel-

lectual enlightenment! We cannot forge an Arab future with the mentality of bygone eras. This is where the great contradiction inherent in the current 'Spring' resides. But given that this mentality is still predominant and enjoys a historical legitimacy and a massive public support, we will have to cross swords with it in one form or another. In other words, we have to criticize it and pull it apart.[10]

He later went on to explain that,

The question is therefore a cultural one, and the battle is, in the first degree, intellectual. If we do not win the intellectual battle for enlightenment against the fundamentalists, we will not at any day win the political battle. And for this very reason the Arab Spring will only turn into a fundamentalist Autumn.[11]

But this also presupposes the need for a new concept of security response, one that recognizes that *the war of ideas is the primary arena of conflict*. Wise heads in the Middle East have been flagging up for some time the need to think outside the "security solution" box and, as the Saudi liberal commentator Mshari al-Dhaydi put it, concentrate on

The intellectual dilemma which constitutes the culture of al-Qaeda and those like it... security should form the 'external' part of the solution, whereas internally, there is a need for intellectual and political reform, as well as a restructuring of Arab society. Unless there is a parallel between the external and internal parts of the solution, we will continue to go round this vicious circle until we wear ourselves out.[12]

The Egyptian analyst Gamal 'Abd al-Rahim Salih goes further, and sees that any amount of solutions on the security, political or economic front will also fail to resolve the main problem since

The root cause of terrorism lies in the intellectual framework which created a state of Muslim mind and sentiment that is not responsible for terrorism alone, but also for creating and sustaining tyranny and economic/social backwardness... We believe that what we can call "the evil triangle" of Backwardness–Tyranny–Violence is a natural product of some negative elements that are deeply rooted in the intellectual and cultural component of Arab and Muslim societies.[13]

For which reason, he argues,

> Instead of eradicating terrorism through initiating democracy, or the use of counter violence, or by dealing with temporary tactical compromises, it is more practical to link it to achieving a program of intellectual enlightenment.[14]

It is because such thinking lies outside the confines of established Western political studies that such thoughts remain in the wilderness. At the same time this courageous focus on the negative influence of deeply-rooted, indigenous ingredients of the cultural dilemma equally steps beyond what Islamists can tolerate and hits raw nerves.

How is it that Arab Muslim intellectuals present such a perilous challenge? It is because, unlike any other voices that are cowed by political correctness, they alone are confident enough to point to the unpalatable fact that educational syllabuses in the Middle East – dominated with a few exceptions by Salafists – bear much of the responsibility for prepriming young Arab minds towards xenophobic rejection of the other and ultimately to violence. "Enclosed, atavistic, fundamentalist thought," laments Hashem Saleh,

> predominates in our schools and universities, and not merely in our traditional institutions and colleges of Shari'a. This thought predominates over the entire Arab Street from the Atlantic to the Arabian Gulf, and indeed the Islamic Street as a whole, from the Far West to Pakistan.[15]

The problem with this atavism's remaining unchallenged is that it provides the underpinning for "the resurgence of movements of self-isolation that pronounce excommunication upon any opening up to the modern, enlightened philosophy on the grounds that it is Western – that is, a 'Satanic abomination'!"[16]

It is therefore unsurprising that Salafists decry the role of progressive intellectuals with bitterness. Indeed, for *Almuslih* author 'Abd al-Hamid al-Ansari, this antipathy is one of the defining characteristics of Salafism, in that they are

> … advocating the suppression of creativity, promoting conflict with liberal thinkers and rushing to pronounce scholars, intellectuals,

artists and poets as "infidel". They make use of mosque pulpits and websites to issue *fatwas* of incitement against "liberals and innovators". The University of al-Imam in Riyadh actually awarded a first class doctorate to a Saudi researcher for his thesis: *Credal deviancy in the modern culture* in which he proscribed 200 Arab intellectuals, describing them as "infidel".[17]

The point is that the accusation of being an "infidel" is an overt call for the person's execution. The thesis was not something produced in isolation, since an earlier work by the Saudi cleric 'Awadh al-Qarni made explicit the Salafist position on the entire infrastructure of modernity. His 1998 publication *Modernity in the Balance of Islam* subjected Arab authors, poets, researchers, philosophers, academics, literary critics and journalists to the accusation of heresy, thus again making licit their killing.[18]

This Salafist-directed educational war against modernity was perhaps most succinctly described by Lafif Lakhdar. Giving as the defining feature of the Salafists their reverence for the ancestors, their thoughts and deeds, he elaborated on the important corollary of this reverence – antipathy to modernity – particularly since this modernity is associated with Jews and Christians, whose ways are to be rejected whatever the cost:

> Ancestor-worship is... manifested in the modernity-phobia which dominates the Arab mentality, modernism being regarded as heresy or imitation of Jews and Christians. This mentality resorts to ... subconscious tricks to evade modernity. The first is religious self-sufficient narcissism which considers itself in no need of any kind of self-renovation, on the pretext that "The first left nothing to the last"... The second trick was adopted by most – if not all – Islamic reformers of the 19th century and is still to the present day advocated. It argues that we should renovate our thought so as to evade French modernity.[19]

The implications of this trick, Lakhdar underlines, is the abdication of the task of fully renovating *fiqh* to cope with the modern environment to one of bypassing modernity as merely constituting "Westernisation". The result is that "these reformists succeeded in eluding modernity, but did not renovate *fiqh* due to a very obvious reason: the core of renovating *fiqh* lies in the adoption of modern legislation, values, sciences, and institutions whose logic and ends are different from those of the *fiqh* of the Middle Ages."[20]

Instead, the "ancestor-worship" has successfully sidelined the humanities – effectively cancelling out studies on the sociology and comparative history of religion – and it stripped the natural sciences of their original role as concepts explaining phenomena in favor of steering them towards religious perceptions of reality. In this environment, genetic research in some Arab countries is banned for representing "an interference by creatures in the affairs of the Creator" and evolutionary theory is written off as an act of apostasy.

The solution for Lakhdar is clear enough, albeit one that eludes many Western observers unfamiliar with the internal infrastructures of Salafist thought:

> The exit from the stormy crisis of modernity faced by the Arab World is through a conscious break with "the commitment to be different from Jews and Christians," especially in the media, education and religious discourse. This implies reconciliation with their modernism – which has become international – without complexes or guilt feelings.[21]

For Hashem Saleh, a core task of the reconciliation process is to resolve the dilemma of "epistemological compartmentalization" that persists in much of the Arab Muslim intellectual class, with their pretensions to cultural self-sufficiency and their assumptions of superiority over other systems of belief and thought:

> If they think that the Arabs (and Muslims as a whole) can overcome their present ordeal without a radical revision of their absolute theological certainties and their shrieking, self-isolating ideological slogans, then they are... deluded.[22]

The revision of these certainties must cross both ideological and cultural boundaries, and the Arab intellectual class would do well to understand the urgency of the task:

> Either we succeed in crystallizing a new interpretation of our faith and our culture – by which I mean a rationalist, enlightened, tolerant interpretation – or we will leave the field open to obscurantist puritans to wander up and down it at their leisure.[23]

The target for the modernist reformers is therefore primarily Salafist interpretations of Islam and the Islamic heritage, and it is worth considering here the focal points of the progressives' attempts to dismantle this trend.

142

Dismissing the Idea of a Single Interpretation

Salafists base their interpretation on an assumption that, though popularly held, is untenable: that the interpretations by classical Muslim scholars are as immutable as the Scripture,[24] and that the implementation of Islamic laws has been consistent throughout history.

It is a deep-rooted position, and it takes a religious scholar of the authority of former Marseilles Mufti Soheib Bencheikh to say that what we are dealing with in this formation of law is little more than the afterlife of bedouin tribalism:

> This static theology we inherited was conceived for an Islam that was the religion of the majority and had sovereignty over its lands. Moreover, it was conceived for tribal societies. This theology was meant for times when nations hardly came into contact [with each other] – and if they did, it was in a spirit of rivalry for dominance. This theology could not care less about living in harmony with other cultures, and knows nothing of pluralism based on universal principles like secularism and religious freedom – [principles that are] applicable to all religions and granted to all.[25]

The progressive scholars' counteraction, therefore, was to embrace the task of combating popular ignorance in the Islamic world as to what an Islamic society should be, and of reconsidering the definition of legitimacy.

We can see this, for instance in the work of Dr. Olfa Youssef. By revisiting the popular conceptions of shari'a, and the Salafists' case, which rests typically on the dictum "the Qur'an is valid for all times and places," she challenges Islamist interpretations of the Qur'anic text and the tendentious use they put it to. If the above dictum itself were true (and it has no pedigree in the writings of the ancients), there is still no case for assuming that it argues that "actual human history must constantly reshape itself to conform to the meaning of the Qur'anic text" – as the Salafists claim. Quite simply, the Qur'an could be equally viewed "as bearing a variety of meanings that are valid for all times and places... meanings which comprehend all the capacities of actual human development down the ages".[26]

Such an interpretation allows for turning the traditional understanding on its head and licensing instead the adaptation of the Qur'an to modernity. The implications for the claimed "authority" of what must now be held to be a human shari'a are clear.

Establishing the Empirical Evidence

The application of the scientific method also gets results. For instance, Dr. Muhammed Sanduk, a regular contributor to the reformist *Almuslih* website, uses his training to provide empirical evidence relating to the results of a historically flawed epistemology, which since the 11th century AD has dictated a steady decline in scientific and cultural output.[27] He notes that Arab thought still looks upon the decline as some form of natural phenomenon "whenever it is not actually casting the blame on historical events and on other peoples". While remarking on this "strange case in the history of human society," he notes the equal strangeness of "contemporary Arab thought, which often supports projects for resurgence and modernization, [but] is failing to make an attempt at studying this historical discontinuity and its causes".[28]

Untrammeled by Western insecurities in the debate, this Iraqi scientist dismisses the blame game exploited by Arab funding institutions, which he holds are themselves responsible for the very collapse that is laid at the door of Western hostility. Instead, Sanduk sees the problem as an entirely internal one, arguing that the sanctification of "conservation" in Muslim societies proved too powerful an instinct to be affected by any programs undertaken by the late 19th century *Nahda*:

> These attempts are no more than cultural tinkerings, made in an ill-considered bid for resurgence. They embarked on the procurement of social, political and military systems that had been established by developed societies. The building up process was therefore a superficial and temporary one and these programs began to collapse. Not only this, the construction and demolition operation went on, and still does, with the result that these societies, after having exited the prison of time, are still confusedly searching for their way.[29]

For all the efforts at combating *alphabetic* illiteracy, he argues, there was no attempt to eradicate the *cultural* illiteracy that was leaving Arab societies ill-equipped for living in the modern age. As a result, in a sharp contrast to the position in other developing societies and cultures, the epistemological deficit in the Muslim world is *actively strengthening* as a class of Muslim intellectuals embark on the Quixotic enterprise of "Islamising" science. This, for Sanduk, is no more than a rerun of the medieval formula that, in contradistinction to the mindset that accounted for the rise of the university system in

Europe, determined the fate of the Mustansiriyya academy in Baghdad: that is, "the conception of knowledge as crystallized by Islamic thought, one which confirmed that no knowledge existed outside the realm of religious thought".[30] As such, this epistemological formula plays to a form of deep Islamic "exceptionalism", "as if the Muslims were a race of mankind with a different mental make-up, one which needs a different reasoning method".[31]

X   Refusing the exceptionalism, and instead discerning an underlying clash of chronologies, progressive Arab intellectuals are left to draw out the implications in "the depths of the tragedy being lived by these Arab-Muslim societies that had been closed off from the world for centuries and were still prisoners to time".[32]

The chronological alienation of Arab Muslim societies presages fatal consequences, according to Sanduk, in that this mental prison risks establishing itself in a state of "post-backwardness," one where the basic cause of backwardness remains deep-rooted, and where so many red lines continue to constrict the space for intellectual freedom and doom any "dithering attempts at awakening" to an unchanging trajectory of failure.[33]

NB   The value of such an unembarrassed empirical approach lies in its unassailable neutrality. By evaluating the performance of the culture on its own terms and pinpointing some specific directions taken by Muslim thinkers (not necessarily to be considered more authentic than any other), all of us, Muslim and nonMuslim, avoid the risk of entering into "clash of cultures" territory. Facts are facts; failures are failures. It is all – neutrally – measurable.

X Introducing to the Muslim World the Study of Comparative Religion

By repositioning the debate in the "clash of chronologies" territory, Arab progressives are able to open up a new, wide and challenging vista in the study of comparative fundamentalism and comparative religion.

A champion of this approach was Lafif Lakhdar, who wrote for the *Almuslih* conference a detailed analysis of how "Islamic" studies of Islam have become "like a drug that has gone beyond its sell-by date" and how this approach is both vital to Islamic reform and deadly to Islamist pretensions, on the grounds that

- It will place Islam on an equal footing with all other faiths;
- It will teach Islam, its holy texts, its legacy and historical personalities through the prism of comparative religion, which will place the relation-

145

ship of Muslims to their faith and their culture on a transparent basis, one that is freed of divine legends, riddles or mysteries.

There are clearly some intriguing possibilities thrown up by this exercise of tracing the influence upon the development of Islamic thought not only of doctrines of Judaism and Christianity, which may be familiar to many, but also of preIslamic Arabia in the Islamic afterlife of the pagan rituals of the *hajj*, and even of Zoroastrian doctrines.[34] Through such a comparative study, Lakhdar asserts,

√ Islam is presented, like any other religion, as but one of the cultural entities that have borrowed its rituals from cultures that preceded them, such as Judaism, Christianity and Manichaeism – from the last of which Islam took many of his doctrines such as "the Seal of the Prophets'"and no less than four of its five pillars of faith: the *shahada* (Declaration of Faith), Prayer, *Zakah* (Alms), and Fasting. This puts it in a position to ask questions and express doubts, and thereby take itself out of the shell of its ancient certainties.[35]

By extricating Islam and its heritage like this from the grip of mytho-history, into history governed by human imperatives and capacities, the establishment of an "Islam of history" will

help us put a stop to the religious narcissism deriving from primitive ethno-centrism, whereby "there is no salvation outside of Islam, the true faith; Islam is the solution to the problems of the Muslims and of the entire world, other religions do not exist; Judaism, Christianity were religious laws that have been abrogated by Islamic *Shari'a*" – and all the rest of this narcissistic delirium.[36]

Ultimately, it will have a direct bearing upon the Islamic Far Right's open warfare against modernity, which has proved to be more than a metaphorical hostility:

- It will generate an Islamic religious rationalism, updated so as to conform to the institutions, sciences and values of the world it is living in and against which it is still waging an open warfare;
- It will produce Muslim individuals that think for themselves and choose their values and their own method of religious belief themselves, so that

they free themselves from the "directors of conscience," and thereby prevent their being dissolved into the "Nation" – all of which generates the
ideology of globalized Islamic terrorism;

- It will cleanse Islam of violence; the violence of the shari'a with its shock-
  ing corporal punishments (over the last 30 years Iran has stoned to death
  approximately 2,000 women), the violence of personal status laws that
  have deprived women of their fundamental rights for 14 centuries, and
  the "legalized violence" that manifests itself in jihad.

The potential of the comparative approach to force through thoroughgo-
ing transformation was eloquently summed up by Mohamed Arkoun:

> It is necessary to open up the Qur'ānic fact by situating it in a com-
> parative approach ... If the present resources of historical enquiry
> allowed it to be established ... that the Qur'ān, when viewed in the ...
> ethno-linguistic, sociological and political theatre of "tribal" life ... at
> the beginning of the seventh century has to change its cognitive sta-
> tus – a whole new field of work will be possible.[37]

Promoting a Deep Re-evaluation of the Tradition

The challenge to the cognitive status opened up by the comparative
approach is indeed a vital weapon in the progressives' arsenal, since Islamists
attempt to found their immunity upon two broad categories. The first is *reli-
gious/cultural authenticity* and the second is the *integrity of the Text.*

On the question of religious/cultural authenticity, the Islamists' skilful
manipulation of this argument certainly affords them strong ideological
resilience. But it is a resilience founded upon weak historical foundations.
"We Arabs are asleep to history," explains Hashem Saleh: "Traditional certainties are the legacy of the decadence of the Middle Ages and they have
smothered Islamic history to make it appear something above history or
superior to it, or even without any relation to history altogether."[38]

The Tunisian reformist intellectual Abdelmadjid Charfi deplores this prevailing interpretative approach, noting that for contemporary Islamist movements

> It is unthinkable to resign oneself to accepting the distance that has
> opened up between the Qur'ān and everyday reality; reality [they

believe] must be changed and the golden age of the early Muslim community restored. The text is not to be subjected to the test of quotidian reality. This position is based on a sort of unhistorical wishful thinking... It has attracted many young people and the oppressed and anxious in society, victims of failed modernisation. However, its theoretical base is weak, and its adherents include many uneducated propagandists.[39]

As the detachment from reality progressively widens, the "narcissistic delirium" demands the employment of ever more strident fantasies, to the point where the disconnect becomes accepted. This detachment, according to Nasr Hamid Abu Zayd, actually rests upon a tacit compartmentalization inherent in the Islamic tradition:

> There exists right from the beginning of Islamic history – including the era of the Revelation of the elaboration of the texts – a permanent conviction that the religious texts have their own domains for intervention, and then there are other domains which are open to the intervention of reason and the human experience, domains which do not apply to the religious texts.[40]

Mohamed Arkoun termed this domain the "official closed corpus" and identified it as the critical arena of the struggle for reform and intellectual emancipation.

In his works *Critique of Islamic Thought* and *Islam, to Reform or to Subvert*, he acknowledges that the forces opposing intellectual revival in the Muslim world are much tougher than many would like to imagine. He laments the difficulty of opening up this closed corpus, and the "dogmatic enclosure" that it perpetuates. The enclosure is both extensive and deeply entrenched:

> The concept of *dogmatic enclosure* applies to the totality of the articles of faith, representations, tenets and themes which allow a system of beliefs and unbeliefs to operate freely without any competing action from inside or out. A strategy of refusal, consisting of an arsenal of discursive constraints and procedures, permits the protection and, if necessary, the mobilisation of what is uncritically called "faith".[41]

This corpus the interpreting community has accepted and will continue to accept for the foreseeable future as a *tanzīl*, a revealed given that abolishes through interpretation and in experience, i.e., in the course of history, the status of the corpus as analysed by historians.[42]

Facing this challenge, progressive thinkers are proposing new forms of interpretation, forms that *prioritize the requirements and achievements of modernity* over traditional Muslim scholarship. Such a process, according to the Moroccan progressive thinker Abdou Filali-Ansari,

> is not preoccupied with following the righteous ancestors; nor does it consider its mission is one of purifying religion and belief from innovation and plagues that have affected its unblemished spirit... The reformers' project of revision is carried out in an intellectually rigorous way, pertinent to the time in which we live.[43]

The salient feature of this time, according to the reformists, is the transferal of emphasis from a collective to an individual identity, which will have a major impact on interpreting the religious heritage. For the Tunisian historian Mohamed Talbi,

> Personal integrity, adoption of freedom as the basis of religion and the following of the moral and human aims of the Qur'ān are all worthier and more important for the Muslim than following the ancestors and legislating according to their legal schools... *Fiqh* (jurisprudence) is to be set aside in favour of a new historical and spiritual approach in the light of the original aims of the Qur'ān.[44]

The perspective provided by the comparative study of religion, the access to the European experience of analysis of its own religious traditions, offers Muslim reformers the prospect of enacting this new approach by applying the same methodologies to the Islamic heritage. The historical-critical method, wherever it has been applied, has promoted an emancipation from traditional authority and fostered renewal through the creativity offered by modernity's open-endedness: "This is the opposite to the traditional theological understanding of belief in Islam, as stated in the hadith attributed to the Prophet: 'The believer is like a camel: when he is curbed, he is led.'"[45]

The most important results of this method are particularly evident in the courageous initiatives of progressive reformers in *historicizing the Qur'an.* Reformers such as Abdelmadjid Charfi are aware that a religion cannot be constructively reduced to its simple historical manifestation, yet they insist that there is nothing to outlaw the study of the Qur'an from an historical perspective, given that

N B

> Neither present-day Muslims nor the generations who came after the "Followers" possess a direct knowledge of the specificities of this discourse, the precise circumstances surrounding it, the individual or individuals concerned ... It was, in fact, subsequent generations who made an effort to examine the circumstances, and they were set down, albeit only partially, at a later period.[46]

As a consequence of this modernist starting point, progressive scholars dismiss the Islamists' claim that the text of the Scripture is to remain immune from re-evaluation:

> Every text, including the Qur'ān, has to be subjected to new interpretations and considered afresh... The crucial point in a religious text is an understanding of its aim and its spirit, not the particular means through which the spirit was communicated in periods of history when prevailing mentality required such means.[47]

By adopting such a position, these scholars seek to safeguard the universal human principles they discern in the Text and bring about the contemporary means of realizing them. The task is an onerous one, however, since the downward pull of intellectual mediocrity and the weight of time has prioritized the letter of the Qur'anic text over the content of its message. Dull minds, Prof. Charfi explains, "took what could be empirically observed as the benchmark by which the unknown and mysterious workings of Providence could be studied, and thus imposed necessarily limited human categories and interpretations on the domain of the divine".[48]

Understandably, this type of research is hitting a raw nerve among Islamists, whose reaction has at times taken a violent turn.[49] This accounts for the level of caution in what, in these early stages, remains a "perilous surgical operation":[50]

> One notices generally that most, if not all, Arab intellectuals tremble in fear and remain on the back foot when it comes to the most important issue occupying the world at present: the issue of a serious critical study of the Islamic religious heritage. To put it another way, they do not dare to enter into the arena of religious and theological

thought itself, the impermeable fortress fenced off for centuries with barbed wire. Consequently they talk about everything else except the one thing that needs to be talked about. The best proof of this is the gifted Moroccan thinker Muhammad 'Abid al-Jabri whose project "The Critique of Arab Thought" enjoyed great success despite its glaring shortcomings. For he fails to deal with the sensitive issue, the most important issue in Arab thought, and instead stays cautiously clear of it.[51]

Yet without a challenge made to this material itself, to its claimed "a-historicity" and eternal, unchanging relevance down to its last Arabic letter – that is, if it is left to the Islamists to define the arena for debate as one that can be held only within the fabric of the Text – then their immunity is upheld. "We can see that the historicization process will not be effortless or easy", argues Hashem Saleh, "since it will have to clash with strong psychological obstacles located deep within the Islamic consciousness. Nevertheless, the battle is joined."[52]

Boldly Scrutinizing the Fabric of the Text

The battle is at its fiercest over the second of the two categories, *textual authority*, since it is the one that constitutes the Islamists' core armory. Both Islamists and militant jihadists justify their positions with constant reference to what they consider to be a non-negotiable primary source material – the Qur'an and the hadith, along with the *sira* (biography of the Prophet) literature – in order to establish that they are replacing a tainted, modernist Islamic pattern with a more authentic one. It is here that the epicenter of the debate is located. According to Soheib Bencheikh, "Any attempt to reform Islam – and Muslim jurisprudence in particular – must disregard its sanctity and reread texts in the light of modern thinking, in quest of a [new] orientation."[53]

This is an extraordinary statement to make (by anyone, let alone a Muslim cleric). Why is this focus on the Text so important? It is because scripturalism is of crucial significance for Islamists. Beyond the obvious fact that they paint themselves as authentic precisely because of their close adherence to the Scripture in their formulation of what true Islam is, the fabric of the Text – particularly its Arabicness – is a fundamental building block of their political ideology, since it assumes the perfection of the nuts and bolts of that source, word for word, letter by letter.

NB The concept of the Text as something sacralized and lying outside the bounds of investigation constitutes a core foundation upon which Islamism, and indeed much of traditional Islam, bases its arguments for a static and unprogressive elaboration of legal authority. These arguments maintain that:

a) the *Qur'anic text is of divine authorship*, down to its smallest Arab phoneme;[54]

b) it is *an uncorrupted text*; there are no alternative readings;[55]

c) the Text is *outside history*; there is no "development" in it;[56]

d) *Islam began fully formed*, and was not the result of a historical process of development.

Challenging this textual immutability, on the other hand, restores the case for the Muslim progressives' creative approach to faith and law. For textual variance would necessarily imply development and the influence of human agency in the transmission of the revelation. This would necessitate an understanding of the Qur'an as a revelation rooted in history, and therefore one that demands a knowledge of context. A contextual approach to interpretation would in turn severely weaken the Islamist case for an unchanging prototype. The implications of calling the integrity of the Text into question may be summarized as follows:

a) *The authority of passive textual referencing in legal thought would be challenged*

The Qur'an would emerge more properly as a text *about* God and hence subject to interpretation.[57] The Islamist technique of plucking verses, or even half-verses out of context (on the grounds that every part of the Text is valid for all time) would no longer be available to them to defend their positions.

b) *The imperfection of the text would impact on the claim of direct divine dictation*

Traditionalist doctrine "particularizes" Islam over other faiths[58] and any challenge to this would establish the role of human agency. A distinguishing feature of Salafist and Jihadi-Salafist thought is to repudiate the concept of a "common humanity" (as a Western modernist concept) by overriding it with a purported Islamic exceptionalism, allowing for ethical nonequivalence. The result of broadening the findings of this research would be to undermine the case for the shari'a as a non-negotiable prerequisite for Islamic identity.

c) A self-confident progressive interpretation of Islam would be promoted

Removing the Qur'an's immunity to internal historical development would open the doors to subsequent development in the religion of Islam, overriding the pattern set by the "Righteous Ancestors" (*al-salaf al-salih*) and the early scholars of *fiqh*.

d) Fundamentalist readings would be delegitimized

If the Qur'an's existence were to be demonstrated as not deriving from a process of immutable inspiration, but rather as a product of intellectual, theological and ethical *development*, this would call into question the authority of the fundamentalist veto against creative interpretation typified by Ibn Hanbal's formula:

> Whoever involves themselves in any theological rhetoric is not counted amongst the Ahlus-Sunnah, even if by that he arrives at the Sunnah, until he abandons debating and surrenders to the texts.[59]

Yet, such precisely are the challenges that are being formulated by progressive intellectuals in the Muslim world who are striving – often at considerable risk to themselves – to demonstrate how the establishment of the Text was a dynamic, selective process replete with revisions and expansions, and one that was carried out in response to the changing concerns and interests of the early Muslim communities.

The historico-critical habit yields still more results. What is it, Abdelmadjid Charfi asks, that we actually mean when we say "the Book"? For many it would simply be what is generally understood by the term:

> That is to say, what is inscribed in the form of a written line on a supporting surface ... [But the Qur'anic terms refer] rather to the content of the message that God saw fit to entrust to the prophets in order that they could communicate it to humankind... There is no clearer proof of this and the way in which the revelation used the term "Book" when the Prophet had not received the complete Qur'ān, revealed in instalments, at intervals of varying length.[60]

In which case, the non-negotiable primary source of the Qur'an as chapter-and-verse reference can also be denied to the Islamists:

KEY

> The term "Qur'an" should really be used only for the message which the Prophet conveyed orally to his contemporaries. As far as what was collected after his death in a particular order "between two covers" is concerned, it is known that the Prophet's Companions were not initially in agreement about the legitimacy of this collection which the Prophet did not carry out or personally order... They were hesitant even about what name to give to the document before they agreed on the term *mushaf* (volume, book), a term they had encountered in Abyssinia.[61]

The only logical conclusion, for Charfi, is that the "reminder" that God undertook to perpetuate

> was the content and not the outer... expressions and words... set down in a particular form and attributed to a particular people. This outer linguistic form has grammar, syntax and grammatical bases which are no different from those of any other language.[62]

From here the ultimate claim to scriptural uniqueness – the "inimitability of the Text" – is similarly challenged. If the style of the Qur'an is distinct and distinguished,

> Great works of art, be they poetry, prose, drawings, sculptures, or musical masterpieces, are all, in their particular way, unique. They cannot, despite the human origins, be reproduced... imitation always represents a decline when compared with the original creative work.[63]

NB

The corollary of this approach to the Text is the destruction of its empirical demonstration of Truth, as imagined by the Islamists. "The divine origin of the text cannot be proved by rational means, leaving faith or unbelief as the only possible choices."[64]

The crucial importance of research on the fabric of the Qur'anic scripture is therefore self-evident. Yet the impact of textual criticism in the Muslim world was limited for as long as the research remained inaccessible in Western languages or written off as the work of insufficiently trained scholars or those considered to have suspect motives.[65] But as the scholarship came to be taken up by progressive Arab and Muslim scholars, whose linguistic facility and *fiqh* expertise are more difficult to call into question, the temperature has risen. This has meant that there is something of the flavor of subversive secrecy attached to the research – or even the perusal – of textual criticism. Dr. Bassam Tahhan gives an indication of the anomaly:

> The German orientalist Theodor Noeldeke wrote several volumes on the history of the various Korans. Today the Arabic translation of his book is being circulated in secret. Jews and Christians readily accept the different versions of their sacred scriptures. Why shouldn't we?[66]

As it stands, advanced textual scholarship on the core texts of Islamic scripture, historically documented editorial revisions of the Qur'anic text,[67] and the existence of manuscripts demonstrating variant readings of the Qur'an (such as the Yemeni fragments[68] and the Munich photographic archive[69]) are calling into question the immutability of the source foundations (the Qur'an, *hadith* and *sira* literature) as justification for the narrowest interpretations of Islamic belief and conduct. And the impact of this research is direct. The Tunisian scholar Moncef Ben Abdeljelil, who is leading a team working on the Yemeni fragments to establish a critical edition of the Qur'an, argues that the differences in the texts from the canonical version are enough to "enlarge our thinking about women's condition, religious tolerance, what we call human rights".[70]

Rehabilitating Orientalism

Bassam Tahhan's observation on Jewish and Christian readiness to engage with the question of textual variants, and the natural extension by the Orientalists of the historico-critical method to Islam, flag up an important nodal point in the struggle for reform and the propriety of Western engagement. "If Westerners want to help us succeed in bringing reform and enlightenment to the Arab and Islamic world," argues Hashem Saleh, "one of the methods would be to translate the works of great Orientalists into the Arabic language." He points to the body of important works on the Islamic heritage – on the *sira* of the Prophet, the Qur'an, the *hadith*, the shari'a and *fiqh* – published in English, French and German, but of which the Arab, Muslim reader remains blissfully unaware:

For the prevailing works that we have at the moment on these sensitive subjects are far more traditional than is necessary and are reverential rather than historical. These works feed the fiery imagination of the fundamentalists. Consequently the translation of these great Orientalists' works and their wide-scale publication in the Arab world will liberate us from puritanical, alienating, ahistorical and obscurantist conceptions of the religious heritage.[71]

Mohamed Arkoun noted the particular value of research endeavor in this field, and voiced his unapologetic admiration for

The pioneering Western researchers in the field of Qur'ānic studies and Islamic thought in general, to a point where I am accused by Muslim colleagues of ignoring or excluding Muslim contributors to the field. [Yet] there is no doubt that Muslims cannot cross the boundaries of the creed based on the *myth of origins* which remains for them the greatest unthinkable.[72]

Just how "unthinkable" can be gauged from the conservative Muslim reaction to such research, which has found itself written off variously as "psychotic vandalism," an act of enmity or at best "reckless rationalism".[73] Remarkably, the climate for Orientalist investigation into the core texts has actually narrowed over the course of the last century, as Arkoun explains:

The taboo that Muslim orthodoxy has always placed on Qur'ānic studies was more easily lifted during the period of historical philological positivism than it is today. The euphoria of scientific reasoning was boosted by colonial rule. Hence the battle for a critical edition of the text of the Qur'ān, including most notably a chronological ranking of the *sūrāt* is not as persistent as it was in the period between the writings of T. Nöldeke and those of R. Blachère. All the same, this subject has lost nothing of its scientific relevance, since it implies a more reliable historical reading, less dependent upon suppositions, hypotheses and the quest for the plausible.[74]

Getting in the way of this logical trajectory of research is what can only be described as an odd meeting of minds between Islamists and a broad strand of Western intellectuals who undertake to devalue the work of European Orientalists. Happily, the broad denunciation of Orientalism (in the West as much as the East), as typified in the work of Edward Said, is being challenged by contemporary Arab voices of reform. "One cannot reduce the function of knowledge simply to pure power relations," argues Hashem Saleh; "indeed we primarily do wrong to ourselves, for Orientalism has no need of us; it is we who have need of Orientalism."[75] The clarity and honesty of this Arab Muslim intellectual on this issue is refreshing:

> We have to acknowledge this considerable backwardness the Muslims suffer from in their studies on their own heritage and their past, as compared to the studies undertaken by Orientalist scholarship ... We are but students in the great school of Orientalism... Our position is indeed somewhat wondrous and strange; we refuse to engage in the scientific historical study of our heritage and at the same time we wish to prevent others from undertaking this task! Instead of thanking Orientalism for its sterling services, we pour the cup of our anger over it and spend all our time cursing it and insulting it.[76]

Unideologized intellectuals such as Hashem Saleh and Lafif Lakhdar[77] have recognized the important contribution European Orientalism has made to the historicization of an Islamic thought that is otherwise steeped head to toe in sanctified, theological certainties and superstition:

> They were able to present a historical picture – a positivist realistic one – of some highly sacralized issues that none had dared touch upon or even approach. And it is for this reason that their researches provoked angry reactions amongst conservative Muslims who held these studies to be an attack on Islam, or even an attempt to destroy it![78]

For which reason, Saleh argues, any differences Arab intellectuals might have with the Orientalists should be restricted to methodology, in contrast to the politico-ideological conflict being waged at present against them: "It is high time that we shift Arab thought on from its ideological stage – a phase of shouting and slogans – to an epistemological phase of sober cognitive responsibility."[79]

The Significance of this Research

What is being challenged by contemporary secularizing intellectuals in the Arab world is the core issue of "authenticity". As we have seen, this issue is obscured by confusion on where to locate the parting of the ways. Traditionalists and Islamists alike will pinpoint the closing years of the 19th century and the ethicizing reforms of the scholars of the *Nahda* as defining the point of deviation from the authentic pattern of the Islamic heritage. Progressive scholars, on the other hand, will see precisely this era as the period when the long task of reinstating the long-buried true message of Islam – smothered at the earliest period by the dictates of dynastic rule and buried again with the defeat of the rationalizing schools in the 10th century AD – was initiated. All of this means that explaining the conundrum of what constitutes "authentic Islam" is largely a matter of where one chooses to date it from.

But for the progressive Arab thinkers, the ceaseless quest for "authenticity" is a fruitless distraction, since the key to rejuvenating and revitalizing Islam lies in understanding and reviving creativity in thought, which must of its nature break free of culturally delimiting patterns. Mohammed Arkoun spent his professional life attempting to extract authenticity from the preoccupations of Arab Muslim thinkers, arguing that the revitalization of humanism in Islam was being hindered by the escapism that this preoccupation offered from the thorny internal challenge of analyzing the texts that underpin Muslim law, and by its unhealthy exteriorization of patriarchal nationalism, fanaticism and xenophobia.

Despite appearances to the contrary, the position of the Islamists is manifestly weak. The pool of "authentic" resources is by nature stagnant, and for as long as Islamists persist in seeing history as immobile and remain blind to its dynamics and movement, they will forever lack the appropriate theoretical bases with which to confront the questions posed by contemporary life. "They are unable to provide coherent responses," argues Abdelmadjid Charfi,

> While the Utopian vision of the Islamist movements has no chance of success. It would condemn Muslim societies to being overtaken by the movement of history and its complexities, far removed from the simplicity of the early Muslim community. The values of the Enlightenment, far from being rejected, are becoming more firmly established. The points of view of... Islamic reformers converge in that they call for part of the message of Muhammad to be retained, while the rest will be set aside or interpreted, without any guarantee that a particular interpretation is more valid than its rivals.[80]

The foregoing pages have demonstrated the vital role played by Arab reformist intellectuals in renewing the "indigenization of modernity" process, which makes their near invisibility in public debate in the West all the more surprising. Their obscurity is not helped by the tendency of Western media to overlook them. As Hussein Haqqani underlines:

N.B.

> For many Americans, the Muslim Brotherhood's version is now the "official" and mainstream version of Islam. If a news organization is looking for a spokesman for the Muslims, they usually go to one of the Brotherhood-linked organizations, marginalizing the opinions of non-radical Muslims.[81]

Rather than encouragement for the voice of liberal thinkers in the Muslim-majority world, a strange bias born of a peculiar type of cultural insecurity has developed, as Ibn Warraq caustically observes: "The West, in its unwillingness to pass judgments on other cultures is far too ready to accept as legitimate spokesmen for the entire world-wide Muslim community the most shrill and public-savvy on matters of Islamic doctrine."[82]

NB This insecurity has had the unfortunate effect of inducing major media organizations – Western or Eastern – to lend center-stage to one side of the argument. Lafif Lakhdar describes the problem:

> The European media – the audio-visual media in particular – which looks to be provocative at any price – presents the supporters of this [Islamist] tendency on any and every occasion. [They present] people like Tareq Ramadan, but it is rare for them to present Fathi Bin Salama, or Malek Chebel, or Taher Ben Jelloun, Ghaleb bin Sheikh, [former] Marseilles mufti Soheib Bin Sheikh, Hashem Saleh, Mohammed Arkoun, or myself, and dozens of other secularising Muslim intellectuals... The Arab media, like *Al-Jazeera, Iqra,* and *Al-Manar* [TV], which have a large audience among European Muslims, act in the same manner. The supporters of the secularist tendency are blocked out of these media.[83]

Nevertheless, it would be over tendentious to lay the fault exclusively at their door. Perhaps the more significant impediment to the propagation of the progressive message is the lack of an effective co-ordination of any response to Islamist propaganda. "There is no institution that unites us," Lafif Lakhdar goes on to lament,

NB

Nor is there any shared program that defines the task and the priorities ... the obstacles are many: first among which is the absence of an institution tasked with overseeing the implementation of the reform program and financing it. All we have left are individual initiatives that are necessarily disorganized. In the absence of this institution the prevailing understanding of reform is fragmentary, and does not comprehend all of its aspects.[84]

If the voices of reason are at present fragmented and isolated, there is no reason why they should remain so, or be left to their own devices. As the embarrassed silences and exaggerated efforts to avoid the elephant in the room eloquently demonstrate, religious doctrine, religious law (the "*fiqh* of jihad") theology – all these are core ingredients of jihadist violence in the Middle East and across the globe. Islamism invokes religion by identifying itself as a movement engaged upon a salvific mission; it portrays and *understands* its opponents in religious terms and in its militant jihadist manifestation justifies its acts of violence through the language and citation of Islamic scripture. If, to recap Mohamed Arkoun's observation, "The theological and spiritual background of religiously inspired movements is rarely mentioned"[85] this is simply because its admixture of totalitarian and religious/doctrinal patterns of thought is proving highly complicating to Western analysts. It is, after all, a new class of challenge, and therefore requires a new type of analytical training, one that is able to accommodate the return of the sacred to the arenas of security and international relations.[86]

For this reason, Westerners and nonMuslims have no reason to see themselves excluded, any more than Arab Muslim intellectuals, from the internal debate on Islam at every level that this debate is taking place. The Muslim cleric Soheib Bencheikh put the case succinctly:

Islam is a message for all humanity. Therefore, it is not the property of Muslims [alone]. Everyone has the right to be fascinated by this religion, to adhere to it, to be critical of it, and even to be hostile to it... To avoid criticizing Islam is a form of segregation.[87]

As Islam is a universalizing message, everyone is entitled to engage in this critical exercise, to intervene with their own voice on how Islamic doctrine is being applied or instrumentalized in a contemporary, globalized world.

The question is: how to engage? On a broad level, Lafif Lakhdar argues, this engagement is already taking place. From his perspective on comparative religion and the Clash of Chronologies ("their past is our present, and their present is our future"[88]), he maintains that we are already fully interconnected:

> Everyone who studies Islam and its historical personalities in comparative religion, irrespective of his nationality or creed, is a participant in the reform of Islam. Even studies on Jewish and Christian texts and their historical symbols participate indirectly in the reform of Islam.[89]

On matters more directly doctrinal, Westerners and nonMuslims naturally have a somewhat large learning curve ahead of them – all the more reason, it would logically appear, to follow closely the unfolding of the debate where it is being conducted at its most internal, by digesting the writings of these progressive Muslim thinkers, who have already carried out the necessary "bridging function" by becoming culturally bilingual and who are therefore able to discourse with authority on what is shared and what is particular.

The problem of course, is gaining access to this debate. As you would expect, the contest in the Middle East is being fought out in Arabic, on blogs and websites and in the printed media (less commonly in the audio-visual media). The names of these progressive thinkers are therefore mostly unknown to the Anglosphere, and their courage in confronting the Islamist advance, often at high risk to themselves, is passing all but unnoticed amid the strident voices of proIslamist state-funded spokesmen. So it is all the more important that these progressive voices are translated for a global readership. The isolation and precariousness of their position demands that their profiles should be promoted in the West and their work financially supported.

The *Almuslih* website – which is the source of many of the excerpts adduced here – is an initial step in responding to this need. It aims to promote a two-way traffic through its publication in two languages, Arabic and English, and to raise the profile of these Arab voices of reform by translating their articles into English. I would highly recommend this type of publishing model as a window onto the trench warfare taking place, for removing the impediments and popularizing the discussion. The enthusiastic reception it has received from Arab writers points to how initiatives such as these can provide a promising response to Lafif Lakhdar's request for an institutionalization of the reform message in both the Arabic and English-speaking worlds.[90]

Some might claim that Westerners lack the cultural context to make sound decisions as to what constitutes the parameters of reform in the Muslim world. If so, who could seriously doubt that observing how one con-

stituency of intellectuals negotiate the parameters courageously and untrammeled by self-doubt is a good way to get up to speed to engage fully ourselves?

At the very least, we will be able to avoid undoing their good work.

Notes

1   The *hadith* of al-Sa'b ibn Jaththamah runs as follows: "The Messenger of Allah was asked
     about whether it was permissible for some people to attack the disbelievers at night, at the
     risk of injuring their women and children? He replied, 'They are from them.' I also heard
     him say, 'There is no protection except for Allāh and His Messenger.'" *Sunan Abi Dawud*,
     Book of Jihad, Vol.15, Hadith 2672.

2   The 11th century AD scholar Al-Ghazali in his monumental work *Ihya' 'Ulum al-Din*
     (*The Revivification of the Religious Sciences*) is adduced into the argument for his assertion
     that "There is no disagreement that it is permissible for the Muslim to single-handedly
     attack the ranks of the infidel and fight, even if he knows that he will be killed... What is
     permissible is only to go forward when he knows that he will not be killed before he kills
     first, or when he knows that he will break the morale of the disbelievers when they see his
     audacity and make them believe that the rest of the Muslims also do not care a whit, but
     love *shahada* in the path of Allah, whereupon the disbelievers' power will be checked."

3   "Only a growing minority is competing with the traditional Middle East studies establish-
     ment, trying to shed light into the 'black holes' in teaching and research programs...
     Reform ... is already happening in small part through the establishment of parallel depart-
     ments not impacted by the Wahabists, such as security, counterterrorism, human rights,
     and new Middle East studies." Walid Phares, *The War of Ideas*. New York: Palgrave
     Macmillan, 2008, p. 194.

4   Mohamed Arkoun, *Islam: To Reform or To Subvert?* London: Saqi Books, 2006, p. 61.
     Previously published as Mohamed Arkoun, *The Unthought in Contemporary Islamic
     Thought*. London: Saqi Books, 2002.

5   "Amplifying Muslim Voices for Reason & Reform", the Rome Colloquium, 7-8 December
     2012. The Rome Colloquium which took as its theme "Amplifying Muslim Voices for
     Reason & Reform" was held at the Pontificia Università della Santa Croce in central Rome
     on December 7-8 2012. The aim was to foster discourse between Islam and the West by
     bringing together leading Western intellectuals with some of the foremost reform-minded
     thinkers in the Arab Muslim world. The report on the Rome Colloquium is available at
     http://www.scribd.com/doc/244144216/The-2012-Rome-Conference-Report (viewed 15
     May 2015).

6   Hashem Saleh, "Mohammed Arkoun on the Golden Age and Beyond", *Almuslih*,
     http://www.almuslih.org/index.php?option=com_content&view=article&id=234:moham
     med-arkoun-on-the-golden-age-and-beyond-2&catid=56:islam-and-rationality&
     Itemid=245 (viewed 20 September 2014).

7   The reluctance to address the religious motivation for acts of terrorism is an interesting
     feature of contemporary analysis of jihadism. The default perception of the grievance fac-

tors driving terrorist groups is limited to left-wing, right-wing or ethno-nationalist/separatist programs. One of the few studies to address this issue is that by David C. Rapoport, "Fear and Trembling: Terrorism in Three Religious Traditions", *American Political Science Review*, 78: 3, September 1984. The author observes that before the nineteenth century, religion was the only acceptable cause for terrorism, providing a transcendent purpose that rose above the treacherous and petty political concerns of humanity.

8 Hassan Mneimneh, "The Islamization of Arab Culture," *Current Trends in Islamist Ideology*, 6, p. 54.

9 "Amplifying Muslim Voices", Rome Colloquium.

10 "Amplifying Muslim Voices", Rome Colloquium.

11 "Amplifying Muslim Voices", Rome Colloquium.

12 Mshari al-Dhaydi, "Is Terrorism Over?" *Al-Sharq al-Awsat*, 1 August 2010.

13 Gamal 'Abd al-Rahim Salih, *Riddle of the Arab and Muslim Societies, The Evil Triangle: Backwardness – Tyranny – Violence, Cultural Framework as the Driving Force*. Unpublished paper.

14 Salih, *Riddle of the Arab and Muslim Societies.*

15 "Amplifying Muslim Voices", Rome Colloquium.

16 "Amplifying Muslim Voices", Rome Colloquium.

17 Abd al-Hamid al-Ansari, "The 15 Characteristics of Salafi Discourse", *Almuslih*, http://www.almuslih.org/index.php?option=com_content&view=article&id=146:the-15-characteristics-of-salafist-discourse&catid=37:salafist-discourse&Itemid=206 (viewed 20 September 2014). The work in question is: Sa'id bin Nasir al-Ghamdi, *Al-Inhiraf al-'Iqdi fi Adab al-Hadatha wa-Fikriha* (*Credal Deviancy in the Culture of Modernism and its Thought*). Jedda: Dar al-Andalus al-Khadra, 2003. It is a doctrinal thesis presented to the University of Imam Muhammad bin Sa'ud. For more on this see Shakir al-Nabulsi, *Sur al-'Arab al-'Azim – ma huwa wa-limadha?* (*The Great Wall of Arabia, What is it and Why is it there?*). Beirut: Siyasa, 2009, pp. 124ff.

18 'Awadh al-Qarni, *Al-Hadatha fi Mizan al-Islam* (*Modernity in the Balance of Islam*). On the publication of this work in 1998, the modernist literary critic Sa'id al-Sarihi lamented, "When the Kingdom's Mufti speaks of the modernists as 'a gang conspiring against the Nation' I think that we are about to face a Holocaust, in that our isolation has become severe, and there is to be a form of cleansing of modernists." (Interview on the program *Ida'at* on the *Al-Arabiya* satellite channel, 8 April 2007).

19 Lafif Lakhdar, "Moving From Salafi to Rationalist Education", *Middle East Transparent*, June 2004, http://www.gloria-center.org/2005/03/lakhdar-2005-03-03/ (viewed 20 September 2014).

20 Lakhdar, "Moving From Salafi to Rationalist Education".

21 Lafif Lakhdar, "Moving From Salafi to Rationalist Education", *Middle East Transparent*, June 2004, http://www.gloria-center.org/2005/03/lakhdar-2005-03-03/ (viewed 20 September 2014). His essay contains a detailed prescription for a reformed system, to include the following units: *Sira* (biography of Muhammad) and *Sunna* (Muhammad's

words and deeds); History of *Fiqh*; History of Religions; Old and Modern Doctrines of Commentary; *Fiqh* and its Fundamentals; Language; Islamic Sects; Sufism; Modern Islamic Thought; Sciences and Arts of the Arab-Islamic Civilisation; Introduction to Linguistics; Introduction to the Study of Law; Scholastic Theology – Research and Philosophical Questions; Comparative *Fiqh*; Comparative Religions; Comparative Religious Research; Contemporary Commentary on Islam and Islamic Thought; History of the Philosophy of the Middle Ages; Sociology of Religion; Methodology; History of Ancient Philosophy.

22 "Amplifying Muslim Voices", Rome Colloquium.

23 "Amplifying Muslim Voices", Rome Colloquium.

24 In most traditional definitions, shari'a is referred to as law based upon the Qur'an, the *sunna* (sayings and actions of Muhammad), and laws enacted through the consensus (*ijma'*) of classical Muslim scholars and analogical reasoning (*qiyas*). The problem here is that this definition lumps together scholarly interpretations (*ijma'* and *qiyas*) with what Muslims believe are revealed Scripture (Qur'an and *sunna*). This is what has led to the false association of the common immutability of all of them. Contrary to the assertion of fundamentalists about the uniformity and divinity of the laws, the implementation of Islamic laws has always differed. This is because these laws were never codified in the way modern secular laws have been. What progressive scholars now face is the weight of centuries of intellectual inertia, since the doors of *ijtihad* were closed during the Abbasid period (750–1258 AD) for political reasons. Since that time Muslim legal endeavour has amounted to little more than commentaries upon commentaries and marginalia.

25 Excerpts from *Marianne et le Prophète: L'Islam dans la France Laïque.* Paris: Grasset, 2006.

26 Olfa Youssef, "Text and Context in Qur'ānic Interpretation", *Almuslih* http://www.almuslih.org/index.php?option=com_content&view=article&id=156:text-and-context-in-qurnic-interpretation&catid=42:ethical-issues&Itemid=210 (viewed 20 September 2014). She cites as an example the Caliph 'Umar's subsequent cancellation of the Qur'anic directive to cut off the hands of thieves, arguing the *force majeure* of poverty. Youssef is celebrated for her provocative work *Le Coran au Risque de la Psychanalyse,* and in her work concludes that Islamic identity has always been subject to change, and that therefore the case for an Islamist policy itself collapses.

27 Sanduk provides a helpful graph to demonstrate the statistical decline in the *Almuslih* article, Mohammed Sanduk, "Freedom and the Progress of Civilisation", http://almuslih.org/index.php?option=com_content&view=article&id=165:freedom-and-the-rise-and-fall-of-culture&catid=56:islam-and-rationality&Itemid=245 (viewed 20 September 2014).

28 See Sanduk's *Almuslih* article , "Intellectual Self-Isolation and the Prospects of Constructing a Culture", http://almuslih.org/index.php?option=com_content&view=article&id=226:intellectual-self-isolation-and-the-prospects-of-constructing-a-culture-2&catid=56:islam-and-rationality&Itemid=245 (viewed 20 September 2014).

29 Mohammed Sanduk, "Reform: A Discourse of Intellectuals or a Rehabilitation?" *Almuslih*, http://www.almuslih.org/index.php?option=com_content&view=article&id=235:reform-

a-discourse-of-intellectuals-or-a-rehabilitation&catid=56:islam-and-rationality&
Itemid=245 (viewed 20 September 2014).

30 Mohammed Sanduk, "Intellectual Self-Isolation and the Prospects of Constructing a
Culture", *Almuslih,* http://www.almuslih.org/index.php?option=com_content&view=
article&id=222:intellectual-self-isolation-and-the-prospects-of-constructing-a-
culture&catid=56:islam-and-rationality&Itemid=245 .

31 Sanduk, "The Islamization of Science and its Intellectual Problem".

32 Mohammed Sanduk, "Arab Society and the Metaphysical Phase", *Almuslih,*
http://www.almuslih.org/index.php?option=com_content&view=article&id=206:arabic-
islamic-society-and-the-metaphysical-phase&catid=56:islam-and-rationality&Itemid=245
(viewed 20 September 2014).

33 Mohammed Sanduk, "Intellectual Self-Isolation and the Prospects of Constructing a
Culture", (viewed 20 September 2014).

34 Zoroastrian eschatological elements provide some particularly thought-provoking parallels, such as the *amar i ruwan* – the reckoning of the souls of the sinner at the *cinwad puhl*
bridge – which provides the model for the Islamic image of the ordeal of crossing the narrow bridge (*al-sirat*); the threefold division of the souls of the dead apportioned according
to the deeds and righteousness of the believer and referenced in the Qur'anic term *barza-
kh,* an extinct Iranian word (from *burz-axw,* "high existence") denoting the idea of a middle abode (termed *al-a raf* in the Qur'an) for the souls of those who deserve neither heav-
en nor hell; the descriptions of earthly pleasures in paradise; the miraculous journey into
heaven by the Zoroastrian priest Arda Viraf under the guidance of an archangel Bahman,
to reach in the seventh heaven the presence of Ormazd, the great deity of the whole universe, who commands him to return to earth as his "messenger" to provide humanity with
guidance, including the instruction to pray five times a day. All of these elements, of
course, are closely paralleled in the Qur'anic tale of the *mi'raj.*

35 Lafif Lakhdar, "Separating the Islam of Faith from the Islam of History", *Almuslih,*
http://www.almuslih.org/index.php?option=com_content&view=article&id=161:
separating-the-islam-of-history-from-the-islam-of-faith-part-2&catid=44:islam-in-
history&Itemid=214 (viewed 20 September 2014).

36 Lakhdar, "Separating the Islam of Faith from the Islam of History".

37 Arkoun, *Islam,* p. 80.

38 Hashem Saleh, "Orientalism and the Historicization of the Islamic Heritage", *Almuslih,*
http://www.almuslih.org/index.php?option=com_content&view=article&id=254:
orientalism-and-the-historicization-of-the-islamic-heritage&catid=44:islam-in-
history&Itemid=214 (viewed 20 September 2014).

39 Abdelmadjid Charfi, *Islam, Between Message and History,* (eds.) Abdou Filali-Ansary and
Sikeena Karmali Ahmed, transl. David Bond. Edinburgh University Press, 2009, p. 56.

40 Nasr Abou Zeid, *Critique du Discours Religieux,* transl. M. Chairet. Paris: Sindbad, 1999.

41 Arkoun, *Islam,* p. 87.

42 Arkoun, *Islam,* p. 82.

43 Abdou Filali-Ansari, *Réformer l'Islam*. Paris: La Découverte, 2003, pp. 238-241.

44 Mohamed Talbi, cited in Moncef Ben Abdeljelil, "Introduction", in Abdelmadjid Charfi, *Islam, Between Message and History*, p. 5.

45 Moncef Ben Abdeljelil, "Introduction", in Abdelmadjid Charfi, *Islam, Between Message and History*, p. 7.

46 Charfi, *Islam*, pp. 49-50. The author argues that although Qur'anic sciences include what is known as *asbab al-nuzul* ("circumstances of revelation"), nevertheless these date no earlier than three generations after the death of Muhammad, so that their texts are in parts marked by confusion and invention.

47 Moncef Ben Abdeljelil, "Introduction", in Abdelmadjid Charfi, *Islam, Between Message and History*, p. 6.

48 Charfi, *Islam*, p. 54. The author notes that "The specialists in *tafsir* went to great lengths in order to explain all the details of the most sweeping and general declarations, and to specify what was meant by every allusion. Symbols became tangible historical facts. It is not the commands and prohibitions relating to prevailing circumstances at the time of Muhammad's preaching which should be studied, but the implicit aims and intentions." Charfi, *Islam*, p. 54.

49 Abu Zayd certainly fell foul of these raw nerves. He was refused tenure at Cairo University owing to the humanistic methodology he applied to Qur'anic hermeneutics. His promotion of the idea of the historicity of the Qur'anic text was considered to constitute apostasy. He was duly declared an apostate by an Egyptian court and was forced to flee Egypt, after receiving death threats. Other famous cases were the defenestration of Suliman Bashear by Islamists enraged by the thesis of his work, which argued that Islam developed as a religion within the historical context of Judaism and Christianity, and of course most famously the story of Taha Hussein and his revisiting of the question on the genuineness of pre-Islamic poetry, and hence the canonical tradition concerning the Arabic idiom of the Qur'an.

50 "Indeed, the application of the historical method to sacred texts and to the persons of the Prophets shocked the traditionalist faithful to the core. You may think of this as a perilous surgical operation or a severe internal bleeding, things which inevitably occur whenever one applies the historical method to the study of the Islamic religious heritage." Hashem Saleh, "Orientalism and the Historicization of the Islamic Heritage", *Almuslih*, http://www.almuslih.org/index.php?option=com_content&view=article&id=254: orientalism-and-the-historicization-of-the-islamic-heritage&catid=44:islam-in-history&Itemid=214 (viewed 20 September 2014).

51 Hashem Saleh, "Mohammed Arkoun on the Golden Age and Beyond," *Almuslih*, http://www.almuslih.org/index.php?option=com_content&view=article&id=234: mohammed-arkoun-on-the-golden-age-and-beyond-2&catid=56:islam-and-rationality&Itemid=245 (viewed 20 September 2014).

52 Hashem Saleh, "Orientalism and the Historicization of the Islamic Heritage", *Almuslih*, http://www.almuslih.org/index.php?option=com_content&view=article&id=254: orientalism-and-the-historicization-of-the-islamic-heritage&catid=44:islam-in-history&Itemid=214 (viewed 20 September 2014).

53 "Quotations by Soheib Bencheikh," http://soheib.bencheikh.over-blog.com/categorie-733578.html (viewed 20 September 2014).

54 The scripturalism of the Islamists entails that the more textually they comprehend God's word, the closer they are to His true will. Islamic law has enshrined this process as a foundation of the faith: *al- ibra bi-'umum al-lafz la bi-khusus al-sabab* ("the precepts are derived from the universality of the expression, not the specificity of the context"). That is, the authority of the text overrides the lessons of life's experience.

55 This position is mandated by following the Qur'anic verse: "Do they not then meditate on the Qur'an? And if it were from any other than Allah, they would have found in it many a discrepancy" (Q 4:82). Such a standpoint was unaffected by the evidence provided by the fact of the Caliph 'Uthman's recension of divergent Qur'ans, as a result of which variant versions were destroyed.

56 The issue of *mansukh* verses (cases where one Qur'anic verse appears contradicted by another, is deemed later in date and is "abrogated") does not alter the unchanging perfection of the Text, since the traditionalist argumentation is not that there is a development towards something better, but that the context to which the Truth is applied is different. That context may again change, calling for the reapplication of the "abrogated" verse. The Truth itself of the verse is never superseded; nor does it go out of date. The key intellectual element behind abrogation is *the avoidance of evaluation.*

57 An indication of this is the *de rigueur* grammatical introductions to religious/legal treatises, and the *de facto* prioritization of obedience to the letter of the text over the workings of the individual's conscience.

58 It would imply, as one author put it, a process that would "amount to copyediting God". Tobt Lester, "What is the Koran?" *The Atlantic*, January 1999, http://www.theatlantic.com/issues/99jan/koran.htm (viewed 20 September 2014).

59 Ibn Hanbal, "The Foundations of the Sunna", April 1991, p. 169, http://www.planet aislam.com/media/usool-us-sunnah%28english%29.pdf. (viewed 20 September 2014).

60 Charfi, *Islam*, p. 52.

61 Charfi, *Islam*, p. 50.

62 Charfi, *Islam*, p. 51.

63 Charfi, *Islam*, p. 51.

64 Charfi, *Islam*, p. 52.

65 A good example of this "defence" is Dr. Maher Hathout's (Islamic Center of Southern California) response. See "MPAC Response to NYT Article on Qur'anic Origins", https://groups.yahoo.com/neo/groups/wanita-muslimah/conversations/topics/28793 (viewed 20 September 2014). This a response to Alexander Stille's article "Radical New Views of Islam and the Origins of the Koran" (alternative title "Scholars Are Quietly Offering New Theories of the Koran"), *New York Times,* 2 March 2002, http://www.nytimes.com/2002/03/02/arts/scholars-are-quietly-offering-new-theories-of-the-koran.html (viewed 20 September 2014).

66 Interview in *Telquel* (Morocco), Issue 229, June 2006.

67 The medieval bibliographer Ibn al-Nadim lists several versions of the Qur'an that were not recognized by the Caliphs. Under the Caliph 'Uthman one version became the standard, after which it was ordered that all other versions be burnt. Some of the Companions expressed their disapproval of his editing, and variant readings continued to be circulated. Several *hadith* refer to the then current text of the Qur'an as "incomplete," or bearing spurious verses, or cite verses that are not extant in the text in circulation today.

68 In 1972, during the restoration of the Great Mosque of San'a, 7th and 8th-century parchment pages bearing variant readings of the Qur'an were discovered. These are some of the oldest Qur'an texts in existence. Some of them are also palimpsests where the text is written over even earlier, washed-off versions. In several cases the organization of the text is different, the *suras* are sometimes in a different order, and there are differences in the text itself. They indicate an evolving text rather than give support to the orthodox belief in a single Revelation to Muhammad. Aware of the potential for controversy, Yemeni authorities are reticent about the work being carried out on these texts by German scholars and have restricted further access to them.

69 The archive is the work of German Orientalist scholars Gotthelf Bergsträsser and Otto Pretzl, who searched out and photographed old copies of the Qur'an in the Middle East, North Africa and Europe in the 1930s. The Berlin University *Corpus Coranicum* project, which aims to provide the ultimate *apparatus criticus* for the Qur'an text, has incorporated these fragments into its research.

70 Jim Quilty, "Giving the Koran a History: Holy Book under Scrutiny, Scholars Draw Techniques of Textual Criticism from those Used to Analyze Bible," *Daily Star*, 12 July 2003, http://www.lebanonwire.com/0307/03071213DS.asp (viewed 20 September 2014).

71 "Amplifying Muslim Voices", Rome Colloquium.

72 Arkoun, *Islam,* p. 72 (emphasis original).

73 S. Parvez Manzoor, "Method Against Truth: Orientalism and Qur'anic Studies," 1987, http://www.algonet.se/~pmanzoor/Method-Truth.htm (viewed 20 September 2014).

74 Arkoun, *Islam,* p. 74.

75 Hashem Saleh, "Orientalism and the Historicization of the Islamic Heritage", *Almuslih,* http://www.almuslih.org/index.php?option=com_content&view=article&id=254: orientalism-and-the-historicization-of-the-islamic-heritage&catid=44:islam-in-history&Itemid=214 (viewed 20 September 2014).

76 Saleh, "Orientalism and the Historicization of the Islamic Heritage".

77 "The translation of works of Orientalists on Islamic heritage – works which were guided by the rationalist science of comparative religion – will play its part in preventing the brainwashing practised by religious stagnation for eight centuries, and which continues still." See "Amplifying Muslim Voices", Rome Colloquium.

78 A typical expression of this conspiracy theory may be seen in the following diagnosis of Orientalist motives by S. Parvez Manzoor: "In order to rid the West forever of the 'problem' of Islam, [Western man] reasoned, Muslim consciousness must be made to despair of the cognitive certainty of the Divine message revealed to the Prophet. Only a Muslim con-

founded of the historical authenticity or doctrinal autonomy of the Qur'anic revelation would abdicate his universal mission and, hence, pose no challenge to the global domination of the West. Such, at least, seems to have been the tacit, if not the explicit, rationale of the Orientalist assault on the Qur'an." S. Parvez Manzoor, "Method Against Truth".

79 Hashem Saleh, "Orientalism and the Historicization of the Islamic Heritage", *Almuslih*, http://www.almuslih.org/index.php?option=com_content&view=article&id=254: orientalism-and-the-historicization-of-the-islamic-heritage&catid=44:islam-in-history&Itemid=214 (viewed 20 September 2014).

80 Charfi, *Islam*, p. 56.

81 Hussein Haqqani, "The Politicization of American Islam," *Current Trends in Islamist Ideology*, 6, p. 93. The motto of the Muslim Brotherhood ought to be enough to clear up any opacity: "Allah is our objective; the Prophet is our leader; the Qur'ān is our law; *jihād* is our way; and dying in the way of Allah is our highest hope." Their alumni include the Afghan jihad ideologue 'Abd Allah 'Azzam and the mastermind of the September 11 attacks Khalid Shaykh Muhammad.

82 Criticising the paralysis inflicted by the heritage of Edward Said's attack on Orientalism, Ibn Warraq notes how Western weakness causes Arab liberals to "look with dismay at us each time we sacrifice one principle after another, in an orgy of self-doubt, cultural masochism, and self-censorship". Andrew Harrod, "Ibn Warraq Takes on Fact, Fiction, and Freedom," *Frontpage Mag*, 1 January 2014.

83 Interview with M. Milson, published on *Elaph*, 8 September 2007, transl. *MEMRI Report* 1729, 2 October 2007, http://www.memri.org/report/en/0/0/0/0/0/0/2409.htm.

84 Lafif Lakhdar, contributing paper to "Amplifying Muslim Voices", Rome Colloquium. One commentator on his paper put it thus: "[Those who support the project of reform] need to stand together and co-operate with each other more ... It is exasperating to see antediluvian thinkers co-operating and standing together while, not long ago, two great scholars of enlightenment thought – Nasr Hamid Abu Zayd and Mohamed Arkoun have now passed away. The geographic distance between them – Holland and Paris – was not great, but did they ever meet? I imagine that that never happened. I give this example to show the psychological gaps separating the bearers of this project. In my view it is high time for some co-operative work and effort, not to say collective work and effort." Yahya Belhasan, commenting on the *Al-Awan* website, 16 December 2012.

85 Arkoun, *The Unthought*, p. 43.

86 On this conceptual problem for international relations and political science, see S. Ulph, *Towards a Curriculum for the Teaching of Jihadist Ideology.* Washington: The Jamestown Foundation, 2011, Part IV, Chapter Six, "The teaching of jihadism in academic institutions".

87 *Le Parisien*, 3 October 2006, transl. *MEMRI Report* 1368.

88 See Hashem Saleh, "The Passing of Lafif Lakhdar, the Arab Voltaire," *Almuslih*, http://www.almuslih.org/index.php?option=com_content&view=article&id=252: the-passing-of-lafif-lakhdar-the-arab-voltaire&catid=38:obstacles-to-reform&Itemid=207 (viewed 20 September 2014).

89 Lafif Lakhdar, "Detailed response to the Almuslih table of questions". See "Amplifying Muslim Voices", Rome Colloquium.

90 It may be providing a model, judging by Lafif Lakhdar's call for "the support of civic society through establishing a website – on the model of *Almuslih* – which would translate into Arabic the most important works on Islam by Western and international Islamologists". See "Amplifying Muslim Voices", Rome Colloquium.

APPENDIX: COUNTERTERRORISM POLICIES AND STRATEGIES (2001-2014)[1]

UN

2001: UN Security Council Resolution 1373, Combating Terrorism

2006: UN Global Counterterrorism Strategy

2008: UN Global Counterterrorism Strategy: Activities of the United Nations System in Implementing the Strategy

2008: 1st Biennial Review of the United Nations Global Counterterrorism Strategy

2010: United Nations Global Counterterrorism Strategy: Activities of the United Nations System in Implementing the Strategy

2010: 2nd Biennial Review of the United Nations Global Counterterrorism Strategy

2011: European Commission establishes the Radicalization Awareness Network (RAN) (over 700 experts and practitioners)

2011: Launch of the United Nations Counterterrorism Centre (UNCCT)

2012: UN Global Counterterrorism Strategy: Activities of the United Nations System in Implementing the Strategy, April 2012

2012: 3rd Biennial Review of the United Nations Global Counterterrorism Strategy

2014: 4th Biennial Review of the United Nations Global Counterterrorism Strategy

Global Counterterrorism Forum (GCTF)

2011: Launch of the Global Counterterrorism Forum (GCTF), New York

2012: 2nd Global Counterterrorism Forum (GCTF), Istanbul

2012: 3rd Global Counterterrorism Forum (GCTF), Abu Dhabi

2012: GCTF launches the International Center of Excellence for Countering Violent Extremism (CVE) in Abu Dhabi, UAE (the Hedaya Centre)

2014: 4th Global Counterterrorism Forum (GCTF), New York

EU

2001: Action Plan on Combating Terrorism

2003: European Security Strategy (ESS), "A Secure Europe in a Better World – A European Security Strategy"

2004: Declaration on Combating Terrorism, March 2004

2005: Counterterrorism Strategy (Prevent, Protect, Pursue, Respond)

2010: The EU Internal Security Strategy in Action

US

2002: First National Strategy for Homeland Security

2002: National Security Strategy of the United States of America

2003: National Strategy for Combating Terrorism

2006: National Security Strategy of the United States of America

2006: National Strategy for Combating Terrorism

2007: National Strategy for Homeland Security

2010: National Security Strategy

2011: National Strategy for Counterterrorism

2011: Empowering Local Partners to Prevent Violent Extremism in the U.S.

2011: Strategic Implementation Plan (SIP) for Empowering Local Partners to Prevent Violent Extremism in the U.S.

UK

2003: Launch of the "Prevent" Strategy (classified)

2006: Countering International Terrorism (CONTEST 1)

2008: The National Security Strategy of the UK "Security in an Interdependent World"

2009: Review of the CONTEST Strategy (CONTEST 2)

2010: The National Security Strategy "A Strong Britain in an Age of Uncertainty"

2011: Review of the "Prevent" Strategy

2011: Review of the CONTEST Strategy (CONTEST 3)

2014: An Annual Report: Pursue Prevent Protect Prepare

Canada

2004: Securing an Open Society: Canada's National Security Policy

2005: Securing an Open Society: One Year Later

2012: Counterterrorism Strategy "Building Resilience Against Terrorism"

2013: National Security Strategy

Spain

2004: Counterterrorism Policy

2011: Spanish Security Strategy "Everyone's Responsibility"

2013: The National Security Strategy "Sharing a Common Project"

Germany

2006: White Paper 2006 on German Security Policy and the Future of the Bundeswehr

Norway

2006: Foreign Policy Strategy for Combating International Terrorism

2014: Action Plan Against Radicalization and Violent Extremism

Bosnia and Herzegovinia

2006: Strategy Combating Terrorism in Bosnia and Herzegovinia (2006-2009)

2010: Bosnia and Herzegovinia Strategy for Prevention and Fight Against Terrorism (2010-2013)

The Netherlands

2007: Polarization and Radicalization Action Plan 2007 – 2011

2011: "National 2011-2015 Counterterrorism Strategy"

2014: The Netherlands Comprehensive Action Program to Combat Jihadism

Australia

2008: The First National Security Statement to the Australian Government
2010: Counterterrorism White Paper
2012: National Counterterrorism Plan
2013: Strong and Secure: A Strategy for Australia's National Security 2013

France

2008: The French White Paper on Defense and National Security
2013: White Paper on Defense and National Security

Sweden

2008: "National Responsibility and International Commitment – A National Strategy to Meet the Threat of Terrorism, 2007"
2012: Updated National Strategy – "Responsibility and Commitment – A National Counterterrorism Strategy"

Denmark

2009: A Common and Safe Future: An Action Plan to Prevent Extremist Views and Radicalization Among Young People

Finland

2009: Finnish Security and Defense Policy 2009
2010: National Counterterrorism Strategy
2012: Towards a Cohesive Society: Action Plan to Prevent Violent Extremism
2012: Finnish Security and Defense Policy 2012

Notes

1 A chronological overview of the counterterrorism policies and strategies in the West (2001-2014) is also available on https://www.scribd.com/doc/242521417/Counter-Terrorism-Policies-and-Strategies-2001-2014.

About the Authors

Anna Bekele

Anna Bekele is a freelance researcher. She received her PhD at the School of Oriental and African Studies (SOAS), University of London. Her research focused on Islamic political movements in Ukraine and Crimea. Anna was a Robert Bosch Fellow at the Russia and Eurasia Programme at Chatham House in 2013. She looked into various transnational Islamic movements in Russia and Crimea.

Robert R. Reilly

Robert R. Reilly is a senior fellow at the American Foreign Policy Council and has written for *The Wall Street Journal, The Washington Post, Reader's Digest,* and *National Review,* among many other publications. A former director of the Voice of America, he has taught at the National Defense University and served in the White House and the Office of the Secretary of Defense. He is a member of the board of the Westminster Institute and of the Middle East Media Research Institute.

Patrick Sookhdeo

Patrick Sookhdeo PhD, DD has been Visiting Professor at the Defence Academy of the UK and Adjunct Professor at the George C. Marshall European Center for Security Studies, as well as guest Lecturer at the NATO School, Oberammergau. He has served as Cultural Adviser to the British military in Iraq and Afghanistan, as well as advising the FBI. He is a consultant to governments and business on security issues and the author/editor of 28 books.

Stephen Ulph

Stephen Ulph is a Senior Fellow with the Jamestown Foundation and is the founder and director of *The Reform Project* and its bilingual (Arabic-

English) website *Almuslih* (www.almuslih.org). He has published a series of works on Islamist ideologization including *Towards a Curriculum for the Study of Jihadist Ideology*, *Islamism and Totalitarianism: The Challenge of Comparison*, *Sacralised Politics and the Politicised Sacred* and *Boko Haram: Investigating the Ideological Background to the Rise of an Islamist Militant Organisation*.

J. Michael Waller

J. Michael Waller PhD is a Senior Analyst with Wikistrat, a crowdsourced intelligence analysis and forecasting company. For 13 years he was the Walter and Leonore Annenberg Professor of International Communications at a graduate school of national security and international relations in Washington, DC.

About the Westminster Institute

The Mission of The Westminster Institute is to promote individual dignity and freedom for people throughout the world. The Institute fulfills this mission by sponsoring high-quality independent research by scholars and policy analysts, with a particular focus on the threat posed by extremism and radical ideologies. The Westminster Institute is a fully independent, nonprofit organization that is funded by contributions from individuals and private foundations. The Institute was created in April 2009 and since that time it has held numerous briefings and events. Recent events include:

Understanding Security in Pakistan's Tribal Areas, with Thomas Wilhelm, Director, the Foreign Military Studies Office.

Islamism and the Future of the Christians of the Middle East, with Prof. Habib C. Malik, Lebanese American University.

How Terrorist Groups End, with Dr. Christopher C. Harmon, Marine Corps Research Center

Lone-Wolf Shooters Motivated by Al-Qaedist Ideology, with Madeleine Gruen, Senior Analyst, NEFA Foundation

Khalid Shaikh Mohammed, Mastermind: The Many Faces of the 9/11 Architect, with author Richard Minter

Arab Spring or Christian Winter? with author Robert R. Reilly

Global Jihad: The Threat Doctrine and Strategic Response, with Dr Sebastian Gorka, Foundation for Defense of Democracies

Combating Terrorist Financing and Illicit Networks, with Celina Realuyo

Lessons from the Battlefield: Counter-Insurgency for Domestic Law Enforcement, with Lieutenant Michael J. Domnarski and Trooper Michael Cutone, Massachusetts State Police

Muslim-Christian Violence in Nigeria, with the Most Rev. Dr. Ben Kwashi, Archbishop of Jos Province, Nigeria

Responding to Islamism: Lessons from Dietrich Bonhoeffer, Karl Barth, and Bishop George Bell, with Dr. Patrick Sookhdeo, Barnabas Fund.

The Rise of Political Islam and the Ideology of Jihad, with Dr. Sebastian Gorka, Foundation for Defense of Democracies

Intelligence and Counter-Intelligence Challenges of Militant Islam, with Dr. John J. Dziak, Dziak Group Inc. Intelligence Consulting.

To receive notification of upcoming events and/or publications, please sign up for the Westminster Institute mailing list, at www.westminster-institute.org. You can also follow us on Facebook.